EVERY DAY WITH JESUS

More New Christian
Devotions for
Every Day of the Year

✄

Companion Edition to:

Daily Walk With Jesus
Daily Word From Jesus
Day By Day With Jesus

by

Robert L. Tasler

Tasler 2018

AUTHOR'S NOTE

EVERY DAY WITH JESUS © 2018, is published by "Bob's Books" and is a companion to the author's other devotionals, *DAILY WALK WITH JESUS* © 2013, and *DAILY WORD FROM JESUS* © 2014, and *DAY BY DAY WITH JESUS* © 2015. All four daily devotionals, together with the author's other published works, are available at *www.bobtasler.com*.

This book is a collection of original devotions, some of which have been published in the author's regular WEEKLY MESSAGE emails. Interested persons may subscribe without cost to receiving WEEKLY MESSAGE through the author's website. The author, a pastor in the Lutheran Church – Missouri Synod, thanks his faithful and talented wife for her assistance in producing this book and many others.

NOTICE OF RIGHTS

Most of the Bible references used in *EVERY DAY WITH JESUS* are from the English Standard Version, 2011 edition, with some verses being paraphrased by the author. The English Standard Version is an updating of the Revised Standard Version of 1971, and it is published by Crossway Bibles. The author allows portions of *EVERY DAY WITH JESUS* to be used in various Christian outlets with his written permission.

FURTHER NOTE

Some of the topics and examples the author uses in this book have been adapted from other sources. These became helpful in creating 365 new daily devotions. The author thanks all others for their ideas he has developed and given an original and personal application. Thanks to all who have so capably written of God's grace in Jesus.

BOOKS BY THE AUTHOR

<u>Daily Devotionals</u>
Daily Walk With Jesus
Daily Word From Jesus
Day By Day With Jesus
Every Day With Jesus

<u>Bible Studies</u>
The Called Disciple (Matthew)
The Loving Disciple (1, 2 & 3 John)
The Faithful Disciple (Colossians)
The Worthy Disciple (Philippians)
The Practical Disciple (James)
The Growing Disciple (Ephesians)
The Hopeful Disciple (1 & 2 Peter)
Old Testament Disciples (OT Prophets)
The Searching Disciple (Ecclesiastes)

<u>Children's Books</u>
The True Story Of Silent Night
Bobby Was A Farmer Boy

<u>Novels</u>
Fun And Games At Palm Creek
Palm Creek Pickles

<u>Other Works</u>
From The Cradle To The Cross (sermon series)
Spreading The Word (rural ministry short stories)
Reflections (personal essays)
A Man's Devotions With God (written for a brother)
Blessings From The Cradle (devotions for new parents)

TABLE OF CONTENTS

JANUARY. . . . . Page 1

FEBRUARY. . . . . Page 33

MARCH. . . . . .Page 61

APRIL. . . . . .Page 93

MAY. . . . . Page 123

JUNE. . . . . .Page 155

JULY. . . . . Page 185

AUGUST. . . . . .Page 217

SEPTEMBER. . . . . Page 249

OCTOBER. . . . . Page 279

NOVEMBER. . . . . Page 311

DECEMBER. . . . . .Page 341

Author . . . . Page 372

PREFACE

I am grateful to the Lord and my loyal readers for the success of my first three daily devotionals, <u>Daily Walk With Jesus,</u> <u>Daily Word From Jesus</u> and <u>Day By Day With Jesus.</u>

It is my hope that people of all ages and walks of life will be blessed by reading my newest and final daily devotional, <u>Every Day With Jesus.</u> It is comprised of more original writings or adaptations of stories and thoughts that hopefully will aid people in finding strength, hope and joy for each day. Although published in a smaller over-all dimension for easier handling, it retains the same type size as the others for easy reading.

The title, <u>Every Day With Jesus,</u> seemed to be a logical sequence as one of four "Daily Jesus" devotionals which many people have been using and sharing with friends and family.

Additionally, I am grateful to be able to write another title which evokes Christian faith and trust in our Lord. These daily devotions are reminiscent of the Weekly Messages I have been writing and distributing online for the past twenty-five years.

May all who read this book be blessed every day by the hope, peace and strength given through faith in our Savior Jesus Christ.

+ + +

Robert L. Tasler, AD 2018
Casa Grande, Arizona
Castle Rock, Colorado

TO ALL WHO LEFT US TOO SOON

…Fritz, beloved brother
…Sandy, my youthful heart's delight
…Jayne, a shining light in the world
…Eric and David, talented and caring young men

EVERY DAY WITH JESUS
in January

✂

JANUARY 1

Happy New Year! Are you grateful for anything special on this New Year's day? I am grateful to help you find a special time <u>Every Day With Jesus</u>. May your New Year be filled with wonderful blessings as God continues to grace us with His presence in our amazing world.

The longer we live, it seems as though time goes by more quickly, and it is actually true. Albert Einstein discovered time goes more quickly if we are at a higher altitude on earth. Scientists proved his theory true. Using the most accurate atomic clocks known, they showed that clocks run faster if they are raised up by just 12 inches.

But anyone hoping to lengthen their life by living in the basement will be disappointed. Life in a basement would add just a quarter second to an 80 year life span. That's about the time of a tiny sneeze.

Better, then, that we should live upstairs, enjoying life and all the blessings God brings us in the sunshine. May this New Year be for you **"The year of the Lord's favor"** (Isaiah 61:2), and may you rejoice Every Day With Jesus, your loving Lord and Savior.

Thanks, Jesus, for all the blessings You've given us.

JANUARY 2

A man realized he had never shown his wife where he had grown up, so he took her to his old home. During the trip there he described to her the house and barn, garden and orchard, the land and the farmyard.

Imagine, then, the man's shock when they came to the old place and found everything gone! The house, buildings, trees, garden and even the farmyard were nowhere in sight. Over the place where he had been born and raised, a field of corn was growing.

Seeing his shock, his wife said, *"There's the bridge where you fished."* *"That used to be our pasture,"* he said, pointing to a field of grain.

"I still dream about this place," he continued, and his wife listened patiently as he described his home, parents and other memories. But the emptiness there now was almost devastating.

Disappointment and disillusionment may shatter our dreams unless we realize there is something greater and more important than the memories of where we've come from. Psalm 77:11-12 says it well: **"I will remember the deeds of the Lord; yes, I will remember Your wonders of old."**

It's important to remember God has been with us, no matter where we are in life. We may focus on our losses, but it's better to be glad for the blessings God gives us now. His mercies are new to us every morning.

Lord, help me remember You are with me always.

JANUARY 3

In January, 1504, Christopher Columbus was in a bad way. On his fourth visit to the New World, his badly leaking ships had left him stranded on today's island of Jamaica. The inhabitants had grown hostile to his crews and threatened to cut off their food supply.

Columbus saw on his astronomical charts that a lunar eclipse was soon to happen. The day before the eclipse, he told the local leaders if they didn't change their minds, the moon would disappear. When the eclipse occurred as he predicted, the locals relented and gave him food. His men and ships were rescued.

Although being deceitful, Columbus did what was needed to save the lives of his people. We should always seek to do what is right, but our choices may involve risk. Desperate people may do desperate things for family or friends.

Due to our sinful condition, we sometimes must choose the lesser of two evils. That is why we need Jesus our Savior to rescue us from sin. He went to the cross to forgive us.

We face complexities in the world today that require us to make wise choices. Such struggles should move us to seek God's counsel and rely on more than only human wisdom. We need God's Word to show us the way.

Isaiah directed us: **"Seek the Lord while He may be found; call upon Him while He is near."** (Isaiah 55:6)

Lord God, please bless our world and its leaders.

JANUARY 4

Jesus is the **"Light of the world."** (John 9:5) Ever wonder how He got that name? The Bible says after God revealed Himself to Abraham, Isaac and Jacob, their descendants became the Israelites. After the Exodus from Egypt, God accompanied them in the desert with the Pillar of Cloud by day and Pillar of Fire by night.

Centuries after conquering the Promised Land, God told King David his son Solomon would build a temple in Jerusalem. He promised to be with them in the Holy of Holies where His Light and Glory would shine to remind the people of His presence.

God's light and glory remained until the Babylonians destroyed the Temple in 587 BC. Ezekiel the Prophet shed tears when he saw the Light of God's glory leave the Temple (Ezekiel 10-11).

But God's glorious Light returned. In 30 AD on Mt. Tabor in central Israel, disciples saw Jesus shine brilliantly as the Light of the World returned. The transfigured Jesus showed that God had returned to His people once again.

Jesus will always be the Light of the World. When God said, **"Let there be light"** (Genesis 1:3) at creation, He planned one day that His glory and power would come to us in the humble carpenter, Rabbi Jesus of Nazareth, whom we believe and worship as the Son of God and Savior of all for gave His life for us.

Help me trust You, Lord, because You truly are the Light of the world.

JANUARY 5

I woke up early one Monday morning and couldn't sleep, so I grabbed my laptop and worked on a project. Later, after having coffee with a friend, I started some office work which took me nearly to noon.

A visitor came by, so then I grabbed a late lunch just before my wife returned home. After a short nap I booked some flights online for a summer trip, grilled pork chops for supper and sat down to watch the nightly news. Only then did I realize I hadn't written my WEEKLY MESSAGE to family and friends, which is always my primary Monday morning task.

So I went back to my laptop with a scowl. I love writing but dislike feeling forced to do it. I once complained of this to a close friend, and he said he liked my devotions even if I didn't like writing them. In 25 years I haven't missed composing the 250 or more words of WEEKLY MESSAGE more than a dozen times.

250 words can say a lot. The Gettysburg Address is 271 words and Psalm 23 only 117 words. We don't need more words in our world; we just need to use those we have more wisely, thoughtfully and carefully.

The Bible tells us, **"Those who seek the Lord shall not lack any good thing."** (Psalm 34:10) The next time you think you need more of this or that, consider the possibility that God has given you enough already.

Lord, help me be content with Your blessings.

5

JANUARY 6

A 92 year-old woman was moving into a nursing home. Her husband of 70 years had passed away, necessitating her move to an assistance facility. She was also nearly blind.

Well dressed and poised as they helped her from the car into a wheelchair, she said with a smile, *"I certainly don't plan to spend all my time in one of these." "I'm just helping you get to your new room, Ma'am,"* the attendant said. *"Thank you,"* she said touching his arm.

As she was being wheeled down the hall, the attendant stopped now and then and described her surroundings: the Office, Dining Room, Library, Exercise Room and other areas. As they went, the elderly woman said a gentle smile, *"I love this place already,"*

"But we haven't reached your room yet, Ma'am" the attendant said. *"That doesn't matter,"* she said. *"Happiness is something I decide on ahead of time. It doesn't matter if my room has a window, how large it is, or even how my furniture is arranged. It's all in how I arrange my mind. Before I even got here this morning, I decided to love it."*

"This is what I try to do every day. I figure I can either spend my time moping about life, or I can get dressed, smile and decide to be thankful for what I still have. Each day is a gift from God for me, and as long as I remember that, I can be happy." Paul said, **"I have learned in whatever situation I am to be content."** (Philippians 4:11) May we be content today!

Lord, give me such an attitude of peace and joy.

JANUARY 7

Yesterday, January 6, was Epiphany Day, also called "Twelfth Night" among many Christians. For millions of Eastern Christians January 7 is Christmas Day, a day to remember not only Jesus' birth, but also the Eastern Magi's visit to the Holy Family.

I once called an Ethiopian pastor friend on this day and asked what he was doing. *"Celebrating Christmas,"* he explained, *"Most Eastern Orthodox Christians still use the Julian Calendar, developed in 45 BC by Julius Caesar. Western Christians use the Gregorian calendar, proposed by Pope Gregory in 1582,"* he said. *"There are 13 days difference between the two. We still celebrate Christmas on our December 25. It's just 13 days later than the western calendar."*

Despite the two calendars creating different days of Christ's birth, Christians all agree on the date of Easter, His Resurrection.

Some think all Christians of the world should agree on everything, but among sinful people, this is not possible. There will always be differences in customs or teachings, but not about its essentials - who Jesus is (the true Son of God) or what He's done for us (died on a cross to save the world from its sin).

Jesus said to His disciples, **"I am the Way, the Truth and the Life. No one comes to the Father but through me."** (John 14:6) His Word assures us we have nothing to fear when we trust Him.

Lord, help me have true faith in You always.

JANUARY 8

On December 8, 1988, Samuel sent his son Armand to school in Spitak, Armenia, with a hug and said, *"Remember, no matter what, I'll always be there for you."* Later that day an earthquake turned that school into rubble.

Samuel ran to the school, found the place where Armand's classroom had been and began digging. One parent asked, *"What are you doing?"* *"Finding my son,"* Samuel said.

Most people left, certain there was nothing they could do, but Samuel kept digging, all through the night and well into the next day. While some placed flowers and pictures on the rubble, but Samuel kept digging into it.

Finally he heard what he'd been hoping for, a small voice saying, *"Help! Help!"* Samuel dug some more until he heard, *"Papa?"* He looked inside with a light and saw Armand.

"Come out, boy!" he said, but his son said. *"Let the others come out first. I know you'll get me."* When Samuel finally took Armand into his arms, the boy said, *"I told the others not to worry because you said you'd always be there for me!"* Fourteen children were saved that day because one father was faithful to his word.

When we are trapped by the debris of life or ensnared by the rubble of hardship, we are never cut off from our loving Father. He has told us in Hebrews 13:5, **"I will never leave you nor forsake you."** In Jesus, He proved this.

Lord, help me be sure You will never forsake me.

JANUARY 9

Living in the latter years of my life, I find there are at least two kinds of people my age: those who work hard to enjoy life as much as they can, and those who are careful, not wanting to do anything to shorten the time they have left.

Someone said these groups represent those who want to flame out, and those who want to rust out. There is a middle ground between the two where I live. I enjoy new experiences, but don't want to break any bones doing them.

I've ridden bikes, pedal or motor, most of my life and a few years ago bought a new bike which I promptly fell off! Grabbing the wrong handle grip, I ended up on the pavement with bruises, but thankfully with nothing broken. Folks my age don't want broken bones!

Bike riding is good exercise, so I still have one. But every time I get on it, I remember that nasty fall. My older cousin Joe raced cars right up to his last breath, dying of cancer only weeks after his last race. He wanted to flame out, and I remember him that way.

God gives us each a life to use, and He wants us to use it for the good of others, whether family or friends, needy or struggling, Christian or non-Christian. Our best help is to share our faith in Jesus with someone who doesn't know Him. In John 6:47, Jesus said, **"Whoever believes in Me has eternal life."**

Please, Lord, help me to live each day by Your will.

JANUARY 10

What do you say when someone asks, *"How are you doing today?"* Our standard response is *"Fine,"* or *"Very good."* If we're unsure, we may say *"Not bad"* or just, *"Okay."* Unless we're in the midst of a life crisis, we probably will give a bland, thoughtless response to what we think is a thoughtless question.

How about responding with something more positive? *"Great, thanks!"* or, *"I'm more good than bad!"* How about saying, *"Better than I deserve!"*

Paul wrote in 2 Corinthians 5, **"If anyone is in Christ, he is a new creation. The old has passed away, and the new has come."** That certainly describes the New Year God has given us. The oldness of the past year is gone now and we can do nothing about it. The future is something we don't know. All we have is now, and Paul says, **"Behold, the new has come."**

Can we be a new creation in this new year? I recently saw a snake skin that had been shed. God made that creature with the ability to get rid of a damaged and worn outer cover so it can spend some of its days with a new one.

God gives us something better – a new life. **"The old has passed away; the new has come."** Can we shed our old worries or resentments, our fears or regrets, and accept God's forgiveness in Jesus so He can make us new again? In Jesus Christ, we are all made new.

Thank You, Jesus, and give me joy for every day.

JANUARY 11

Time goes by quickly, doesn't it? Commentator Ben Stein writes with humor and common sense, making him interesting and worth reading. In a November, 2011, Newsmax article, Stein wrote, *"Of all life's mysteries, the most cruel and unyielding is that the moment, which seems to be permanent and fixed today, passes and is gone forever."* He concluded his comments, *"The only thing I can do about it is to cherish the time I have left and appreciate it while I still have it."*

"Tempus Fugit" - time flies. 1 Peter 1:24-25 says, **"The grass withers and the flower falls, but the Word of the Lord will last forever."** Some people seem to delight in speculating publicly that this new year will be cataclysmic, that something will happen to change the course of human history.

Maybe it will be so and maybe not. But if we trust in God for all of life, then, **"No evil shall befall you, no scourge will come near your dwelling."** (Psalm 91:10) This doesn't mean we will avoid all evil, but trusting in Jesus, we won't be crushed if something bad happens.

We meet the new year best by renewing our trust in Jesus and rededicating ourselves to holding His hand in faith, no matter what happens. He assures us, **"Whoever believes in Me has eternal life."** (John 6:47) We know not the future, but Jesus will be there when it comes, and there's no better companion.

Lord, help me cherish my fellow travelers in life.

JANUARY 12

I once officiated at a wedding on a Saturday in January that was made memorable by a snowstorm the day before. The afternoon of the wedding day was peaceful and the earth was lovely, all covered in new, white snow.

It would have been a fine wedding day except for the snow drifts on the roads that kept most of the family and friends from attending. The young bride shed tears of sadness when only 14 people were able to attend, including myself.

However, five years later I received a Christmas card from that young woman, now mother of two, telling me how happy she and her husband were. Despite a disappointing ceremony at the beginning, she said they were happily married now.

The finest of ceremonies does not guarantee a good marriage, a loving relationship or even a mutual partnership. It is a blessing that God brings man and woman together to form a good union, and it's always made better when God Himself is included.

Although people are capable of living alone more easily today than ever, it is still very true that God has said, **"It is not good for man to be alone."** (Genesis 2: 18) So He gave us marriage.

Yes, our Lord Jesus remained single, but He blessed marriage with His Word and presence. He is the groom for His bride, the church. He knows it is not good to be alone in life.

Thank You, Jesus, for all my blessings, even snow.

JANUARY 13

Paula Fox, in her fine little book, <u>The Second Mile</u> (Inspired Faith, 2009), writes that *"going the second mile"* has its roots in first century Palestine where a Roman soldier could compel a subject to carry his pack for him one mile. Resenting this rule, Israelites obeyed by going one mile, but not one step more.

In His Sermon on the Mount, Jesus counters this, saying, **"If someone forces you to go one mile, go with him two."** (Matthew 5:41) Going the Second Mile represents a higher law of kindness, of generosity and love. Going the Second Mile means living above the norm, treating people with gentleness and respect, regardless of what we feel they may deserve.

This concept deserves consideration since this is surely not how most people live today. Little thought is given to following rules, much less going beyond them to help someone.

Going the Second Mile is based not on emotions but on choice. We can choose to be kind, not because someone deserves it, but because we want to live as Christ directs us.

Our world today is filled with anger, jealousy and selfishness. The antidote to such negative feelings is not resentment, rage, or demands. It is the **"Love, joy, peace, patience, kindness, goodness, gentleness, faithfulness and self-control"** that Paul speaks of in Galatians 5:22-23. With such attitudes, life is much better.

Lord, forgive our selfishness; help us care for others.

13

JANUARY 14

Well do I remember my boys playing T-Ball games when they were small. Whoever dreamed up that game was brilliant. Every kid gets a chance at the fun and joy of the game.

In T-Ball, a baseball is placed on a rubber tee about waist high for five and six year-olds. When the batter is "up," he or she swings the light bat until the ball is hit, and then takes off running around the bases.

In a T-Ball game years ago, a little batter hit the ball surprisingly far into the outfield, and every player on the field from every position ran out to get the ball! When someone reached it, there was no one left to throw the ball to. They were all in the outfield! There they all stood, cheering that they'd found the ball while the little runner rounded all the bases.

Wouldn't it be wonderful if Christians could have such exuberance together, giving praise to God for Jesus? Most worship services are quite reserved with those present following what comes next in the Order of Service.

Long-time Christians may forget the joy of new-found faith. During a sermon I preached many years ago, a man said loudly, *"Hallelujah! Praise the Lord!"* Later he told me that's what they often say in his church in Africa. It was a true expression of joy! God wants us to **"Make a joyful noise to the Lord!"** (Psalm 100:1) even if we aren't sure how to express it.

Jesus, help us have joy in praise of Your love!

JANUARY 15

A member of a family had died while doing her duties as a nurse. The medical helicopter she was in crashed during an emergency run, and there were no survivors.

She left behind her husband and sons, as well as the others in the family, all of whom had already lost an adult member, either through death or divorce. Weeks after her death, the remaining family members had gathered for Sunday dinner and were talking about how much they missed her.

In a quiet moment of reflection, the grandfather spoke: *"Someone said we are all passing time, and each of us occupies our chair very briefly. The time we had together with her was a gift, and we are all the better because she occupied her chair so well. Some may say we have had more than our share of loss, but I see God's light in this family every day. And though I may not understand it, I trust in His plan for us all."*

During the past year I've received word of several beloved people who have passed into eternity. We've all experienced the loss of a loved one, someone precious to us who has "occupied a chair" of life among us. It is a blessing of God that we are allowed to do so.

Our Creator God has a plan for us all, and although we may not understand it, we can trust that His plan is good for us. **"Give thanks to the Lord for He is good."** (Psalm 106:1)

Thank You, Jesus for all Your blessings in life.

15

JANUARY 16

Some writers have given names to the younger generations. Those born from 1946-64 are "Baby Boomers," and then come "Gen X," "Millennials," "Gen Y," and even "Centennials."

Being born in 1945, I am not in any of those. People born from 1925-45 are "Traditionalists," or the "Silent Generation." With all the homes that were built during those years, it might be better to call us "Builders."

Although I've never built a complete house, I've added a room on two of my homes, doing all the planning, buying, hauling, measuring, hammering and sawing myself, all except the electrical. I also helped build a church from the ground up with the help of the Good Lord.

Just before retiring, I built our sunroom, finishing it in five months. Quite a job for days off during a Colorado winter. I love that room and have written some of my books there. I've taken some great naps there, too.

The Bible says, **"Unless the Lord builds the house, those who build it labor in vain."** (Psalm 127:1) When we bought our last house, we didn't know we'd be living here longer than in any other house before.

We had a house blessing when we moved in and have prayed together there every day. A house blessing is a wonderful event, for in it God is invited to be part of your home.

"Bless This House, O Lord, we pray,
Make it safe by night and day."

16

JANUARY 17

A few years after retiring, we had the joy of paying off our house mortgage, making us debt-free for the first time in nearly forty years. When my Dad sold his farm he still had a small debt on it after forty years. I decided I'd never wait that long, and yet almost did.

It's not easy to pay off a mortgage for various reasons. It's even harder to be "debt-free" in life. Christians know they have a debt to God for all He has done for them, and they rejoice knowing that their debt has been *"Paid In Full"* by our Savior Jesus.

Some people think God keeps a record of our sins, something to use against us if we don't obey Him. But that's not true of those who have faith in Jesus. Because of Christ's suffering, death and resurrection, all who trust in Him are forgiven. Their relationship with God is *"Paid in Full."* No more worries about this or that sin. God's mercy covers them all.

This doesn't mean we can sin all we want. In Romans 6:1-2, Paul says, **"Shall we go on sinning so that grace may increase? By no means! We died to sin, so how can we live in it any longer?"** We are free from sin's debt and free to follow Jesus, but not free to sin against Him.

Our debt to God is paid by Jesus, so we can praise and serve Him who has freed us from all our debts of sin. Jesus taught us to pray, **"Forgive us our debts."**

Jesus, may we live "debt free" because we trust You!

JANUARY 18

Among the more enjoyable things of life is solving a stubborn problem. When you've tried hard and finally figured it out, it's a sweet feeling.

I bought a used car with a code panel on the driver's door that would open it without a key (if you had the code). I could not find the code in the car documents and had been told it would cost $50 for a mechanic to find it. So I tried all the internet solutions, none of which worked. I spent five frustrating hours, unsuccessfully trying to find that door code.

One online source said if all else failed, take the door panel off and the code would be inside. I managed to get the panel off and there it was! My car's door code! I made sure the code worked and wrote it down. My wife patted me on the back, and later said I smiled all the rest of the day. It is a great feeling to finally solve a difficult problem!

I wonder if God the Father smiled when Easter finally came. His only Son Jesus had accomplished an impossible task, living as a human without sinning and dying on the cross to forgive our sin. When Jesus said, **"It is finished"** and rose again from the grave, He'd done it! It must have been a sweet feeling to know He had solved the worst problem in the world.

There may be some problems we can never solve, but we know Jesus solved the hardest one, and He did it for each of us.

Thank You, Jesus, for finishing our salvation.

JANUARY 19

My wife and I enjoy eating at a café now and then, but we don't always like the same place. There are at least two places I don't take her because she has had bad experiences there. One is a local place and the other is a chain where you can get all you want to eat for about $9. She cares for neither place, but I occasionally will lunch at one of them with a friend.

A restaurant once advertised, *"Help Yourself to Happiness."* Wouldn't it be nice if a cheap meal was all it would take to become happy? But no restaurant can fulfill that promise, unless that person was starving, of course.

Happiness is elusive. People pursue it with food or drugs or a host of other things, but in the end, happiness stays just outside our grasp. Being happy requires more than food or goods.

The reason for this is that the earthly things we pursue will not give us what we're really seeking. We may find momentary fun or pleasure, but our deep needs are still unmet.

Psalm 146:5 tells us, **"Happy is he who has the God of Jacob for his help, whose hope is in the Lord."** Sure and certain hope in God is a far greater source of happiness than anything we can buy or own.

Only when we entrust ourselves to God by faith in our Savior will we be able to find the happiness we seek. Our hope and help can only be found by trusting Him.

Help us put You first, Lord, that our happiness may last.

JANUARY 20

One of the joys grandparents can have is seeing their little ones in a Christmas program. No matter where these are held, in a hall, classroom or the church sanctuary, the place is abuzz with family and friends, awaiting the program to start.

When the children come in, some are looking at the teacher, but most are looking at the audience, hoping to see or be seen by a familiar face. They've been reminded to pay attention, but they're looking all over.

They may wave when they see us, but they sing or speak together when it's their turn, because this is their time. It may be a program about Jesus, but they think it's about them.

Some adults feel the same about church. Instead of worshipping Jesus or doing a good deed for their Lord, they want to know if people are paying attention to them or helping to provide their needs.

Even strong Christians can be self-centered. After the resurrection, Apostle Peter heard Jesus say he would be required to give his life for Him. But Peter pointed at John and said, **"What about him?"** Jesus answered, **"What is that to you? You must follow me!"** (John 21:22)

We may get distracted by what others are saying or doing, or we may think God has a better plan for their life than for ours. But His plan for each of us is the same: to follow Jesus.

Lord Jesus, help me follow You, no matter what!

JANUARY 21

On this date, January 21, in …

1542, Count Mykos of Zrinyi fought the Turks.

1793, Russia and Prussia divided up Poland.

1813, Hawaiian pineapple was first planted.

1880, First sewage plant was used in Memphis.

1915, Kiwanis International was founded.

1962, President Kennedy arrived in Paraguay.

This may seem a strange and unrelated list, since not all events are of equal importance. Yet in each of those events, the people involved felt it was extremely important. And these events all fell on January 21.

Which of these is most important to you?

+ The day you graduated from High School?

+ The day you were married?

+ Your birthday?

+ The day you were baptized?

To me, they are all important, but I'll choose two: my birthday and my baptismal day. On one day I was given physical life by my mother and father, and on the other I was given eternal life by my Heavenly Father.

Baptism is God's blessing to make us part of His eternal family. In it, He adopts us as His child. Faith in Jesus is necessary, of course, but the gift of Holy Baptism is what only God can give us by the Holy Spirit. Jesus told His disciples, **"Baptize all nations in the name of the Father, and of the Son and of the Holy Spirit."** (Matthew 28:19)

Thank You, Jesus, for being our divine Brother.

JANUARY 22

Chuck, a Christian man, was having a conversation over coffee with Bill, a friend who was angry at organized religion. Chuck wanted to encourage Bill and perhaps share his faith with him. Yet he didn't want to come across too strong and "turn off" his friend.

In the middle of their conversation, Chuck asked, *"Hey Bill, do you know where sinners go?"* *"That's easy,"* Bill replied. *"You're going to tell me they all go to hell."* Chuck replied, *"Actually, no, my friend. They all go to church!"*

Bill was quiet a moment, not expecting that answer. *"You mean all people in church are bad? I thought they were supposed to be holy – like you!"*

"Naw, Bill," Chuck said with a grin. *"You know I'm not holy. In fact, you know I'm sinful. I go to church to be forgiven by Jesus, not to parade around like some saint."*

Bill was unsure what to say next, so Chuck continued. *"Jesus forgives people; the church doesn't. I know you've been hurt by some church stuff in the past, but I go there to worship Jesus, the only really holy person who's ever lived. I ask Him to help me live better. I sure don't worship the church. It's filled with sinners – just like me."*

The church is not a perfect place. It's a hospital for sinners, not a club for the holy. We go there because we have faith in Jesus, our holy Savior. **"By grace you have been saved through faith."** (Ephesians 2:8)

Lord, help me live so others will see You.

22

JANUARY 23

Willard S. Boyle, Nobel Prize winner in physics, was the co-inventor of the "electronic eye" in the digital camera, as well as the Hubble telescope. He was once at a store in Halifax, Nova Scotia, seeking to buy a new digital camera. The young salesman tried to explain its complexity to Boyle, but stopped because he felt it was too complicated for him to understand. Boyle then bluntly said to the young man, *"No need to explain. I invented it."*

Jesus' disciples followed Him for years, and they were amazed at His knowledge, His wisdom and His ability to perform miracles. Yet they often tried to correct Him.

When Jesus wanted to heal a girl, they told Him not to bother because she was dead. When He said He wanted to go to Jerusalem, they warned Him it was dangerous. But Jesus said, **"Don't be afraid; only believe."** (Mark 5:36) He was actually saying, *"No need to explain, I know what I'm doing."*

God often needs to remind us that He has "invented" life when He created the world. If we're tempted to tell Him how life should work, let's remember, He knows what is going on, and He will make sure we're okay.

God doesn't need our advice, just our faith. The Creator of the Universe knows that we struggle, so He reminds through Jesus, **"Don't be afraid; only believe."**

Jesus, remind us that You know what's going on.

JANUARY 24

A good night's sleep is necessary for good health, no matter what our age. Scientists may debate the actual reasons for why we need sleep, but they all can point to problems that come when we don't get enough.

As I aged, I began struggling with getting enough sleep and came to depend on daily naps to compensate for lack of nightly rest. My doctor cautioned me about this, saying it is far better that I get a good night's sleep than to accumulate sleep time during the day.

Then my cardiologist pointed to problems with my heart and said I needed to get a sleep machine that delivers "Constant Positive Air Pressure", known as CPAP. I resisted this for months, but finally gave in when the Doctor told me I'd live longer if I used one.

Now I use it almost every night and have benefitted from it in several ways. It took time to adjust to its use, but knowledge of how it helps convinced me I could do it.

We humans can be stubborn and like to have proof. Most people know we need God but we want to do things ourselves. Our *"Can-Do"* attitude may help in some things, but it can harm us if it leads us to do the wrong things.

Jesus came to be our Savior, our Spiritual Doctor. If we place our lives into His hands, He will make things better for us. He tells us, **"See, I am making all things new."** (Revelation 21:5)

Lord, how can I thank You for all You do for me?

JANUARY 25

Living in cactus country is different from the Midwest. Cacti are highly adaptable and will root down from a cutting planted in a little soil, with a little water for growth.

But one cactus that will not sprout roots from a cutting is the giant saguaro. It grows from the seeds of the berries of its large flowers which are spread around by the birds.

Of the thousands of cactus varieties, most will grow in any soil. Saguaro, however, grows wild only in a certain type of soil. They will often suddenly appear in the desert as if a line is drawn in the sand. One side has them, the other side does not. These giants can weigh tons and live a hundred years in the Sonoran Desert.

Most cacti have thorns that should be removed quickly if they stick us. Even the fine, soft ones can go deep into the skin, causing rash or infection. Thorns are not to be trifled with.

They're like sins we get caught up in, our secret acts, addictions or destructive behaviors. If we let them continue and don't stop them, they will cause problems and harm. Thorny, sinful activities implant themselves in us and become entrenched in our lives.

God sent Jesus to help us get rid of destructive elements in life. He said, **"I came that they might have abundant life."** (John 10:10) Jesus offers us more contentment and peace in life than we can imagine.

Lord, help me stop those sins that trouble me.

JANUARY 26

On a winter day in 2011, an accident occurred in West Valley City, Utah. Aryann Smith, 24, was crossing a street when a city bus ran over her. She was pinned completely beneath the bus with two broken legs.

Officer Kevin Peck was the first responder on the scene. Hearing someone was under the bus, Peck crawled on the icy ground to check for a pulse. The woman was alive and conscious, but she asked him not to leave her. He gently assured her he would not let go of her hand until help came.

An emergency crew was able to jack up the bus, slide a backboard under her and bring her out. *"She was afraid she was going to die,"* Officer Peck said, *"I just prayed she'd make it, so I told her I'd stay with her until we got her out."* The young woman lived, in part because the officer stayed with her in her most dangerous time.

There may be times we are *"under the bus"* from ill health, bad relationships, faulty finances or foolish decisions. But Jesus will be there with us to hold us and help us through it all. He has promised to be our Immanuel, which means, **"God with us"** (Matthew 1:23).

We need not fear what will happen today. Jesus will hold our hands and make sure we get the help we need. *"Jesus"* means Savior, *"one who rescues."* Trust Him and give thanks that He is with us when we need Him.

Thank You, Jesus, for never leaving us.

JANUARY 27

What risks are you willing to take to get what you want? One 17-year-old boy wanted a new laptop computer so badly that he was willing to sell one of his kidneys to get it. His desire to get something unimportant overcame the risk of his surgery. Fortunately, his parents stopped him from doing it!

Why do people, especially the young, take such risks? Some do it because they feel invincible, and others because they want excitement in their otherwise dull life. Some take risks to fit in with a group, and some because they think it will make them feel better.

But some risks are worth taking. A soldier or policeman may risk life and limb for someone in danger, or a parent may be willing to risk his or her life for a child. The founders of the United States were willing to risk their *"lives, their fortunes and their sacred honor"* to be free. (from the Declaration of Independence)

Stephen in Acts 7, took a serious risk when he publicly told of his faith in Jesus, and he lost his life because of it. Willingness to remain faithful to God has always been a risk for believers. History tells us that except for John, all Jesus' Disciples were martyred for their faith.

Our example is Jesus Himself. He gave His life rather than avoid His work of bringing salvation to the world. **"The Son of man came to seek and save the lost."** (Luke 19:10)

Thank You, Lord, for taking the risk of saving us.

JANUARY 28

One of the phenomena of modern times is our compulsion to watch sports, especially the professionals. Baseball, football, basketball and a dozen other sports draw millions of people to spend billions of dollars watching thousands of athletes getting paid millions simply to play games. Why?

I'm sure it's the excitement of performance, but it's also that spectators are able to watch others do something they can't. Humans often enjoy living vicariously through others. Like the Olympic saying, *"The thrill of victory and the agony of defeat."* It's a thrill to watch them.

Life is often like sporting events. There are shocks and surprises, fears and frustrations, joys and sorrows, and all the while we are unsure of the outcome. Believers in Jesus, though, have it better. Although many of life's situations are uncertain, our eternal outcome has been settled by the work of Jesus.

The Apostle John wrote, **"These things I have written to you who believe in the name of the Son of God, that you may know that you have eternal life."** (1 John 5:13)

Life will give us many surprises on this earth, but because of Jesus, we can have peace that everything will be okay in the end. Because of His suffering, death and resurrection, we have the chance to live with Him forever. What a great blessing to know this!

Lord, help me not be worried when I trust You.

JANUARY 29

In July, 2011, former First Lady Betty Ford was laid to rest. During the service, her son Steven gave this tribute.

"She was the one with the love and the comfort, and she was the first one there to put her arms around you. Nineteen years ago my mother...gave me one of the greatest gifts, and that was how to surrender to God and how to accept the grace of God in my life. In her arms I felt like the Prodigal Son coming home, and I felt God's love through her. And that was a very good gift."

The story of the Prodigal Son is a parable which most of the world understands. It is about how the father (God) is willing to accept back the son who has left home and squandered his inheritance foolishly (all sinners).

The father's response of unconditional love has amazed humanity since Jesus told this story. Instead of lecturing or punishing the wayward son, the father took him back into his home and honored him with a party. Why? **"Because my son was dead and is alive again; he was lost and is found."** (Luke 15:24)

Steven Ford ended his tribute with the words, *"Thank you, Mom, for loving so many, loving your husband, loving us kids, and loving this nation with the heart of God."*

May God also give us grace to open our hearts and arms to those who return home to receive forgiveness.

Help us, Lord, to be loving to all people as You are.

JANUARY 30

I read a lot, mostly light stuff by Robert B. Parker, J. A. Jance or Louis Lamour. Lately I've tackled more serious authors and topics such as Lee Strobel's The Case For... series, as well as some astrophysics texts and Churchill's History of the English Speaking People.

The former British Prime Minister was a remarkable person. When he passed away at the age of 90, millions of viewers around the globe watched on January 30, 1965, the largest state funeral the world had ever seen at the time. Not surprisingly, Churchill had planned the service himself with his favorite hymns and scripture readings.

After the benediction at the end came his most personal touch. A bugler played "Taps" *("Day is done, gone the sun...")*, and then immediately followed it with "Reveille" *("It's time to get up...")* The two military bugle calls showed his commitment to the Christian belief that a Christian does not merely die, but is also given resurrection by the work of Jesus.

Existence on earth is not all there is to life. God created human beings to experience both an earthly life here and eternal life there with Him forever. Apostle John said, **"In Him was life, and the life was the Light of men."** (John 1:4)

God shows His grace by giving sinful people a second chance through Jesus. When we have finished life on earth, it's time to live again!

Lord, give us faith to trust in You for all things.

JANUARY 31

In our modern world, most of us are blessed with ample (some say too much) time for entertainment. Computers have made it possible for us to see amazing images that look so very real but are only imaginary.

I recently saw a commercial for a computer game based on Greek mythology with heroes, quests, war and even mythological gods. To take part in this game, you must register online, choose your god and build your empire.

"Choose your god?" Now there's a truly imaginary idea! It could lead a person to think we might actually be able to do it.

Actually, all of us do choose our own god. While there is only one true God who created the universe and mankind, people create all kinds of other gods for themselves, many of whom they trust in life.

There are many known names of false gods – Buddha (buddhism), Allah (islam), Elohim (mormon), Krishna and Vishnu (hindu), to name a few. Few would say we believed in those gods.

But there are other, very real gods - money, fame, sex, drugs, power or pleasure. These are real gods too. *"God is whatever we value for the highest good in life."* (Martin Luther) But Isaiah 45:5 reminds us saying, **"I am the Lord and there is no other. Besides Me there is no god."**

May we always seek the True God, Father, Son and Holy Spirit, to be our only God in life.

Lord, help me follow You and avoid all other gods.

EVERY DAY WITH JESUS
in February

✂

FEBRUARY 1

A big tree fell over in a farmyard during a windstorm. The old giant had stood strong for decades, but that day it fell over. A close examination revealed a rotting center had been weakening the tree. Outside it looked strong, but inside the tree had been slowly dying.

Cleaning up after a fallen tree is fairly easy. We cut it up and haul it away. But what do we do when a human life collapses? People don't live alone, but in a world of interdependence. We mingle in each other's lives, inter-twine our roots and come to depend on each other. How do we deal with a life that has collapsed?

Some of us may seem fine, but we don't let people know how we are inside. An unhealthy habit, a dependency or a small but deadly sin grows within us and attacks our heart. If kept secret or excused, it weakens heart and soul.

When a human collapse occurs, many may feel the damage which can linger for years. Thanks be to God there is hope for this. Jesus said, **"Those who are well have no need of a physician, but those who are sick."** (Luke 5:31) If you know of someone in danger by "hidden" sin, pray for them and let them know you care.

Jesus, keep me always from hidden sin and danger.

FEBRUARY 2

One of humanity's quests is to do better. We try harder and hope we can get it just right. Not everyone does, of course, but some do. Whether it's inventing a better tool, formulating a better theory, composing better music or writing a better story, most of us want to get it done as well as possible.

When a writer puts his words into print, he wants to see something good, not glaring errors. Whenever I find a mistake in my writing I wonder how I could have missed it.

When I hit the "Send" key to a thousand emails on Monday morning, I wonder what error someone might find. At one of my former congregations, I told members the bulletin usually contains at least one mistake, so if the sermon gets too boring, they could try finding where it was. A few times I was handed a corrected copy!

Only God is without sin. He created people perfect, but they soon placed their indelible blotch of sin on the world. Praise God that Jesus fixes our foolish foibles. Paul wrote, **"For our sake God made Jesus to be sin who knew no sin, so that in Him we might become the righteousness of God."** (2 Corinthians 5:21)

What part of your life is the most difficult to control? What is the hardest to get right? Remember that Jesus was human also, and He overcome sin so that we might be forgiven.

Thank You, Jesus, for forgiving our sins.

FEBRUARY 3

Some people love to go shopping but I don't. I usually go to help carry things my wife buys. Sometimes I say that I'm her mule.

A large clothing store near us had an annual sale on January 1 with low prices, so I went along. The parking lot was packed and inside we joined hundreds of eager shoppers who ravaged racks of slacks, jackets, tops and anything else men and women might want.

The clerks' hands flew, removing hangers, scanning price tags and stuffing treasures into bags as fast as they could. This sale helped make the store's annual sales quota.

At one point my wife handed me a blouse on a hanger and told me to stand over by a men's table while she kept shopping. The table was next to some mannequins, so I decided to become one. I stood up straight, hung the item she'd given me on my collar, looked straight ahead and tried not to move a muscle. Of the people who looked at me, most smiled knowingly, but a few actually came up to look at my outfit, being startled when they saw I was alive. It was fun!

We can treat others like store mannequins, noticing but not really seeing them or caring about them. Jesus wants us to do more. He said, **"Love one another as I have loved you."** (John 13:34) He knows what is in our hearts and wants us to trust Him. He wants us to value each other as precious persons.

Lord, help us see each other as real people, as we are.

FEBRUARY 4

President Lincoln once said, *"Let reverence for the laws be breathed by every American mother to the lisping babe that prattles on her lap... Let it be taught in schools, preached from the pulpit, proclaimed in legislative halls and enforced in courts of justice."* (January 27, 1838)

Why has it become difficult for Americans to obey laws which have been duly passed? Even Congress may pass a law and its leaders choose to ignore it. People may know a law, but if they don't agree with it, they won't follow it.

Abraham Lincoln had a great idea in his words. *"Reverence for the laws"* means we revere them as important enough to follow. It means we hold them above public opinion which is usually a poor determinant of right or wrong.

Of course not all laws are equal in goodness. But if each of us thinks we can be the judge of the rightness or wrongness of a law, we are walking on the dangerous ground of lawlessness. Better that we should follow the law or change it than picking and choosing.

The Bible mentions "law" 542 times. Matthew uses the word two dozen times, nearly every time quoting Jesus. He says in Matthew 5:17, **"Do not think that I have come to abolish the Law or the Prophets; I have come to fulfill them."** People must take care not to uphold only the laws we agree with. We are also bound by the ones we don't like.

Help us, Lord, to hear Your Word and keep it.

FEBRUARY 5

The Super Bowl had one quarter left and the lopsided score made the game seem over. The young quarterback was running the show, and the aging quarterback didn't appear to have the stuff to win it. Or so it seemed.

Somehow the other team came back from a huge deficit, tied the game and won it in overtime. The "old" quarterback won his fifth Super Bowl ring, proving he arguably was the best NFL quarterback of all time.

After the game ended, the old QB went to his knees, face down, right in the midst of the pressing crowd. Whether giving thanks or weeping in disbelief, when he rose up, he did so as a great winning athlete.

I saw a lesson in that game: God's plans aren't always our plans. The team with a poorer record wins the Big One, an unwinnable candidate becomes president, or an old quarterback wins the Super Bowl.

A Yiddish proverb says, *"Mankind plans, and God laughs."* With each stage of life, we may think we know how things will go. But then we get there and find things are very different.

God knows the future and His plans may be not be our plans. Jeremiah 29:11 says, "**I know the plans I have for you, declares the Lord, plans for good and not for evil, plans to give you a hope and a future.**" God's plans are best, and we must have faith in them each day.

Thank You, Jesus, that Your plans are best of all.

FEBRUARY 6

"The Music Man" was a successful musical and movie in the early 1960s. Set in the 1800s in Iowa, Prof. Harold Hill comes to a small town to convince people to invest in band uniforms. He says they will keep their children out of trouble, such as at the local Pool Hall. It's all part of a scam which he later regrets. One of his signature speeches has these words:

> *"My friends, ya got trouble, right here in River city! With a capital "T" and that rhymes with "P" and that stands for Pool!!"*

The story may be imaginary, but life can be filled with genuine trouble. Illness, untimely death, bad decisions, or financial reversals can bring us a tsunami of sorrow. We may hope the new year will bring us less trouble, but it may bring even more.

John 16:33 says, **"In this world you will have tribulation."** Following Jesus does not promise a life of ease, prosperity or good health, yet we are never alone when trouble comes. God encourages us, **"When you pass through waters, I will be with you."** (Isaiah 43:2)

When we have troubles of any kind, God is with us. He never leaves us. Although we don't always understand His purpose in our trials, we still trust Him because we know He always loves and cares for us. God loves us, no matter what. We have His Word on it!

Thank You, Jesus, for being with us every day.

FEBRUARY 7

How family life in America has changed in the past 50 to 75 years! Few young families now have a mother at home while father works, and household duties are no longer as clearly defined as before. The availability of prepared foods and advancements in technology have made life simpler, leading to some changes in roles of men and women whether married or single.

Also in the church there have been changes. People seek to change what God's Word means or how the church goes about ministry. It is true what they say, *"It's not your parents' church any more."* Indeed, it often feels like, *"It's not even our parents' country any more."*

But while everything seems to have changes, nothing really has changed. It's only how we perceive change. People are still born, grow up, work, have families, invent things, get sick, get old and eventually die, just as they have always done. Those are things we can count on.

Even better is that God doesn't change. In Malachi 3:6, God says, **"I, the Lord, do not change."** Through the prophet's words, He says people may change, but He does not. His Law and justice, as well as His mercy and faithfulness, always continue the same.

Hebrews 13:8 affirms this when it says, **"Jesus Christ is the same yesterday, today and forever."** People may try to change God, but fortunately, He is unchangeable.

Thank You, God, for Your unchanging love.

FEBRUARY 8

The huge clock tower at Westminster contains the clock known as Big Ben. It is London's most iconic landmark and for decades it has chimed a tune called "The Westminster Chimes," composed by Joseph Jowett and John Randall. Few know it is based on an aria from Handel's <u>Messiah</u>. The actual words of the tune are on display in the clock room:

> *"Lord, through this hour be Thou our Guide*
> *So by Thy power no foot shall slide."*

Installed in 1859, "Big Ben" got its name from Benjamin Hall, the engineer who oversaw its installation. In 2017, Big Ben went silent for repairs for the first time in 158 years and will be heard again in 2021 when repairs are completed.

Time is one of the most important elements of creation. In the beginning of time, God created the universe. Then, **"In the fullness of time, God sent forth His Son, born of a woman, born under the Law, to redeem all those who were under the law, that we might become children of God."** (Galatians 4:4-5)

What an incredible gift mankind was given at the time God chose! Time has a purpose, not merely to know how many moments are left, but also to know God is with us each moment.

God knows our needs all the time. A man challenged me how God could possibly know this. I said, *"Because He is God and we are not."*

Thank You, Jesus, that You came into our world.

FEBRUARY 9

Our age of technology never fails to amaze me. Among the many "Apps" (applications) for computer, ipad or iphone, one helps us to track airline flights. If someone you know is flying on a commercial airplane, the App not only tells you where that plane is, but where it came from and whether or not it is on time. The next App will probably tell names of the flight crew and what is served for lunch!

Why should we care about location or other details of an airplane in flight? Perhaps because we care for someone on that flight. A loved one or business associate may be onboard, or we may be interested in the political stability of that region. We know more of what is going on in the world today than at any other time in history.

Psalm 32:8 tells us God's concern for us. **"I will instruct you and teach you in the way you should go; I will counsel you with my eye upon you."** God knows the details of our life, as well as the lives of those we care about. His promise to us is that He will *"keep an eye on us"* as my Dad used to say. God cares about us.

Whatever happens today, we can be assured that God is watching over us. Some think that's impossible, that God can't possibly keep track of us all. But if a computer system can direct an App to tell us where airplanes are in the world, cannot God also keep track of us?

Thank You, Heavenly Father for caring for us.

FEBRUARY 10

Galway is located in western Ireland on the northern side of a huge natural seaport that is very important to Ireland's shipping industry.

St. Nicholas Church in the center of the city has a long history as the oldest church in Ireland. Its church tower not only shows the church's presence, it also provides guidance to ships' captains as they navigate their way safely in and out of Galway Bay. For centuries this tower has shown sailors the way out or back.

We all need points in our life that help us know if we are on the right course. At every turn of life, we need God's guiding hand to help us go the right way. We also need our Lord Jesus to forgive us when we fail to do so.

Jesus told His disciples in the Upper Room, **"When the Spirit of truth comes, He will guide you into all truth, for He will not speak on His own authority, but whatever He hears He will speak, and He will declare to you the things that are to come."** (John 16:13)

It's an amazing gift from God to know that in a world of confusion and fear we can always count on Jesus to show us the way. We can be easily blown off course as we hear the world's voices, but the Spirit will guide us if we let Him.

Jesus gave us His Spirit to help us. We can pray to the Spirit to guide us as we go, today or any day. If we set our course by our Savior, the Holy Spirit will keep us on it.

Dear Lord, help us follow You in all things.

FEBRUARY 11

I read of a private investigator whose first method of finding the truth was to knock on a door, show his badge and say, *"I guess I don't have to tell you why I'm here."* The reaction of the person very often was a stunned look followed by, *"How did you find out?"* The person then described a criminal act committed long ago. Some call this the "Tell-Tale Heart."

Edgar Allen Poe wrote a short story by that name about a man who had killed someone in the past, burying him under his floorboards. He was kept awake by a thumping sound which he believed was the dead man's heart. It's a story of guilt and how it can accuse us.

We all have some guilt over past actions that can accuse us even if we have confessed our sin to God. Apostle John wrote to those struggling with an accusing conscience, **"Whenever our heart condemns us, God is greater than our heart, and He knows everything. Beloved, if our heart does not condemn us, we have confidence before God, and whatever we ask we will receive from Him."** (1 John 3:20-22)

God will help us deal with a tell-tale heart if we ask Him for forgiveness and believe He has removed all our sins through Jesus on the cross. He came into the world to give us abundant life, not to live in constant guilt.

God loves us no matter what, and He will take away all our burdens, no matter what!

Lord, take my hand and lead me today.

FEBRUARY 12

History is filled with stories of its heroes, whether Odysseus and Achilles of Greek mythology, Gideon and Deborah in the Old Testament, or Alfred the Great and Martin Luther of the Middle Ages. Heroes give us motivation to live more fulfilling lives, and they also give us some good stories.

But not all heroes have memorable names. Othniel was one of the Old Testament Judges. Of him, the Bible says, **"God raised up a deliverer; the Spirit of the Lord came upon him, and God delivered Cushan, the king of Mesopotamia, into his hand."** (Judges 3:9-10)

I'll guess most of us have never heard of Othniel. We have no T-Shirt with his name on it, nor have we heard exactly how he did his heroic deeds. You see, the Bible doesn't describe Othniel; it rather tells us what God did through Othniel. He helped His people get back on the right track, at least for awhile.

A hero may have special qualities or powers greater than the average person. Just as often a hero is a regular person who acts beyond what he or she thinks is possible. For example, when we share our faith in Jesus, God makes us heroic helpers for other people in their daily walk through life.

Othniel was just a regular guy who obeyed God and helped His people. We can all do that and know what it's like to be God's hero.

Jesus, help me follow You today to help others.

FEBRUARY 13

A man was shipwrecked on an island and lived alone twenty years before he was rescued. To keep his sanity the man occupied himself with building a village, complete with houses, a store and even a church. Before leaving, he showed his rescuers around. *"This was where I lived, there is where I worked"* he said. Pointing to a building with a cross he said, *"This is my church." "I thought that building back there was a church,"* said on the rescuers. The man said, *"Oh, that was the church I used to attend."*

The story might seem silly or even old, but it points to problems of disunity in the church. Apostle Paul saw this, even in the early church. At Ephesus there were rich and poor, Jews and Gentiles, slaves and free people. And they didn't get along very well.

In Ephesians 4 he urges them to walk together in a manner worthy of their calling. **"With humility, gentleness and patience, bearing with one another in love, eager to maintain the unity of the Spirit in the bond of peace."** (Ephesians 4:2-3)

How can we help with unity in church? By expressing opinions carefully and patiently. Apostle Peter urged people to share their faith **"with gentleness and respect."** (1 Peter 3:15)

The Holy Spirit will help us with this if we ask Him. Truth is important, and so also is living by God's love.

Lord, help us show love to others in all we do.

FEBRUARY 14

Valentine's Day is a time to show love to special people in our lives. For those who take this task seriously, it can be frustrating if they can't figure out how to show that love in an appropriate way. What is the best gift? What's the best way to give that gift?

As we all know, an entire industry has been created to move people to give a gift to that special loved one. The ads usually speak of the "perfect" gift, or the "best" gift. One even spoke of the "supreme" gift to give on that day. Really heady stuff for the true romantic!

One year, Valentine's Day fell on Ash Wednesday, which happens to be a great day to talk of love. It is all about God's love for us in sending Jesus to be our Savior. I told my wife I knew the absolute best gift for her, she asked, *"What's that?"* I said, *"Based on what Jesus did, I'd say my best gift to you is my life!"*

Remember what Jesus said: **"Greater love has no man than this, that he lay down his life for his friends."** (John 15:13) Jesus truly makes His life the supreme gift, and we are grateful to Him that He gave to it us.

I was really glad when Carol said she didn't want that gift from me. So I gave her flowers and a little devotional book. We read a devotional each day, and we gave the daily devotional book to our son and his wife. Great gift!

Thank You, Jesus, for giving us Your supreme gift.

FEBRUARY 15

I have been blessed to enjoy many of life's pleasures, including snow skiing. My wife and I were introduced to this enjoyable sport, which I enjoyed until into my 60s when the high price of lift tickets and some physical problems brought those winter fun days to an end.

I was fortunate not to have injured myself as some do on the slopes. During a Montana winter outing with friends, one of our more experienced skiers fell the first day and broke his collar bone. He spent the remaining days of our group trip on a sofa with something named Jack Daniels.

Healing a physical injury can take time, but I am amazed how quickly professional athletes seem to heal. An NFL quarterback broke his collar bone early in the season, but was able to play again nine weeks later. Incredible!

God has given us amazing bodies, able to heal injuries of bone or muscle with special cells already built into our body. The Psalmist tells us, **"I praise You because I am fearfully and wonderfully made; Your works are wonderful and I know that full well."** (Psalm 139:14)

Sometimes it takes an injury or sickness to remind us of God's marvelous design that we carry around in our bodies. If you should happen to be injured in the coming days, rather than only be angry or piteous like my friend, praise God that He has given you a body that can heal itself so efficiently.

Thank You, God, for giving us amazing bodies.

FEBRUARY 16

Human language is very important. It is the method by which we communicate to each other the information, concerns or emotions we have. We use some words very often, for example, saying *"hello,"* in greeting or *"goodbye"* as we leave them.

In most languages there are single words that can be used to mean more than one thing, depending on when and where it is used. For example, the Hebrew word *"shalom"* can be used when greeting as well as when leaving someone. The same is true of the Hawaiian *"aloha"*, or the Italian *"ciao"* or *"ya'at'eeh"* (yehtaHEY), a Navajo word often used both when greeting or leaving someone.

Most of us take for granted the words we use each day without realizing their root. *"Goodbye"*, for example, is a contraction from the Old English phrase, *"God be with ye."* That phrase would be nice to hear coming or going, but we use it only when going.

God has blessed us with languages. This is especially true when the words tell us of His love for us in Jesus. **"This is love, not that we love God, but that He loved us and gave His Son as the means by which our sins are forgiven."** (1 John 4:10) That is a favorite verse of mine.

Words may also hurt us, but we are blessed when we use them for good. Think of how you are blessed by the words you say and hear today.

Lord, help us use words to build others up today.

48

James, the half-brother of Jesus, wrote, **"Let everyone be quick to hear, slow to speak and slow to anger."** (James 1:19) Some days I have had to remind myself of that verse. Early in my ministry I wrote a sermon based on that verse which was titled, "Listen!" I was surprised at getting some compliments, mostly from women who heard it. I shouldn't have been surprised.

We men certainly can be poor listeners, and not just because we have poor hearing, but because we don't always listen to what others are saying. I once heard something my son told me and assumed he wanted me to fix a problem he had. When I tried, he was embarrassed, and he later told me, *"I didn't want you to do something, I just wanted you to listen to me."* That was a learning moment for Dad.

When a person's hearing deteriorates, older people may try others' patience when they ask for something to be repeated often. Older people ask this, not to criticize how others speak, but to be sure they know what is said. James words, **"Be quick to hear, slow to speak and slow to anger"** are very meaningful then.

Understanding the Bible, which is God's Word, requires careful reading and listening. God doesn't blast His important messages at us, but usually gives them in gentle words or phrases. May we be quick to listen today as we deal with others at work or home.

Lord, help me carefully listen to others today.

FEBRUARY 18

My wife and I were at a small gathering, a party for oldsters, and, as usual, men were in one group and women in the other. All of a sudden there was laughter from the women's group and one of the guys said, *"I think one of us guys is getting talked about."*

A good laugh can help a person's attitude. If we can laugh at a humorous situation or even at ourselves, the heart is made lighter. The Psalms say, **"The LORD has done great things for us, and we are filled with joy."** (Psalm 126:3)

My mother told me, *"Laugh with people, but not at them."* I've also heard it said, *"It's okay to carry on, so long as you don't get carried away."* The joyful person can share that joy. Laughter and joy can rub off onto others.

It's easy to look only at the sorry side of life, at the sourness instead of the sweetness. Our sinful natures seem drawn to the bad instead of the good. But God would have us be joyful, for He has done great things for us. That's the truth, not just some talk.

Jesus attended wedding receptions and probably joined in a dance, and even tasted a little of the good wine He made at Cana. The disciples were surprised that He played with children, because most Rabbis did not. Maybe it's because children are often filled with the most joy.

Like the man said, *"It's okay to carry on, so long as you don't get carried away."*

Thank You, Jesus, for sharing Your joy with us.

FEBRUARY 19

I often spend time in the pharmacy line to get the right things to refill my pillbox. Certain meds are for the morning and others for the evening. Half are prescription drugs with names I can't pronounce and the other half are over-the-counter items, like vitamins or fish oil. Even with insurance, meds can cost a lot.

I used to think my wife took too many pills, but I now take more than she does, so I keep my mouth shut. Regardless of cost, I appreciate getting them because they keep my heart and other things working better.

Each medication has its purpose and each does its own work, but I'm amazed they don't work against each other more often. A retired pharmacist told me many medications "fight" each other, so he developed a company to help people, especially the elderly, make sure their meds cooperated and didn't do harm or cancel out the effects of the others.

Wouldn't it be nice if we had just one pill to fix everything? No more forgetting which to take or when, or having to pay for them. How nice that would be, especially if it was free!

As sinful human beings there is one solution that fixes everything – our Lord Jesus. His death and resurrection cover all our sins, and He has paid the price. Life with God costs us nothing. **"The wages of sin is death, but the free gift of God is eternal life in Christ Jesus."** (Romans 6:23)

Many problems, but just one good solution, Jesus.

FEBRUARY 20

I'm always amazed to see farmland in the desert southwest. Only a ten miles east of Casa Grande are five dairies surrounded by irrigated fields of alfalfa, corn, barley, sorghum and even cotton. Thousands of black and white Holstein cows produce a river of milk, some of which you may find on your own table.

There are even flocks of sheep. They are moved between fields of alfalfa or small grain, nibbling enough to sustain themselves and nourish the soil. Electric fencing keeps them on the field, assisted by the shepherd and his dog.

The church we attend has a shepherd. He came from serving in Hawaii to Arizona, from paradise to the wilderness, and he's been doing a good job of sharing God's Word for those of us who are significantly older than his former parishioners in Honolulu.

"Pastor" is the Latin word for shepherd. A Christian shepherd guides his flock, making sure they have the right things to eat, and working to keep them spiritually healthy.

Have you been fed by God's Word, nourished and blessed by its divine content? Paul told young pastor Timothy, **"You will be a good minister of Christ Jesus, nourished on the truths of the faith and the good teaching that you have followed."** (1 Timothy 4:6)

Recall those who have helped you know God's Word, and give thanks for them.

Thanks, Jesus, for faithful teachers of Your Word.

FEBRUARY 21

My wife loves murder mysteries and reads or watches movies about them all the time. One day I told her we should find another kind of movie, so I found one about the Three Stooges. Sounds fun, right? In it they solved a murder!

If a visitor from another planet read novels in our libraries or watched our television shows, they'd think nobody here dies a natural death – they're all murdered!

Death may be fascinating to some, but it is not so with others. I have worked in hospitals and seen people die and have officiated at a couple of hundred funerals, so death to me has never been fascinating. Its finality, no matter how peaceful, reminds us we are mortals and it comes to us all because of sin.

The only positive thing about death is that it takes us from a sinful world to be with God. God gives us life, but Satan wants our death. Eternal life means being with a caring Creator God forever. But as long as we are here on earth, death is our enemy.

Jesus Christ came into the world to save us from eternal death. Apostle Paul says, **"Where, O death, is your victory? Where, O death, is your sting?"** (1 Corinthians 15:55) Jesus came to give us abundant life on earth and eternal life in heaven. May we always find joy in knowing Him as our Savior and friend.

What a friend we have in You, O Jesus!

FEBRUARY 22

During the 1970s and 1980s, thousands of refugees came to America from Southeast Asia, a result of the Viet Nam war. Congregations all over were asked to help sponsor families or individuals, and my congregation sponsored a family of eleven from the country of Laos.

Ly and Chanh Keohavong stepped off the plane in Fargo with their nine children one cold February day, and the children immediately wanted to know what the cold white stuff was under their feet. The following months were filled with many "firsts": first snow, first big house, big car (station wagon), English school, first shopping for groceries and warm clothes.

One of the firsts for me was the baptism of ten in one service. Chanh had a baby whom I was asked to name. I called her Sarah, and later found they had hoped I would adopt her, a custom in large Lao families.

They moved to New Orleans, and we heard little of them until recently when Sarah, now mother of two, emailed me. We are in contact now and have a nice relationship. Sarah means **"mother of nations,"** (Genesis 17:16) and she is the only child I have named other than my own.

In Isaiah 43:1 God says, **"I have called you by name; you are mine."** In Baptism, God gives us the name of His Son, CHRISTian. Our new name has the promise of a special relationship with God forever. What wonderful news!

Thank You, O Christ, for giving us Your holy name.

FEBRUARY 23

The congregation that sponsored the Lao family also had a member family from Germany. As a son of German immigrants, I connected with them right away. Many were the visits and meals we had with John and Ella Marek and Klaus and Irma, their son and his wife.

For our tenth wedding anniversary, my wife and I flew to Germany, travelling around by train and visiting, among other places, Elmshorn, the small city north of Hamburg, from which the Mareks had immigrated.

Among the many unforgettable sites was the view of Hamburg from the tower of old St. Michael's Church. There we saw photos of the city's WWII devastation, and how it has been amazingly rebuilt. But the effects of two World Wars there will never be forgotten.

Fighting wars began in the Garden of Eden when Cain killed his brother Abel and acted as if he had the right to do so. Sin has brought a great strain on this world through the devastation of war. War can be a just thing if fought to defend the innocent, but most wars come from selfish, power-hungry people.

Psalm 46 says, **"God makes wars to cease unto the ends of the earth."** Jesus says wars will remain until the end of time. Praise God for sending Jesus to give us salvation despite the cruelty and injustice of sinful people. May our earth never again see World War – ever!

Lord, keep war away from us and our loved ones.

FEBRUARY 24

When is it the right time to "move on" in life? About this time of year, we hear that some of our friends are selling their retirement homes here and choosing to stay all year at their permanent residence in another state. Most do so for health reasons or to be near loved ones.

But some move home to make life simpler. Most people move into retirement with goals or plans they hope to follow. If they are blessed with enough funds and health to attain those plans, it can be a joy.

But it can also be a joy to move out of that plan, to stay home and live one's final years in peaceful surroundings amid familiar faces.

In Malachi 2:5-6, God says of Levi the priest, **"My covenant was with him, a covenant of life and peace, and I gave them to him. He walked with me in peace and uprightness, and He turned many from iniquity."** What a great thing that God might say of us.

God calls us into a covenant with Him, so that we will trust Him as our loving God who forgives us and provides us all our needs. When we complicate life with so much stuff, so many plans and so much activity, we may find ourselves lacking the one thing needful, the peace and joy of just trusting God each day.

Life will always have its problems and sad days, but with faith in Jesus, those days need not overcome us. He will be with us always.

Thank You, Jesus, for being with us every day.

FEBRUARY 25

Have you ever had a time when God seemed far away, a time when your faith felt so weak that you wondered if you still had any? Or, have you had times when you were on a spiritual "high" and felt very close to God?

Our Christian faith is not a static thing. It changes often, depending on events that come to us. Sometimes we feel propelled to the heights, and other times we feel robbed of the energy to make it through the day.

Our faith does not depend on our feelings. Feelings can be fickle, whether about people, ourselves or even God. It is far better that we look to what we can know in God's Word, that God loves us and cares for us, no matter what happens or what we have done.

After Moses died and Joshua had become leader of the Israelites, God assured him he'd be up to the task. God told him, **"Be strong and courageous. Do not be frightened, and do not be dismayed, for the Lord your God is with you wherever you go."** (Joshua 1:9)

I have kept those words of promise in front of me during most of my pastoral ministry. Right now I see them at the top of my computer monitor. What God tells us in the Bible is true, so it doesn't matter if we are having a good or bad day. God is with us, no matter where we are or what is happening. He will never leave us nor forsake us.

Lord, help us trust that You are with us always.

FEBRUARY 26

Years ago the residents of Hawaii heard that a nuclear missile was approaching their islands and would be there in minutes. Fortunately it was a false alarm, but hearing this jarred the Islanders from the safety of their normal lives. It took days to shake off their fears.

Similar events can also alarm us. Fires burning homes and mudslides burying people, terrible accidents taking lives and a neighbor killing his family can shake us to our roots.

An aged pastor, speaking privately to friends, related how depressed he was when his native Germany was destroyed by war. He'd been part of the Hitler Youth, but realized he was duped by the Nazis. He moved to Canada, studied to become a teacher but lost interest through fear of nuclear war. He idolized President Kennedy, but was devastated by his murder.

"The music of the sixties almost destroyed my soul," he recalled, *"but God saved me through a Bible verse."* It was Hebrews 13:8: **"Jesus Christ is the same yesterday, today and forever."** Realizing this truth of Jesus and praying for guidance, he became a pastor, serving decades in the Midwest.

We must take care not to be alarmed at world events. Paul said, **"What business is it of ours to judge those outside the church? Be concerned with those inside the church. God will judge those outside."** (1 Corinthians 5:12-13). God knows our needs and will protect us from all danger.

Thank You, Father God, for Your justice and mercy.

FEBRUARY 27

In Herman Wouk's fine novel, <u>The Caine Mutiny</u>, there's a little scene that shows how life can change. A young man from a wealthy family has enlisted in the Navy during World War Two, and the family has begrudgingly accepted his decision. On the day of the boy's induction, his mother drives him there in her luxury car and kisses him goodbye.

As the boy enters the building and the door closes behind him, his mother suddenly worries he will need more money. So she runs from her car up to the door, but is stopped by a guard. She demands to be allowed to enter, saying, *"He's my son!"* The guard removes her hand from the door and says, *"I know Ma'am, but he belongs to Uncle Sam now. He's a sailor."*

There are a number of similar situations in the life of a parent. After graduation, the boy leaves home to be on his own. In marriage, the son becomes part of a new family. True, parents may wish to hold fast to their adult child, but there is also a time to let go.

In a similar way, when we follow Jesus, we are under new authority. We now belong to Him. He doesn't demand or control us, but He is Lord of our life, and we should welcome it. In the First Commandment God says, **"You shall love the Lord your God with all your heart and with all your soul and with all your might."** (Deuteronomy 6:5)

Thank You, Jesus, for guiding me through life.

FEBRUARY 28

Today is the day before Leap Year which comes once every four years and is caused by a wobble in the earth's revolution around the sun. We needn't worry since there's nothing we can do about it, and we humans did not cause it.

I wouldn't be surprised, though, if someone out there will tell us we did. Every day we are warned about dangers lurking around that we've surely caused: global warming, overpopulation, racism, transfats, obesity, cruelty to illegals and transgenders, just to name a few. Many of those are our fault, but most will happen no matter how good people are.

Hearing all these problems, a newcomer to our planet might think life on earth is on the brink of extinction! Not true! People today live better now than any time in the past.

Life a hundred years ago was far worse than we think. War and disease decimated populations and destroyed cultures. Today we don't chop wood, work fifteen hour days or apply home remedies just to stay alive. All kinds of diseases back then would kill us today.

Since sin came into the Garden of Eden, people have lived with danger. The Bible says, **"Trust in the Lord with all Your heart, and don't depend only on yourself."** (Proverbs 3:5)

Rather than living in fear, let's trust in Jesus and let Him carry our burdens. He will bring us safely through life to our eternal home.

Thank You, Jesus, that we can always trust in You.

EVERY DAY WITH JESUS
in *March*

⚜

MARCH 1

An unusual list appeared in the online publication 24/7 Wall Street. It was called, *"The 100 Least Powerful People in the World."* Among the people listed were corporate executives, sports figures, politicians and celebrities, all of which share a common trait – they used to be powerful but no longer were.

Some were victims of circumstances or were ruined by the actions of others. But most of these people lost their influence due to poor business decisions or moral failure. Whatever the reason, these formerly important people no longer seemed to matter.

The Old Testament is filled with names of forgotten kings who failed in their duties, having lost power by disobedience. A few names of failed rulers do stand out, but as examples not to follow: Ahab, Pilate or Herod.

Paul warns, **"Let him who thinks he stands take need lest he falls."** (1 Corinthians 10:12) All people are tempted, but God gives us Good News in the next verse: **"He will not let you be tempted beyond what you can bear... He will also provide you a way out."** Jesus forgives all who have failed in life and need a Savior.

Help us, Jesus, to keep from falling away from You.

MARCH 2

Have you ever been the one in the middle, caught between two others? Perhaps it was in a family quarrel, a work dispute, or trying to keep two people from fighting. Being in the middle can be uncomfortable or even dangerous.

Jesus died on the cross, the Son of God between two thieves, but being in the middle was where He intended. The Holy One was between God and humanity, giving His life to bring people back to God. The *"Man in the Middle"* was where He was destined to be.

Two thieves were crucified with Him, but only one recognized He was more than just a man. Most criminals watch their surroundings, seeing others and what is taking place. Both of those thieves knew they belonged on a cross, but only one realized that the *"Man in the Middle"* shouldn't have been here.

Despite his hopelessness, the observant thief didn't want to die alone. He rebuked the unrepentant thief and reached out to Jesus, the One who did not belong there. Jesus offered him eternal life, and He does the same for all who realize they need His forgiveness.

The Bible says, **"There is one God, and there is one Mediator between God and humanity, the man Christ Jesus."** (1 Timothy 2:5) A mediator brings factions together in peace, and no one has done that better than Jesus. Sin separates us, but the Son of God unites us.

Thank You, Jesus, for being in the middle for us.

MARCH 3

Despite being a fairly level-headed person, there have been times when I've been restless, looking for something else, wondering if there were better decisions I should have made or things I should have done differently. Maybe you've had such times as well.

Just before I retired, my oldest son gave me a birthday gift of a wooden wall hanging. In huge 6" high letters it said, **"BE STILL."** Inside the large letters were smaller letters ones that continued, **"and know that I am God."** I hung it in a prominent place in our sunroom as a reminder of my son, as well as the God we all serve in our family.

The words come from Psalm 46:10. Seeing them helps me to know my need to stop impatiently rushing around, and know God is still with us, in our home and in all of life.

In Hebrew, the word STILL means to cease striving. It's the idea of putting your hands down and letting God intervene in your life without interfering. It's an interesting idea, since we often use our hands to protect ourselves, make things or even push things out of our way so we can live our own way.

But when we drop our hands and let God take over, we learn to trust Him more. Another wall sign says it similarly: *"Let Go and Let God."* Stop struggling and wait on the Lord. In any circumstance, we can know peace through Jesus.

Lord, help me let go and be directed by You.

MARCH 4

If you've ever been to Mitchell, South Dakota, you've surely seen the Corn Palace. It's one of the most unique of that state's tourist attractions. The outside of the huge building is decorated with all kinds of pictures, birds in flight, animals, covered wagons heading west, native American villages and rural scenes.

The pictures are all beautifully detailed, but what makes them unique is that they are all made from seeds – corn seeds and cobs, sunflowers, wheat and other grain seeds and even native grass seeds. These outside wall murals are replaced each year with new pictures and a new theme, in part because the birds land on the walls and eat the seeds.

Jesus told a parable about a farmer who planted seed in a field. Some fell on the road, others among weeds, and still others in dry, sandy soil. Most of those seeds were eaten by birds or choked by the weeds. Only the seed that fell on good soil produced a good crop.

"The seed is the Word of God" (Luke 8:11) Jesus said, and it is the basis of our faith relationship with God. Satan wants to separate us from God and each other. He uses cares of the world, deceit, lies, evil events and temptations to put a wedge between God and each other.

The good soil is all believers anywhere in the world who are willing to trust Him for all that happens in life. The good seed grows abundantly!

Be with us, Lord Jesus, every day of our lives.

MARCH 5

There is a long wooden cedar fence near our Colorado home. It is old by most standards, standing twenty-five or more years. Yet it is remarkably straight and strong, as it surrounds the yard which it guards.

If you look closely at the fence, you can see why. The original upright posts and brace boards are old and weathered, but the fence is strong due to a second set of brace boards next to the old. And on the reverse side you can see square posts holding the fence sections in place, fastened by bolts set in concrete.

Because of the extra bracing, the old fence still stands straight and strong. It would take a big windstorm or a careening automobile to knock this fence over because it has been strengthened by additional materials.

Do you feel some days like a sagging fence? Do you wish you had something or someone to help you be stronger, stand taller or work better than you've been doing?

Jesus told a story about the two houses, one built on sand and the other on a rock. He concluded by saying, **"Whoever hears these words of mine and does them will be like a wise man who built his house upon a rock."** (Matthew 7:24-27)

God's Word is important, but believing it is essential. It is the key to holding up in life's storms. It is never too late to build on Jesus.

Lord, help us stay close to You as we live each day.

MARCH 6

Which do you think is better? Fixing up the old and or replacing it with the new?

After retiring, I bought a new bicycle and enjoyed riding it until one day when I lost my balance and fell onto the street. By God's grace I broke nothing, but the deep bruises moved me to sell my new bike and stick to whatever has four wheels. One wants to ride anything that might break a leg at this age.

But I love riding a bike and a few years later picked up a sturdy old one left behind by someone. The bike was small but mechanically sound, so I gingerly resumed riding. Slowly, of course, and away from traffic.

It was looking tattered, so I put on new tires and repainted the frame. I added a new seat, a basket, a rear view mirror and a bell to tell others I was coming, but it cost nearly $100! Perhaps I should have bought a new one. Then again, my last new bike left me with bruises.

When God saw the earth He'd created, now riddled with sin, He knew something must be done. So He started all over again, sparing only Noah and his family to begin His new world. God's rainbow was His promise never to totally replace the world again. (See Genesis 6-9)

Centuries later God saw the world needed further repairs, so He sent His Son Jesus who tells us, **"Whoever believes in Me has eternal life."** (John 6:47) Jesus makes us new people!

Lord, help us live as Your new people by faith.

MARCH 7

We live in an ever-changing world, and one change that affects people all over is the advent of online shopping. Those with a laptop can enjoy the ease of finding what they want and ordering it delivered to home or workplace. For those who dislike shopping, having items delivered to our doorstep is a pleasure.

This is not an American phenomenon. For many centuries merchants have brought us desired goods from other places, by wagon or freight train. In "The Music Man", the little boy is excited about what the "Wells Fargo Wagon" will be bringing him.

What has God provided for you in His amazing ways? From the fruit of nature to the goods developed by human genius, we are blessed to have so much at our fingertips. If we were left only to our own abilities, life would be much more difficult than it is.

The Psalmist praises God for these blessings, saying, **"You have made people a little lower than the angels and crowned them with glory and honor. You made them rulers over the works of Your hands; You put everything under their feet."** (Psalm 8:5-6)

Christians wait for Jesus to come to this world again. In His grace and mercy, we can all enjoy His new heaven and new earth. Isn't it wonderful to be expecting blessings? What are you hoping will come to you?

Lord, make us grateful for all our blessings.

MARCH 8

Today there is a battery for everything, and many of them are rechargeable. From the tiny silver battery that powers your watch, to the heavy lead battery that starts your car motor, they can be bought at the store or ordered online and delivered to your door. Where have we heard of that before?

Batteries all need to be charged. Their metals and chemicals need to be connected by liquid or gel to generate the electrical power to light our home or power our things. Friends of ours get their power from solar panels and wind chargers. At over eighty years old, they have been "off the grid" for thirty years. Amazing!

Spiritually we need to be connected to God's power grid. Sin has taken away our desire to be close to God, so the Holy Spirit gives us the power we lack. The Spirit's work is to inspire us to believe in God and trust His Son Jesus.

Satan wants the opposite. He wants us to try living off the grid, away from God's power and strength. But our frailties remind us of our need for His power every day. Without God's power, we will fail.

The prophet Samson needed God's power. Blinded, he prayed for strength to conquer the Philistines, saying, **"Please, Oh God, strengthen me just once more."** (Judges 16:28) God heard Samson and gave him strength to show God's power and defeat the enemy.

Lord, give us the strength we need to live for You.

MARCH 9

The angry young man said to the pastor, *"Why should I pray? What has God ever done for me? My whole life has been just one failure after another. If there is a God, He doesn't care about me."*

Have you ever felt defeated by life? Who of us has not felt like a failure? Another relationship goes bad or health fails us again. We make another stupid mistake or we see evil prosper and triumph over the helpless.

In our sinful world it is easy to forget God is still in charge. His ways may clash with ours, but He is still in control.

Jesus told a story about workers in the vineyard who grumbled against their master thinking he paid some of his workers more than they deserved. Instead of remembering their agreement to work for the same wage, they saw only injustice. *"We worked harder, so we deserve more,"* they said. (See Matthew 20:1-16)

But we forget that God owes us nothing. He has given us earthly life and salvation in Jesus. He generously sends us the Holy Spirit to help us trust Jesus and be prepared for eternal life. Yet even the most seasoned believer can become angry and grumble in times of trial.

When times get hard, we must turn our eyes to Jesus and find our strength in Him. The apostle wrote, **"Let us run with perseverance the race marked out for us, fixing our eyes on Jesus."** (Hebrews 12:1-2)

Lord, help us look to You in all our troubled times.

MARCH 10

My first bicycle was a heavy model with no gears. Its big tires helped ride over the pebbles in our farmyard, its pedal brake brought me to a quick stop, and it once took me ten miles to town and back on the last day of school.

My next bike had three gears, and I used them all around college in St. Paul. Years later I was given a big red road bike with fifteen gears, most of which I never used since two or three were usually enough.

Some gears are for climbing hills, some for leisurely riding and others for speed on the road. Although I didn't use all of them each ride, I might need them another time.

The same is true of the spiritual gifts and abilities God gives us (discernment, teaching, sharing Gospel, wisdom, prophesy, etc.) We never know when we will need to use them. But God gives them to us, and they are ours whether we use them often or not.

Paul wrote to Titus, **"Be ready for every good work."** (Titus 3:1) That little thought reminds us we should always be ready to use our gifts, and we can start by learning what they are. We may not use them often, but if we know they are there, we'll be ready to use them when needed.

Jesus' life shows us His gifts. He was a wise teacher, caring servant, loving friend, strong leader and a healer. He loved us enough to give His life to forgive us. Jesus is amazing!

Lord, help me know my gifts and use them wisely.

MARCH 11

People from the Midwest can be known for their pessimism, even when they should know better. One winter Wednesday years ago, we were in the midst of a January Thaw and the sun warmed the air. My secretary returned from lunch saying, *"What a gorgeous day! It is so nice outside."* How did I respond? Like a true Minnesotan: *"Yes, but they say it's going to snow tomorrow."* What a pessimist!

My comment was foolish and ungrateful. Anyone can find something to complain about. But when there is cause for joy, why must we spoil it? Why not experience it?

Apostle Paul wanted his readers to be grateful to God for what He had given them. In his writings he used the word "thanksgiving" 23 times, and we can learn from him about being thankful. My favorite verse of Paul is, **"In everything give thanks!"** (1 Thessalonians 5:18)

Paul's thanksgivings were always directed towards God. He thanked Him for people and their gifts, and he showed God as the source of all blessings. God cares for His creation and does all things for our good.

We may be aware of this but still find some reason to grumble or complain. But think of it - who cares if it's going to snow tomorrow? If today is sunny and warm, let's rejoice in its blessings right now! Pessimism never raises our hearts like optimism does.

Thank You, Father God, for all Your blessings to us.

MARCH 12

Have you ever had someone say to you, *"I don't love you anymore"*? I truly hope you haven't heard or said that. A mountain of hurt and pain can follow those five words.

Such a declaration can end a relationship, break a heart and shatter dreams. Hearing this has caused many a person to lash out in anger or pull back from future relationships, guarding against further hurt.

We know God loves us in His Son Jesus, but could it ever happen that He would say these words to us? Why or how could it ever be?

The prophet Jeremiah experienced these terrible feelings that left him emotionally empty and exhausted. Lamentations tells us how God's people had rejected Him despite repeated calls for them to follow Him. At one low point Jeremiah said, **"My strength and my hope have perished from the Lord."** (Lamentations 3:18)

Yet in his darkest hour, Jeremiah did not give up on God's unfailing love. **"Through the Lord's mercies we are not consumed, because His compassions fail not. They are new every morning; great is Your faithfulness."** (vs. 22-24)

Despite all the unfaithfulness he had seen, Jeremiah's hope remained in the Lord. Such strong faith had been repeated earlier by Moses when he said to Joshua, **"He will not leave you nor forsake you."** (Deuteronomy 31:6) God's love for His people knows no bounds.

Lord, never leave us nor forsake us, no matter what.

MARCH 13

Most people know the story of the Titanic and how it sunk. My mother came to America with her family in 1912 only months after that world-renown incident. I asked if she knew about the Titanic back then. *"Everybody did,"* she said with a note of sadness.

There's another story not as well known. Englishman Mark Wilkinson bought a 16-foot boat and christened it the "Titanic II." On his maiden voyage, he was leaving Dorset Harbor when his new boat began taking on water. Soon he was clinging to the rail of his capsized boat, waiting for rescue.

Weeks after the incident, he told a reporter, *"It was all a bit embarrassing. And I am getting tired of people asking me if I had hit an iceberg."* An eyewitness to his rescue was quoted as saying, *"It wasn't a very big boat. I think an ice cube could have sunk it."*

The original Titanic's sinking shows the danger of misplaced trust. Its designers and builders were certain their ship was unsinkable, but how wrong they were! Jeremiah the prophet wrote, **"Cursed is the one who trusts in man and his strength, whose heart departs from the Lord."** (Jeremiah 17:5)

We are all tempted to trust in ourselves. How often do we need to be reminded not to do so? What happens when we entrust ourselves to something other than God?

Jesus, help us trust You, rather than only ourselves.

MARCH 14

Ever wonder where that new gadget came from or who invented it? Most new things are dreamed up in the mind and then crafted to make life easier or more useful. Some help get things done faster or more safely. I guess I could say I've invented two such things.

One I made to rapidly get rid of a dusting of dry snow on our driveway in the winter. It is tempting to walk or drive on it, but tracks press it into ice, making it dangerous. So I bolted two snow shovels side-by-side, and now my "Colorado Super Shovel" cleans off my driveway in mere minutes.

Another thing I made was a rigid large curved tube to attach to my leaf blower to clean out our house gutters. That makes my wife happy because it keeps me off the roof.

Our mind is an amazing gift from God that can help us create, work and enjoy life. It can also think up ways that are wrong. There's nothing so good that can't be made bad or harmful if our sinful mind is given its way. That's why we need His mercy.

The Psalmist tells us, **"I praise You because I am fearfully and wonderfully made; Your works are wonderful and I know that full well."** (Psalm 139:14) Our minds are the greatest of God's gifts, only surpassed by His mercy and forgiveness in Jesus Christ our Lord. Using them well gives us great blessings.

O Jesus, help me use my mind only for good things.

MARCH 15

Have you ever needed to hide something? That question may conjure up something bad, such as hiding a theft, an indiscretion or some other form of sin. But not all things we hide from each other are bad.

When cell phones were invented, there was a need for many towers to transmit the signals around the world. Such towers were usually not tall, but being filled with so many antennae and wires, they were unsightly, even ugly. Someone came up with the idea to camouflage phone towers to look like trees, church crosses or small buildings that disguise their actual use.

Mike Slattery built a fake barn with vinyl panels that allow the radio waves to pass through them. His efforts eventually turned into a company that builds all sorts of structures to hide phone towers for aesthetic and security purposes. Most of Mike's neighbors have no idea what is the reason for his original barn.

Most of us may try to keep something hidden in life. It may be a harmless basement clutter or a toxic moral or spiritual failure. We try to hide all kinds of things from God.

King David tried to hide his affair with Bathsheba, but later confessed to God, **"Against You, You only have I sinned and done what is evil in Your sight."** (Psalm 51:4) God forgave David, and He will forgive all our hidden sins as well, if we let Him.

Thank You, Jesus, for forgiving and accepting me.

MARCH 16

During my years of ministry in rural North Dakota, I took many long trips over flat roads. Being a young father and busy minister, I was often tired and had trouble staying alert or awake driving, especially at night. Being drowsy at the wheel can be dangerous.

During one night trip I was startled by a flash of brown in front of my lights, followed by a "bump". I had hit a skunk at seventy miles an hour! Fortunately, the car was not damaged, but the smell stayed with me for days. I never bothered to stop and look around. The critter was dead. Needless to say I was fully awake for the rest of that trip!

Apostle Peter said we often may need a "wakeup call" in life when he wrote, **"Be sober-minded; be watchful. Your adversary the devil prowls around like a roaring lion, seeking someone to devour."** (1 Peter 5:8)

His words are a call to look around, see possible danger, and be ready for Satan's attacks. If we are honest about life and have our eyes open, we can see some problems before they harm us or our loved ones.

Jesus knows this and through His Holy Spirit helps us with His Word to stay awake in a world that tries hard to put us asleep. Satan wishes us either to deny his existence or be frightened of him. We must always know he is around so we can resist him with Jesus' help.

Lord, keep us safe from Satan's temptations.

MARCH 17

An amazing invention that affects nearly everyone these days is the GPS – the "Global Positioning System." One of my cars has one built into the dash and my "smart phone" has one that I carry along with me. No matter where I am, that GPS can show my presence. Some GPS systems can even speak electronically to give you directions as you drive.

I must confess, though, that I use a map more often than a GPS. In fact, the only time I don't use a map is when I don't have one detailed enough to show me where I should go. Either a GPS or a map helps me get my bearings so I can know where I'm going on my journey. We all a spiritual map for our journey through life.

Jesus was once telling His disciples that He needed to leave them and that later they would come to be with Him. Thomas, ever wanting to make sure of the details, said, **"Lord, we do not know where You are going. How can we know the way? Jesus said to him, "I am the way, and the truth, and the life. No one comes to the Father except through Me."** (John 14:5-6)

Following Jesus is the surest way to follow God and His will. If we want to know God, we need to follow Jesus. This means trusting that He will take us in the right direction, no matter how difficult that way may seem. When we are following His Son, God is ever beside us.

Thank You, Jesus, for showing us the right way.

MARCH 18

Awhile back I read that Mitch Miller died. To those who may not recall who he is, Miller had a popular 1960's television music program, "Sing Along With Mitch" where his all-male chorus sang beloved, popular songs with the words appearing on the screen so viewers could sing along. Just follow the bouncing ball!

Miller's chorus was so popular because its singers were so ordinary. Miller once said, *"I always made a point of hiring singers who were tall, short, bald, round, fat, however every-day guys looked like."* From such a variety of men came beautiful music in which everyone was invited to participate. I often sang along.

Unity - being together as one – can be a very good thing. Apostle Paul said this was one of the hallmarks of the Christian faith, so he wrote his desire, **"that together you may with one voice glorify the God and Father of our Lord Jesus Christ."** (Romans 15:6) Continuing his letter by citing some Old Testament passages, Paul spoke of Jews and Gentiles being together and singing their praises to God.

That kind of unity has often been considered impossible, or at least unlikely, but God can bring people together, no matter how diverse they may be. We live in a fractured society today, angry and disagreeing on many things. We long for unity, and so we praise God that we can have it in Jesus, His Son and our Lord.

Help us, Jesus, always to agree that You are Lord.

MARCH 19

I love hymns or other good Christian music, especially when it is sung or played well. I especially enjoy the music of the masters who lived centuries ago, but whose beauty still stirs the soul with a lovely melody and a meaningful message.

Music has been around since mankind spoke with God in the Garden of Eden. Today's music is much different from that of Bach or Mozart, Verdi or Puccini. Not many new hymns today thrill the soul like the old ones do. The words may seem poetic, but the melody is hard to sing.

A pastor was surprised when his usually joyful congregation could barely be heard singing a new hymn. *"What happened?"* he asked an usher after the service. *"The words were good, but nobody could figure out the tune,"* said the usher. After singing it a few more times, the members loved their new hymn.

Songs of praise to God are welcome in any age and from any culture. Whether played with instruments or sung with voices, God loves to hear us make joyful noises to Him. Whether old hymns or new praise songs, God welcomes our musical offerings.

Psalm 149:1 tells us, **"Sing to the Lord a new song, praise Him in the assembly of the godly."** God knows our hearts and hears our faith in the songs we offer Him. Jesus sang at home, synagogue and temple. We can, too.

Accept our songs and prayers to You, Lord Jesus.

MARCH 20

The young husband was weary from work and distracted by his thoughts. During dinner his wife told him what happened that day, but he tuned her out, buried in his own thoughts. He was jolted back to reality when his wife squeezed his arm and asked, *"Have you heard anything I've said?"*

Listening is an important part of any relationship, including our relationship with Jesus. He wants to be our friend, and a friend listens when a loved one speaks. He said to His disciples, **"No longer do I call you servants, for the servant does not know what his master is doing. Now I call you friends."** (John 15:15)

It is, however, just as easy to tune out Jesus as it is a family member. Worries and cares may keep us from hearing His Word, and pleasures keep us from seeing Him. Gadgets seem more interesting than someone talking with us, but gadgets get old, or break and run down their batteries. Jesus, our Good Shepherd, wants His beloved sheep to hear His voice in the Bible and listen to what He tells us.

Just as listening attentively to a spouse or child shows we value and love them, paying attention to the words of Jesus shows we value and love Him also. Let's put aside distractions that tune out His voice and drown out His Words. Then let's tune into His message of hope and grace, and pray to Him often.

Jesus, speak Your Word to us and help us listen.

MARCH 21

A small boy was asked to pray at the end of his Sunday School class. His teacher noticed he had not been attentive and thought this would teach him something. Folding his hands the boy thought a moment and then said,

"Dear Jesus, keep us all safe on our ride home today, and keep me and my friends safe playing football this afternoon, and keep my Mom and Dad safe at work tomorrow. And Jesus, You be safe too, because if You get hurt, we're all in trouble, amen!"

That's a great prayer! Although only focused on safety, he included his class, his friends, His parents and even his Lord. That young man may have been paying attention more than his teacher thought.

Can you recall some of the prayers you learned as a child? Have you prayed today about safety, healing or the care of someone? The writer of Psalm 72:15 spoke words that may also be ours: **"May prayer be made for him continually and blessings invoked for him all the day."**

Prayer does more than just make things happen. Prayer shows we trust someone besides ourselves. God likes to hear from us, just as a parent likes hearing from a child, no matter how old or what the concern may be.

Prayer is a show of faith in God. When we open up to Him, He listens. Prayer is our gift to Him, and His answer is His gift to us.

Father, thanks for taking time to hear and answer us.

MARCH 22

A recent new TV program has become quite popular. Jamie Colby, host of "Strange Inheritance", tells stories of people who have become heirs to all sorts of things, from doll and gun collections to tourist attractions and pets, from historical treasures to warehouses full of tractors. She signs off each show with the same words: *"Remember – you can't take it with you."*

How true, and the Bible agrees with her. Apostle Paul reminded young Timothy, **"We brought nothing into the world and we cannot take anything out of the world."** (1 Timothy 6:7) It's so logical, and yet so many of us accumulate, get and hang onto things like they will haul it to heaven with them.

People, especially heads of households, have often kept in mind what kind of legacy they will leave to their heirs. Christians do well if they leave a legacy of faith, for it is of greater importance than a bank account. Faith is something valuable you can leave behind.

There is one vital inheritance we can all keep, eternal life with God because of Jesus. Paul told Titus, **"So that being justified by His grace we might become heirs according to the hope of eternal life."** (Titus 3:7)

All who trust in Jesus as Lord have a precious inheritance - life with Him forever. By faith in Jesus, WE CAN TAKE IT WITH US! How about that for planned giving?

Thanks, Jesus, that we have eternal life awaiting us.

MARCH 23

Carol and I once went to visit friends in Tucson. They'd bought a new house and invited us to have dinner there. We were acquainted with Tucson, but their address was unfamiliar, so I put it into my car GPS, assuming it would take us there by the best route.

Instead, it directed us to go by the shortest route, right through a dense, tangled housing area. Slowly turning this way and that, we eventually got to our destination, but it was confusing. Our friends told us of a better way to travel there next time.

When I don't follow the GPS's directions, it tells me to turn around, or says in large letters, "RECALCULATING" which is a warning that we are going the wrong way.

What does God do when we are going the wrong way? Sometimes He lets us go that way and get into trouble to teach us a lesson. Sometimes He gives us a big warning that we should not go our own way. His Word is filled with such warnings.

David wrote, **"Commit your way to the Lord, trust in Him and He will make it happen."** (Psalm 37:5) Those words are very good instructions to follow.

But even the best student can still make mistakes. Jesus instructed His disciples many times during the years they were together, and when they failed, He gently forgave them.

Dear Jesus, help us heed Your Word always.

MARCH 24

I've had a lifelong desire to learn to fly an airplane, but by the time I had enough money for lessons, I no longer had the courage. I decided to heed a pilot friend who told me that at my age I'd better leave flying to the experts.

I do, though, have some fun with a Flight Simulator on my laptop. With it I can fly several planes all over the world. Best thing about it is no matter how many times I crash, I always walk away unharmed and fly again.

The prophet wrote, **"They who wait for the Lord shall renew their strength; they shall mount up with wings like eagles."** (Isaiah 40:31) The word picture of flying with wings helps us envision how God will bring us to Himself one day. Such a flight cost Jesus His life, yet it is ours free for the asking.

Isaiah also wrote, **"He gives power to the faint, and to him who has no might He increases strength. Even youths shall faint and be weary, and young men fall exhausted."** But we know that by faith in Jesus, **"They shall run and not be weary; they shall walk and not faint."** (Isaiah 40:30-31)

What is making you weary and tired these days? Have you taken on more than you can bear? Are you waiting to get your strength back? What kind of help do you need?

God gives us strength for each day. He will not let us be overcome. He will hold us up.

Lord Jesus, hold onto us in life. Please save us!

MARCH 25

One Sunday at church one of the hymns we sang was, *"Precious Lord, Take My Hand."* Hopefully you know that the composer, Thomas A. Dorsey, was not Jimmy Dorsey's brother, but an African American pianist who wrote it after his pregnant wife and their one-year-old child had died back home.

Dorsey founded the first black gospel music publishing company and was the founder and president of the National Convention of Gospel Choirs and Choruses. He died in Chicago at 93. One of his verses is so very true:

> *Precious Lord, take my hand,*
> *Lead me on, let me stand,*
> *I am tired, I am weak, I'm alone.*
> *Through the storm, through the night,*
> *Lead me on to the Light,*
> *Take my hand, Precious Lord, lead me home.*

There is a longing in most of us to go home, to return to a place where it is safe and we are loved. For the Christian, that home is with our Heavenly Father. There He will take us in and give us all that we need.

King Solomon wrote of elderly life, **"Desire fails, because man is going to his eternal home."** (Ecclesiastes 12:5) We know our life will end, but the Christian wants the Lord at our side, guiding us to the place He has prepared for us. Dorsey was battered by life, but he never gave up his faith.

Lord, help us stay faithful to You, and lead us home.

MARCH 26

"Stay the course!" That was the advice a long-time member gave when his congregation was calling a new pastor. The people had been served by a loyal and caring man for two decades and the Call Committee was taking information as to the kind of pastor the congregation would like for the future. *"The pastor we had served us well, so let's get a man who does likewise. Let's stay the course!"*

That can be good advice unless the old course doesn't work any more. Speaking to the Corinthians, Apostle Paul spoke of staying faithful in one's Christian daily life. He urged the people to live faithfully, not aimlessly, saying, **"I discipline my body and keep it under control, lest after preaching to others I myself should be disqualified."** (1 Corinthians 9:27)

Sadly, I have met some pastors who gave up their faith. Whether by bad decisions, moral failures, overwhelming struggles or giving in to doubts, Christians can and do fall out of faith. Paul tells us he worked at controlling his habits and life so he would not fall away.

Doubt is not a sin, but letting doubt have its way without prayer and God's Word can lead to great sin. Satan works to kill faith in people of all ages. We must ask God for help.

Jesus our Lord took time to pray. The harder He worked, the more time He spent in prayer. That's a good method that will work for us, too.

Jesus, help us stay with You, no matter what.

MARCH 27

In our techno-crazy world, too many of us have become obsessed with our gadgets. If you sit in a waiting room for only minutes and you'll see nearly every one looking at a "smart phone." What do they want to see? Are they expecting an important message?

Nicholas Carr, in his book, <u>The Shallows; What the Internet is Doing to our World,</u> writes *"The sense that there might be a message out there for us is increasingly difficult to resist."* I suppose that's why we can't go anywhere without bringing the internet with us.

But sometimes the message comes when we're not expecting it. Young Samuel heard someone call his name as he slept in the tabernacle near Eli, the priest who was training him. Samuel told Eli he heard a voice and Eli realized God was speaking to him. "(1 Samuel 3:1-10) He told Samuel when it happened again to say, **"Speak, Lord, for your servant hears."**

Are we listening for God's voice in our lives today? Or are we more drawn to our smartphone than to God and His Word? The Holy Spirit can speak to us in many ways, even in our dreams, telling us God's special message. Will we listen, or stay glued to our screen?

Young Samuel heard God's voice often during his years as one of the great prophets. Because he did, God blessed us all. May we also listen for God's voice.

Heavenly Father, help us be alert to Your voice.

MARCH 28

In 1957 our farmhouse caught fire. My parents quickly got my brother and me out of the house, and in less than a half hour, a dozen or more firemen and neighbors were fighting the blaze. We watched them work from inside a warm car. Flames broke through our roof, but nearly all of our house was saved by the prompt and willing assistance of others.

Seven decades later and I can still remember the warmth of the car, the flames on the roof and my mother's tears. Most of all I remember the heavy smoke smell in our clothing because we had to wear what they salvaged for us to attend school the next day.

Gratefully, no one was hurt, most of our possessions were saved, and we were able to move back into our house a few weeks later when repairs were made and the house had been cleaned and painted.

Fire is always a fearful thing. Maybe that's why it is so often used in the Bible as a symbol of the suffering and punishment in hell of those who have rejected God. Jesus said, **"The one who hears you hears me, the one who rejects you rejects me, and the one who rejects me rejects Him who sent me."** (Luke 10:16)

The most serious consequence of all comes to the one who rejects Jesus as Savior. Unbelief separates us from God eternally, but Jesus welcomes us back whenever we repent.

Help us, Jesus, to believe and trust in You.

MARCH 29

It's always tempting to find fault with the Internet. True, it can be abused, but it has many more ways to help us than harm us. One of the good ways is through information we otherwise might never be able to see.

The Dead Sea Scrolls were discovered in the late 1940s and contain the oldest known copies of the Old Testament, written 2,000 years ago.

For decades these scrolls have been guarded and restricted to scholars where they are stored in Israel. But now it is possible to see parts of them online. Google has partnered with the Israel Antiquities Authority to show those ancient fragments online and in high-resolution.

This is good news for Bible students and scholars all over the world. The writings of the Old Testament are part of God's Holy Word, and we treasure them. The Psalmist says, **"I will never forget Your precepts, for by them You have given me life."** (Psalm 119:93)

Reading the Bible is good for us to do every day. It takes effort, though, because there are so many other things that distract us from doing it. I love to read books, but I need to take more time each and every day to listen to what the Good Book has to say.

I do not need to read the Bible in its original languages to know its main message: that Jesus is the Savior God promised to us ages ago in both the Old and New Testaments.

Lord Jesus, help us open Your Good Book each day.

MARCH 30

I'm sure we all know someone who has had cancer. Perhaps you reading this are one of those victims. I have known some who had it and lived decades, while others lived only months after being diagnosed. Some families have a long history of the disease, and many of its members are careful to be tested regularly.

One of my nieces was diagnosed with cancer and yet lived a joyful life more than ten years. As wife and mother of four, Jayne taught public school over thirty years before the disease took her. During her teaching years she rarely missed school and was usually able to schedule her treatments during the summer vacation. Living on a small farm and being a Grandma kept her busy during the summer also.

Some people will complain over a hangnail while others can smile after nausea. Jayne may have grumbled, but few ever heard it. Instead, she joked about losing her curly hair and how she never had to worry about being overweight. I officiated when she was married, and she and her husband enjoyed their 35 years together.

God's Word says, **"Do not think it strange when the fiery trial is upon you,... but rejoice when His glory is revealed."** (1 Peter 4:12-13) God is gracious, despite hardship and disease. He mercifully grants us strength to handle what life gives us. Not all of us handle problems well, but we give God thanks for those who do.

Lord, Jesus, thank You for people like Jayne.

MARCH 31

I read a humorous passage in a book. *"I've gone all day and haven't sinned once!" said the plain-spoken cowboy trying to impress a pretty woman. The girl looked at him a moment and said, "Mister, the way you looked at me a few minutes ago when you walked through that door, I already knew you were a sinner!"*

That girl knows her Bible! She may have had other things in mind with her comment, but what she said is true. Every one of us is sinful, all the time. I don't mean that everything we do is a sin. Of course that's not true. But our whole human nature is sinful.

The Bible says, **"For all have sinned and fallen short of the glory of God."** (Romans 3:23) Because of mankind's fall into sin, everyone born is a sinner already. Sin is a condition that shows itself in wrong actions, and sin can kill us. Romans 6:23 says, **"The wages of sin is death."** That's the truth of God's Law.

Thanks be to God there is more to that Bible verse! It continues, **"But the free gift of God is eternal life in Christ Jesus our Lord."** We've all sinned, but we can all be forgiven by Jesus. His free gift is life with God the Father forever.

Some folks think if they haven't done any evil action today that they haven't sinned. But sin is a condition, and Jesus covers our whole life with His grace. God sees our sinful condition and loves us anyway.

Thank You, Jesus, for loving us no matter what!

EVERY DAY WITH JESUS
in April

❧

APRIL 1

Is the world a better place because you are in it? It's doubtful most of us have ever given that idea much thought. Some may have, especially if they're depressed about life and wonder what's going to happen next.

On the other hand, some may feel the world is privileged to have them. In a "Peanuts" cartoon the ever-confident Lucy declares, *"How could the world be getting worse with me in it? Ever since I was born the world has shown a distinct improvement!"* That's a lofty opinion, but some may think so. The Bible says it is better to be humble than proud.

In his letters, the apostle Peter sought to give people hope as well as help them know how to live Christian lives. He says to his readers, **"Keep your conduct honorable among the Gentiles that they may, by your good works which they observe, glorify God."** (1 Peter 2:12)

If people know we are Christian, they will look for evidence of our faith. If they know little about our faith, perhaps our deeds of mercy, forgiveness and kindness will help them see Jesus in us. We can't change the world single-handedly, but we can make a difference.

Lord Jesus, help us show our faith by our kind deeds.

APRIL 2

"What's going on in our world? Who is doing this to us?" Such questions swirl around like the wind as the stock market bounces up and down. People asked the same kind of questions during the Great Depression (1934), after Pearl Harbor (1941), or when the Twin Towers went down (2001).

What makes our world unstable? Perhaps we should look to see what we're doing to make it that way. People have always sought less troubled times. When peace finally comes, or life is more prosperous, or medicine brings a disease under control, then we feel better. We want life to be more predictable.

King David's reign gave people hope because he sought God's will, despite his sins and the rebellion of his son. King Solomon's reign brought prosperity and peace, but that ended when his government disrespected God. The people then may have asked, *"What's going on in our world? Who is doing this to us?"*

We must never trust in human rule alone. **"Put not your trust in princes, in a son of man in whom there is no salvation."** (Psalm 143:3). Peace and prosperity may occur for a time, but sinful ways always bring back instability.

Rather, we should **"Trust in the Lord with all your heart, and don't depend only on what you know. In all your ways acknowledge Him and He will direct your paths."** (Proverbs 3:5-6)

Lord Jesus, direct us in life and give us peace.

APRIL 3

Every year since 1900 during the second week of August, the tiny community of Britt, Iowa, celebrates "National Hobo Days". It is the largest known gathering of hobos, rail-riders and tramps in the nation.

There is a parade on the Saturday morning where anyone can let their "hobo spirit" soar. It has bands, floats and crowning the Hobo King and Queen. The parade is described, *"Some in rags, some in tags, some in velvet gowns."* While only 75-100 there are actual hobos, spectator attendance is in the thousands.

Everyone is welcome to join in community meals, and nearby fields are open for camping since there are no motels in Britt. The guests of honor need not prove they are hobos, just stand in line for the meal provided by the Britt people and others who contribute.

When Jesus gathered with His disciples on Maundy Thursday, the meal was memorable, not because they were worthy or special, but because Jesus provided His holy blessings in the bread and wine. He said, **"This is my body...This is my blood, do this to remember Me."** (Mark 14:22ff)

Compared with the sinless Son of God, we are all hobos, all in need of cleansing and nourishing. Ever since the night of that first meal, our Lord has blessed millions of hobos who come, *"Some in rags, some in tags, some in velvet gowns."*

Lord, help us see our need for Your mercy.

APRIL 4

Americans have always been shoppers. The things that stores sell and the ways they inspire people to buy are amazing and inventive. The Friday after Thanksgiving has long been considered the first official day of Christmas shopping and recently it has become known as "Black Friday."

Some think it is so named for the color of the sale tags, while other believe it's the first time all year some businesses make enough profit to be "in the black." A year or two ago some stores began holding "Spring Black Friday", certainly to spur on sales as well.

Christians know, however, that there has been a spring "Black Friday" ever since Jesus was here. The Friday He died on Calvary's cross was very black, because the world put to death the innocent Son of God. We now call it "Good Friday" because it was a good day when Jesus atoned for the sins of the world.

Surprisingly, one of the first to realize Jesus was more than just a man was the Roman Centurion beneath the cross. He said, **"Truly this man was the Son of God."** (Mark 15:39)

The Holy Spirit moves people to see Jesus for who He really is. This soldier had seen many crucifixions but in that moment he realized this man on the cross was different. He was no criminal, but someone from God who might bring light into a world of darkness.

Lord Jesus, help us always see You as God's Son.

APRIL 5

Do you buy your drinking water? Here in the U.S., we've been on a bottled water binge for years. Even though most people have a safe supply of water that's free and available from their faucets and fountains, they still buy bottled water at the store.

Paying for something that we can enjoy at no cost makes no sense. Probably some think buying bottled water is safer, or others believe paying for a product makes it somehow superior to water that is free.

This attitude can show itself in other areas of life, including our relationship with God. If we want to be pleasing to God, we think we must work for it, or pay for it. Getting in God's good graces shouldn't be free, we think. We must do something to merit His favor.

God's Word says the opposite. **"The wages of sin is death, but the *free gift* of God is eternal life in Christ Jesus."** (Romans 6:23) Another Bible verse says almost the same thing. **"To the thirsty I will give from the spring of the water of life *without payment.*"** (Revelation 21:6) It's free - Jesus already paid the price.

God loves us with an everlasting love. He grants us such wonderful blessings on earth that it's almost breath-taking. Life on a beautiful and fruitful planet is ours in the midst of a hostile universe. That makes us recipients of the greatest life ever!

Lord, we can never give You enough thanks!

APRIL 6

One of the most embarrassing things can be forgetting an important event, and it happened to me again recently. We'd told folks we'd be attending a church function and forgot all about it. One of the people there said later they expected us to walk through the door all evening, but we never showed up. How embarrassing to have forgotten!

It also happens in my relationship with God. I make a promise and realize after a time that I've done what I promised not to do, or failed to do what I promised I would.

Apostle Paul knew of this frustration. He said, **"I do not understand my own actions. For I do not do what I want, but I do the very thing I hate."** (Romans 7:15) Paul here is speaking of sin, but it can apply to all kinds of failures, including being forgetful.

People may be forgetful, but God is not. He remembers His mercies to us every day, so we must not forget His daily benefits. We may remember certain sins in our past, but God lets go of that sin and gives us another chance. In fact, the Gospel is all about giving us another chance in life. Jesus forgives us, so we have another chance each day.

It's not a chance to be perfect, but to trust Him who was perfect for us. A perfect memory will never be mine, but, **"Thanks be to God through Jesus Christ our Lord!"** (Romans 7:25)

Lord Jesus, thank You for forgetting our sins.

APRIL 7

One of the reasons I love living in our small house each winter is because it is next to a golf course. It's not that I love playing golf so much or love the free and easy life of the rich and famous (haha!). It's because we have a beautiful green backyard and someone else mows it.

I always wanted a lovely green backyard, and God has given us several, But I confess I no longer enjoy caring for it as I once did. A nice lawn means someone must mow it, and lots of trees and shrubs mean trimming and leaves to bag in the fall. So I changed things and now pay someone else do the mowing for me.

Age robs us of youthful energy. Even ten years ago I would never have dreamed of having someone else take care of my yard. But life often pushes our pride aside and replaces it with gratitude.

Pride can be a good motivator, but it can also be a stumbling block. We may believe we have earned all we have, worked hard to deserve it and won it all by our own cleverness. But honesty tells us we've had help. Without God's mercy, we'd have nothing worthwhile. Without Jesus, nothing would really matter.

But we do have God's mercy, and it does come to us through Jesus. Apostle Paul reminds us of this: **"By grace you are saved through faith... It is a gift of God, not of works, lest anyone should boast."** (Ephesians 2:8-9)

Lord, help me boast in what You have done for me.

99

APRIL 8

This time of year we may be thinking of Easter, the high point of the Christian church year. Without having Easter, our Lord's glorious resurrection, we could not have the hope for life now and eternal life to come.

A contest was held for Fourth Graders at an elementary school. All the children were to participate, and the contest involved both physical and mental activity. The First Prize was quite unique – it was the chance to able to compete all over again. The twenty children all worked hard, but one small boy was very motivated. His answers were the quickest and his legs ran the fastest. When he was announced the winner, he jumped up and down and shouted, *"Hooray! I get to try it again!"*

I'm not sure I would have been as excited about that prize, but the little boy was, because he was the winner. When we win, we are excited even if the prize isn't very big.

Paul says that in Christ are all winners. He lists all kinds of things that may be problems. **"Who shall separate us from the love of Christ? Shall tribulation, or distress, or persecution, or famine, or nakedness, or danger, or sword?"** (Romans 8:35) He concludes, **"No, in all these things we are more than conquerors [winners] through Him who loved us."** (vs. 37)

In Jesus we get a second chance. He makes us all winners because of what He's done for us.

Dear Jesus, thank You for making us winners.

APRIL 9

In the springtime of the year, the weather can surprise us, especially in Colorado. The warm sun can melt the snow and turn trees and lawns green, but then it can snow again! We usually return there late enough to avoid spring snow, but every year we usually still get some. One year it snowed May 12th. Springtime in Colorado can break your heart.

But it's not really all that bad because the snow doesn't last long. Give the sun a day or two and it turns that white stuff into water for the soil. And as they say, *"We can never have too much moisture in the Centennial State."*

God tells us in Isaiah, **"For as the rain and the snow come down from heaven and do not return there but water the earth, making it bring forth and sprout, giving seed to the sower and bread to the eater, so shall My word be that goes out from My mouth; it shall not return to Me empty but it shall accomplish that which I purpose, and shall succeed in the thing for which I sent it."** (Isaiah 55:10-11)

There is a great lesson in these words. God sends the earth rain and snow to help it give food to all living things. In the same way He sends His Word out into the world and it brings spiritual life because all people need it.

Jesus is at the heart of it all. He came to be our Savior and forgive our sins. His gifts to us are eternal and give us joy and peace.

Dear Jesus, thank You for feeding us what we need.

APRIL 10

An agnostic and a Christian were debating the central Christian belief that Jesus rose from the dead. As their debate drew to a close, the agnostic gave a lengthy summary of reasons he believed proved his case. He ended, *"So, you can see Jesus could not have come back to life after being dead more than two days."*

Rather than presenting a lengthy refutation, the Christian simply asked, *"What if you are wrong? What if Jesus really did come back to life? What then?"* The agnostic hesitated and said, *"Well, I guess that changes everything!"* How true! The resurrection does change everything! It proves Jesus is who He said He was.

To some doubters in Corinth, Paul wrote, **"If Christ has not been raised, your faith is futile and you are still in your sins...and we are of all people are to be pitied. But in fact Christ has been raised from the dead, the first fruits of those who have fallen asleep. For as by a man came death, so by a man has come also the resurrection of the dead."** (1 Corinthians 15:17-21)

Jesus' resurrection changes everything. After contradicting the Jewish leaders and Pilate, Jesus knew He'd signed his own death warrant. But His resurrection changed everything.

If you've wondered about the resurrection, consider how Jesus' returning to life has changed all of human history, and also yourself. Christ is risen! He is risen indeed!

Lord, help us know that Your resurrection is true.

APRIL 11

When I helped my sons learn to drive, I included some instruction on basic auto maintenance. I stressed the need to change oil regularly because oil is cheap and engine repair is expensive. I showed them how it was done, and later when they each had a car, they showed they'd learned their maintenance lesson well. They both decided to take their car to an oil change shop – wise indeed!

A Christian's life also needs maintenance. Faith does not come with a warranty. It must be exercised through worship of God, praying often, reading God's Word, and doing our best to follow what it tells us. Time spent in prayer may be easy, but failure to do so can result in lost faith which can make one's life arduous and even painful. maintaining our faith is easier than fixing it.

David the Psalmist wrote, **" I will sing aloud of Your steadfast love in the morning, for You have been my fortress and refuge in the day of my distress."** (Psalm 59:16) It is good to begin each week with worship, each day with a prayer for guidance, and each meal with a prayer of thanks.

It is good each morning to read the paper and check email or our financial accounts. It's much better first to pray and read from God's Word. This helps maintain our faith as we navigate the road of life each day. It won't remove all the ruts, but it will make the road easier.

Lord, go with me and help me stay with You today.

APRIL 12

At 6,288 feet, Vermont's Mt. Washington is the highest peak in the Northeastern United States. Although small compared to most other mountains in America, it held the distinction of having the fastest recorded surface winds in the world, a speed that could blow a truck off its top, if it were possible to get one up there.

On the afternoon of April 12, 1934, the Washington Observatory recorded wind gusts up there of 231 miles per hour, making it one of the most dangerous peaks in the world to climb. It would be 62 years before a new record, 253 mph, would be set by winds from a typhoon in Australia. Who knows when another new wind speed record will be set?

Notorious for its erratic weather, Mt. Washington periodically experiences several weather patterns that will come together at the same time, creating a monstrous wind. Some may call this a "perfect storm," but it's really an evil one. It can be a killer.

When several unfortunate events come together in life, we cry for God's help. Within a short time, David was caught in adultery, faced a rebellion, and lost his favorite son. From a cave he wrote, **"With my voice I cry out to the Lord; I plead to the Lord for mercy."** (Psalm 142:1)

Some of us may be caught in a perfect storm, but most of us just get blown around. God is there to keep us from being blown away.

Lord Jesus, when evil winds blow, hold my hand!

APRIL 13

It is wonderful to wake up each morning, living in our great nation. It has its problems, as it has always had, but it is a good country God has given us, and for that we are thankful.

It's also wonderful to wake up refreshed and rested. Last winter my doctor convinced me to use a CPAP machine (Continuous Positive Air Pressure) which takes pressure off my heart to produce adrenalin every time I stop breathing at night due to sleep apnea. I had resisted it with all kinds of excuses, but after a month of enduring the mask, I began sleeping longer and better each night. It feels good to be able to sleep for so many hours now.

We all need our rest. Our bodies usually need more rest than we give them. There is little pride in thinking we need less sleep. If you're always tired, find a way to rest better, even if it means using a CPAP machine.

The Bible often speaks of Jesus going away for rest and renewal. Mark 6:31 tells us, **"Jesus said to them, 'Come away by yourselves to a desolate place and rest a while.' For many were coming and going, and they had no leisure even to eat."**

We've all had times when we're burdened with work or family, dealing with problems each day. But we can still be like our Lord. He took time because it was needed. We all need time to get enough rest for each day.

Lord, help me to find time for rest and renewal.

APRIL 14

One April day a few years ago in Titusville, Florida, a boy saw something he wanted at a store - a stuffed toy. But it was inside a large "claw" machine with other toys, so the boy somehow crawled inside, found his toy and then couldn't get out. He frantic mother called the firemen who quickly came, opened the machine, and got the boy out.

That same year, newspapers reported at least three other cases of small children crawling into those machines to get toys. Why were Firemen called in each case to rescue the tots? Because no one on site had a key!

Many thoughts come to mind here: the urge of a child to possess a toy, the fear of a parent when they feel unable to help, or the lack of something obvious, a key. Gratefully no story has come forth where there was injury.

Children are not the only ones who go to such lengths to get what they don't have. How many times have adults trapped themselves when trying to get stuff? They, too, can find themselves trapped by debt, fear or obsession.

God's Word gives us direction: **"Keep your life free from the love of money, and be content with what you have."** (Hebrews 13:5), **"Do not be frightened, and do not be dismayed, for the LORD your God is with you wherever you go."** (Joshua 1:9) **"Cast all your cares on Him, because He cares for you."** (1 Peter 5:7)

Lord, help us when we feel out of control in life.

APRIL 15

It is "Tax Day" again and perhaps a good time to re-examine our principles. We may do so for personal reasons, but also because we're citizens of our nation.

Equality for all is a good concept but it can be misunderstood. In a scene from the recent movie about Abraham Lincoln, Representative Thaddeus Stevens of Pennsylvania states he did not believe in equality "for all" because that was impossible to achieve. He said he believed in equality "under the law" for all, which gives the groundwork for people to achieve in life as they are able. Equality under the law gives people an equal chance.

God gives us spiritual gifts, but not equally. **"To one is given the working of miracles, to another prophecy, to another the ability to distinguish between spirits, to another various kinds of tongues. All these are empowered by one and the same Spirit, who gives to each one individually as He wills."** (1 Corinthians 12:10-11)

Although God has not endowed all people equally, nations should work to give all people equal rights. This is part of the principle of taxation. Even though paying taxes is rarely viewed favorably, it is still necessary.

The Bible says, **"Pay to all what is owed to them: taxes to whom taxes are owed, respect to whom respect is owed, and honor to whom honor is owed.** (Romans 13:7)

Lord, help us be grateful for living in our nation.

APRIL 16

Self driving cars – are you ready for them? My first car was a used 1963 Ford Galaxie 500, two-door hardtop, yellow with black interior. I drove it for three years and still dream about it. Driving a car is one of life's pleasures. To drive on roads we choose to places we like, alone or with people we love, makes cars a blessing.

Society is now developing self-driving cars. I've already seen a few of the bubble-top sedans in the city, and I'm sure one day laws will mandate this method of travel, removing another freedom for the sake of safety and efficiency, but I've barely accepted the idea of an electric car!

Mankind may develop a car that drives itself, but it can never solve the problem of sin. Humanity has tried for thousands of years to do this and failed. The fallen state of our world needs a divine solution, and God has given it in our Lord Jesus. All other religions depend on humans coming to God, but the Bible tells of us God coming to us in Jesus.

While blessing his sons, old Jacob said, **"The blessings of your father are mighty beyond the blessings of my parents. May they be on the head of Joseph, on the brow of him who was set apart from his brothers."** (Genesis 49:26)

While God gives each generation various earthly blessings in history, His eternal blessings are the same: life with Him forever.

Lord, keep us in Your faith that brings us salvation.

APRIL 17

What are your non-negotiables? What ideas, principles or even possessions are you not willing to part with? Experts tell us we all have some truths or things we refuse to give up. We should check to see if our non-negotiables include anything about God.

I've made myself some promises of things I hoped never to do. Of course, I eventually did them. One was that I would never take God's name in vain. I broke that the day I got beat up by a bully and I cussed at him. A friend said I then started to cry, not because I was beaten, but because I said words I'd promised myself I wouldn't say. Years later he told me he never forgot that moment, although I had. I can recall the beating, but not what I said.

I'm guessing that all of us have abandoned a non-negotiable. When it happens, we must turn to God for His mercy, and also help that when the next temptation comes, we will be more ready for it. God will give us strength to resist.

Some non-negotiables can cost people their lives. Prisoners, even under torture, may choose death rather than give up information or betray a country. The Bible says, **"Jesus spoke not a word"** before both Pilate, King Herod and the High Priest (Mark 14-15). That cost Him His life.

Jesus chose death rather than give up the purpose for which He came, and because He did, we have God's forgiveness.

O Lord, how amazing You died for us. Thank You!

APRIL 18

I saw the movie premier of "The Case For Christ," written by Lee Strobel, a best-selling author and former investigative reporter for the Chicago Tribune. This story chronicles Strobel's journey from atheism to faith. It all started with his wife's conversion to Christianity after a Christian nurse helped them through a near tragedy. Strobel also became a believer as he examined the life of Jesus.

The movie is well written, realistically acted and moves along at a good pace. Gratefully, it doesn't have a syrupy ending as do many Christian movies. It merely presents Strobel's personal journey from unbelief to faith, and lets the Holy Spirit do His work with the audience.

If you have ever wondered about whether Christianity is true, Strobel's books can be very helpful. His most popular works, The Case For Christ, The Case For Faith, and The Case For a Creator, are thorough and interesting, based on interviews with experts in their field.

Apostle Peter urges us, **"Always be ready to make a defense to anyone who asks you the reason for the hope that is in you."** (1 Peter 3:15) Lee Strobel does this in his writings. He is now an ordained clergyman who knows how to explain the Gospel well.

I give both the movie and the book, "The Case For Christ", two thumbs up. Check it out. I think you'll be glad you did.

Lord, help us take care of the bodies You've given us.

APRIL 19

What are we willing to sacrifice for those we love? Would you be willing to move out of your house because you had a bad cold and didn't want to give it to your spouse? I did that for a day or so, and it worked.

Each winter my wife seems to get a cold just before an important event that she's worked hard for, such as a Chorus Show or a vacation. One winter she made it through December and January with no such episodes, but a week before a trip we'd planned, I got the sniffles and cough.

Realizing she would also catch my cold, I moved out of the house. Well, not completely, just into our guest room across the breezeway. Choosing to live apart for this reason was a "first" for us.

This took some adjustment. At lunchtime the second day, I knocked on our door and said, "*Can a poor man have an apple, Mum?*" She smiled and handed me an apple, crackers, chicken salad and more tissue. What a nice lady!

The Bible says, **"When the time was right, God sent forth His Son, born of a woman, born under the law, to redeem those who were under the law, that we might become children of God."** (Galatians 4:4-5)

Jesus was willing to give up His home for a time so that we will be blessed eternally. Now He's back there waiting for us to come to Him.

Lord, thank You for coming to earth to save us.

APRIL 20

When is the cost of living too high? When does it become too much for us to bear?

A certain teenager felt that the cost of living with his parents was too high. They said he had to wear the clothes they bought him, sleep in the bedroom they provided and clean up after himself. When they said he had to go to school, be polite, tell the truth and go to church with them, he argued with them. But still he stayed with them until he graduated from high school.

Later in life he laughed at how ridiculous he had been. His parents never charged him a cent for living at home, because his only cost was his obedience. Even when he didn't obey them, they still didn't kick him out. They just kept reminding him that their rules were meant to help and not harm him.

That's the way it is with our Heavenly Father. The rules He gives that seem restrictive and harsh are given to help and protect us. The Ten Commandments are for our good, not to make our life unbearable.

Some people think the Bible has too many rules. Yet God has told us, **"Be careful to obey all these regulations I am giving you, so that it may always go well with you and your children after you, because you will be doing what is good and right in the eyes of the Lord your God."** (Deuteronomy 12:28)

God's rules are always worth following.

O God, help us to see Your rules as worth keeping.

APRIL 21

In 1852, a young man and a woman leading a horse approached a humble cottage in the Scottish highlands. They had gotten lost on their ride and now a gusting wind and rain had started. The old couple inside the cottage invited them to the warmth of their fire, gave them supper and the use of their on bed for the night.

The next morning the older couple was surprised to see a group of soldiers walking across the fields towards their house. The group commander came inside, saw the young woman and bowing, said, *"Your majesty!"* The old couple, without knowing, had given refuge to Queen Victoria and her husband, Prince Albert who had gotten lost. One never knows who God will send us that might need assistance.

The Bible gives tells us, **"Do not neglect to show hospitality to strangers, for some have entertained angels unawares."** (Hebrews 13:2) God shows us people in need. How shall we respond?

Few of us will ever be called on to help a world leader, but all of us can help someone in need. Most large cities have people on street corners with signs asking for help. We may not always be able to give them something, but sometimes we can. It's good to help if we can.

Helping people in need is what God wants. Whether or not they will use our gifts rightly should not be the determining factor in our giving. God will return our gifts to us.

Father God, help us help others when we can.

APRIL 22

Life can drag us down at times, and we may not be sure of the reasons. Our plans can be lost or we can get bogged down in problems of work, health, relationship or even forces we cannot identify.

Prayer and patience help, but sometimes we need to seek out a qualified counselor, pastor or a good friend who is willing to listen to us and be truthful with us. Perhaps then we can find the source of our struggles.

I've never owned a large boat, but a boat owner once told me how his boat began losing power and acting sluggishly. An examination of the motor and mechanics showed them to be in fine condition. There were no leaks, but the boat seemed to sit lower in the water. Despite being only ten years old, it was aging quickly.

Another fisherman told him the problem was barnacles. The bottom of my friend's boat was covered with nearly half a ton of tiny shell creatures that were slowly weighing down and ruining his boat. Having them removed saved his boat, because the barnacles could have ruined it.

Barnacles are like sins we ignore or deny. Lies, obsessions and evil ways threaten our soul unless they're removed. John says, **"If we confess our sins, He is faithful and just, and will forgive us our sins and cleanse us from all unrighteousness."** (1 John 4:7-8) Jesus forgives us, no matter what we've done, barnacles and all.

Thank You, Jesus, for forgiving me on the cross.

APRIL 23

Despite all of our amazing human technology, it is still possible a problem might never be solved. As obvious as that statement sounds, there are people who believe otherwise.

Last year I directed that a large check from my IRA be sent to our church, but the check was intercepted by someone who deposited it electronically into his own personal account. After this was discovered, it took several weeks for the bank to find out what happened and determine a course of action.

A tech-savvy young man once told me, *"Everything is possible; some things just take longer."* I think he really believed technology could solve anything. However, he was wrong, because he wasn't taking into account the sin and evil which affect our world. Some things are impossible.

Modern culture tries to teach us there is no such thing as sin, just problems to solve. The Bible, however, tells us sin is at the root of the world's troubles. Unless we accept this, we will never understand why things go wrong.

Jesus tells us, **"In this world you will have trouble, but take heart; I have overcome the world."** (John 16:33) Troubles of this world will never go away this side of heaven, but Jesus can and will help us overcome them. As long as we live in this world, we will need Jesus. He alone can give us the strength and solutions we need for each day.

Lord, give us faith to trust You for everything.

115

APRIL 24

Our son and his wife have a new dog that has been trained well. When Papi is given certain commands he will usually do as they want, even when he is tempted to do what he wants to do. They can put a tasty snack near him, tell him "no" with stern voice and wagging finger, and he will sit there, looking longingly at it, but not grabbing the snack. When he hears "okay", then Papi grabs what he wants.

Papi knows he will get what he wants if he waits long enough, but if "okay" didn't come, I wonder how long it would be before his doggy nature got the best of him.

It's a basic human weakness to give in to temptation. We want certain things, and when they're within reach, it's hard to deny ourselves. Our human nature, our impulses fueled by sin, make it difficult at times to say "no". The Bible says being tempted is not a sin, but giving in to doing what is wrong is sinful.

Apostle Paul says, **"No temptation comes to you that is not common to all. God is faithful, and He will not let you be tempted beyond your ability, but with the temptation He will also provide the way of escape, that you may be able to endure it."** (1 Corinthians 10:13)

We all need to follow God in doing what is right. Our culture's morality does not always equate to God's Word. As Peter said, **"We must obey God rather than men."** (Acts 5:29)

Lord, help us to follow You in our decisions always.

APRIL 25

A number of years ago my wife and I visited England for a week. Instead of my usual choice of renting a car, we chose to travel by bus, train and taxi. Our reason? The Brits drive on the left side of the road there, and I didn't care to do it myself. It was a good decision.

About 35% of the world drives on the left side of the road. Why? Some say it came from feudal times to make using a sword easier, as most soldiers were right-handed. Others say it made driving horses and hauling loads easier.

Whatever the case, by the late 18th century, most civilized nations had chosen one side of the road for dealing with oncoming traffic. Today England and most of its former Asian, African and Australian colonies use the left side. If you drive there, don't drive right, drive left!

Driving on the wrong side can lead to injury and death, much the same as going against God's commandments can do. They are given for our benefit and protection.

Apostle Paul wrote, **"For you were called to freedom, brothers. Only do not use your freedom as an opportunity for the flesh, but through love serve one another. For the whole law is fulfilled in one word: "You shall love your neighbor as yourself."** (Galatians 5:13-14)

God blesses us with freedom of choice, but not all freedoms are beneficial. Jesus came to forgive us for our unwise choices.

Lord, help us to see wisdom in Your commandments.

APRIL 26

In America certain days are set aside to observe almost anything. April 2nd is "National Ferret Day" and April 11th is "National Cheese Fondue Day". Today, April 26th, is "National Pretzel Day" and tomorrow, April 27th, it will be "National Babe Ruth Day." Strange!

People usually try to observe their birthday or wedding anniversary, and some Christians also remember their baptismal birthday into the Church. What special days of yourself or others do you like to remember?

History has honored Jesus by dating most modern calendars before and after His birth. "B.C." means "Before Christ", and "A.D." stands for "Anno Domini", Latin for "Year of the Lord." Whether or not people trust in Jesus, most all date their activities based on His birthday, which is a nice way to honor Him.

No one in all history has affected as many people as Jesus of Nazareth. In today's world of seven billion people, about 2.5 billion follow Him as Lord and Savior. They believe He is, **"The Way the truth and the life: no one comes to the Father except through Him."** (John 14:6)

People need hope to live, and Jesus gives us hope for every day. When we follow and trust Him for life, health and daily bread, we are given peace of heart and mind that can come from no other source. Jesus is our Helper, our Hope and our Joy for all of life.

Lord, help us trust You always for all things.

APRIL 27

I like to help keep our house clean and neat, and my wife is glad that I do. She insists on doing the laundry but is happy to let me clean floors and wash windows when needed. Most days I'll put my clothes away, help make the bed and even do the ironing (giving thanks for new fabrics so easy to iron). I don't cook often, but baking a morning coffee cake will earn me a smile. (There's one baking in our oven right now!)

I enjoy a nice home because we didn't have much extra growing up on the farm. We had all we needed, but I always wanted to live in a home that was nicer. Our home today is not large or fancy, but it is so much better than the one my parents had.

Yet they made sure we had essentials and more. They fed and clothed us the best they could, took us to worship God every week, and made sure we had an education. They taught us to appreciate what God has given us and to share with others in need. So much of what I've taught our boys comes from what I learned from my parents. That's as it should be.

The Apostle Paul wrote, **"Fathers, do not provoke your children to anger, but bring them up in the discipline and instruction of the Lord."** (Ephesians 6:4) Despite being the Son of God, Jesus was also son to Mary and Joseph. He is a good example of an obedient child and shows us how to obey our Heavenly Father.

Lord, show us how we can teach our children well.

APRIL 28

My father used to give us boys a haircut with a silver hand clipper. Covering us with a small sheet to catch the clippings, he would squeeze those hand clippers, moving it back and forth and trimming our hair until we looked better. He also used a sharp barber shears and brush. I'm told he put a bowl over our heads a time or two, but Mom put a stop to that saying we looked better without it.

In Junior High I graduated to the barber shop and for twenty or more years was trimmed by men and women with varying degrees of skill. Thirty years ago my wife came home with an electric clipper set and cut my hair for the first time. In remarkably fast time, she became very good. Once again I now have my hair cut by someone who loves me.

The Good Lord gives us all kinds of blessings in life. It may be easy for some to think life is just a lucky string of accidents that work together, but I am certain God has His hand on our lives every moment of the day.

For those who think God can't possibly keep track of us all, they need to consider how even a simple computer can make sense of billions of bits of information. If it can, so can God. After all, He gave us the ability to invent computers.

With the Psalmist we should say, **"I praise You, for I am fearfully and wonderfully made. Wonderful are Your works."** (Psalm 139:14)

Lord Jesus, we praise You for all our blessings.

APRIL 29

Because God loves us, it's always possible to begin again. A young man called Joey joined a gang when he was in the sixth grade and ran away from home. After living on the streets for three years, Joey was able to return home to his parents, but he was not allowed to return to his former school system.

Joey enrolled in a new high school, and a teacher took an interest in him, encouraging him to write about his experiences rather than feel guilty and possibly repeat them. Joey took up the teacher's challenge and experienced a new start in life, excelling in his studies, graduating and entering college.

God encouraged the Jews in exile to think about making a new beginning. He told them, **"Do not remember the former things, nor consider the things of old."** (Isaiah 43:18) God told them to stop dwelling on their past and all that happened back then. While still being captives, He urged them to focus on Him and what He would do for them when they left there and went back to their homeland.

Because God loves us, it's always possible to begin with Him again. With His help in Jesus we can let go of the past and start over by trusting all His promises. Our Lord gives hope to all who trust Him, no matter what wrong road they have taken in life.

"O God of new beginnings and second chances, here I am again."

APRIL 30

A television news report on the problems refugees face told of a family hoping to return to their war-town country. A ten-year-old girl was featured who showed a determination rarely seen in one so young. She said, *"When we go back, I'm going to visit my neighbors, and I'm going to play with my friends. My father says we don't have a house there any more, but I told him, we will find one and fix it up to live in."*

Some might think the girl is living a fantasy, and perhaps she is. But she had a goal, to return to her country and make a home there again. There is a place for determination and tenacity. When our faith is rooted in Jesus Christ and His love for us, we can do amazing things.

Ruth and her mother-in-law Naomi were widows who returned to Naomi's homeland. Although Orpah, Naomi's other widowed daughter-in-law, stayed behind, Ruth went back with Naomi. She said, **"Don't ask me to leave you. Where you go, I will go, and I will live with you and your people."** (Ruth 1:16)

Naomi was determined also. She told her daughter-in-law to find a relative named Boaz and glean his grain field so they'd have food. Ruth did so and God blessed her determination by becoming Boaz' wife. Their descendants include King David and Jesus of Nazareth.

When we trust in our Lord, even the most difficult situations can become a blessing for us.

Thank You, God, for giving hope to Your people.

EVERY DAY WITH JESUS
in May

✤

MAY 1

In past days, May 1st has held a charming tradition. People wrapped flowers in pretty paper, along with a small gift or piece of candy, and hung it on the door of a special friend. While attending Country School in the 1950s, we always brought May Baskets on this day.

It was also a way for a romantic young fellow to let a girl know he cared for her. He would hang his May Basket on her doorknob, knock on the door and run away. If the girl liked him, she would try to chase him down and give him a kiss. If he saw her coming, he would not run very fast.

Awkward scenarios might arise in this custom. In 1889 an unfortunate fellow walked a mile and a half to present his May Basket to his sweetheart, only to find someone else's basket already hanging on her door. This custom is unfamiliar to youth and most adults today.

"God so loved the world that He gave His only Son." (John 3:16) God showed His love for us by the gift of His only Son Jesus, and His Son showed us His love for us by giving His life on the cross that we might be forgiven. God loves us all, and He wants us all in His Father's House. His love is our best gift in life.

Lord Jesus, thank You for Your forgiving love.

MAY 2

What do you think heaven will be like? The Bible gives several word pictures of being with God in eternity, singing with angels, being in everlasting peace and joy, walking streets of gold, and feasting with God and all the saints.

Personally, I think heaven will be like one huge glorious reunion, gathering all those who have departed in the faith, knowing they are eternally at peace and all truly loved by our Heavenly Father.

Before graduating from Concordia Seminary in St. Louis, Missouri, in 1971, nearly all the hundreds of students and faculty participated in a worship service with Holy Communion in the Field House. That day it occurred to me I had attended eight years of college and seminary with most of these men, so I shook hands with my friends as they walked past, going up the center aisle to receive the Lord's Supper.

Realizing this was our last worship service together, I quietly wept sad tears knowing many of us would never see each other again.

Heaven will be a glorious reunion with all those who have departed in the faith. Apostle John saw a vision of **"a multitude that no one could number, from every nation and tribe and people, standing before the throne and the Lamb, clothed in white."** (Revelation 7:9)

We will all be filled with joy that we are there together with no more strife. Wow!

Lord Jesus, prepare our hearts for that glorious day.

MAY 3

I love a good story, especially when it's true. I once got locked in a zoo. It's really true! It happened to me. I *was* locked in a zoo.

During my final year at the seminary, my wife and I took my aged Aunt Marie to visit the Forest Park Zoo in St. Louis. On a pleasant October evening we parked across from the entrance gate and visited the animals about an hour before my Aunt said she was tired.

As we began walking from the far side towards the gate, I noticed no one else was there. We were alone, and the gate was locked!

I saw a police phone, so I called about our predicament. After a few chuckles, the dispatch person told me of the turn style a half block from the gate. When I told of my aged aunt being quite agitated, she told us to wait, that a squad car would soon come. Within minutes, a police car came in the back, lights flashing. And a young seminarian, his wife and aged aunt took their first ride in a police car. Years later my Aunt Marie, then 95, recalled this and said of the officer, *"He was such a nice young man."*

God delivers us from eternal harm and danger when we come to Him in faith because of our Savior Jesus. Life may bring us peril or pain, but it will not last. He will send His angels, sometimes dressed in blue, to help us. That's why we pray the words He gave us, **"Deliver us from evil."** (Matthew 6:13)

Thank You, Jesus, for delivering us from all evil.

MAY 4

It's good that we pray for each other, no matter what the circumstances. This is especially true when it involves our children.

Carol and I attended the weekly chapel service at Christ Lutheran School, Phoenix, where our grandchildren attend and our son and his wife are teachers. Our son Chuck was leading the service with over 600 children and adults. During the prayers, he included a petition for God's protection on those in the northeast who were experiencing an enormous snowstorm that day.

How wonderful that children in sunny Arizona would pray for those children in a Boston snowstorm! I wonder if Bostonians would pray for Arizonans caught in a deadly dust storm which can occur any time of year.

Apostle Paul tells us, **"Pray without ceasing, give thanks in all circumstances, for this is the will of God for you in Christ Jesus. Do not quench the Spirit. Do not despise prophesies, but test everything. Hold fast what is good, abstain from every form of evil."** (1 Thess. 5:17-22)

Prayer is not merely an exercise in faith or psychology. It is calling on God's will and power as we lay before Him our petitions, adorations, confessions or thanksgivings, no matter when offered or by whom. It is invoking the blessings of God through Jesus who has given us life now and for eternity.

Lord God, accept our humble prayers to You always.

MAY 5

Now and then I am still asked, *"How did you know you wanted to be a pastor?"* Every pastor has his story, and most of them show that God works in interesting ways to call pastors. I started thinking about it at a very young age.

Mrs. Emma Papke was Kindergarten Sunday School teacher at our church for decades. A stern and stately widow, she treated us all as if we were her children, reminding us of Jesus' love and our need to follow Him. One day after her class, I heard her tell my mother, *"Robert should become a pastor."* I was six years old.

That made me feel pretty good. Pastors were respected, and I loved to sing and talk, and it was interesting being around people. So I decided maybe that's what God wanted me to do. Family and friends knew this, so they were not surprised when I entered eight years of college and seminary and was ordained in 1971.

There were some curves in the road that made other work seem attractive, but I found true what another pastor told me, *"If you want to do something else, go ahead and try!"*

Amos left his sheep to follow God's call, Hosea had to marry a prostitute, and Jonah ran away. I didn't have to go to such efforts. I just went to North Dakota. We are all, **"A royal priesthood, a holy nation, called out of darkness into His marvelous light."** (1 Peter 2:9)

Lord Jesus, wherever You lead, help us to follow.

MAY 6

The Bible calls God's people sheep, primarily because the people of Israel were so familiar with sheep and the shepherd. Jesus, our Good Shepherd, once told His disciples, **"My sheep hear my voice and I know them and they follow me, and I give them eternal life; and they will never perish, and no one will snatch them out of my hand."** (John 10:27-28)

Sheep are not the only animals God has made to recognize the human voice. Other animals can also learn to recognize it, especially when there is a benefit for them. Consider how a cat may react when it hears the can opener, or the dog's reaction when it hears food poured into its dish.

This can even happen with cattle. As a young pastor in rural North Dakota, a farmer once asked during a visit if I would like to help feed the cattle. On a cold, windy Sunday afternoon, he and I loaded hay on his rickety old truck and drove it through a gate into a vacant pasture.

At least I thought the pasture was vacant. When he started honking the truck horn, cattle appeared from behind bushes, out of ravines and over the hills. As we pushed hay bales off the truck, those whiteface cows and calves came to the farmer, fully expecting food. They would have followed us anywhere for that hay.

So also, God's people will follow His Son's voice to receive His blessings. We know God has blessings for us when we hear His Word.

Help us, Jesus, to hear Your voice and follow You.

MAY 7

Our word, "friend" probably comes from "freond", an old Indo-European word meaning "to love." Friends are wonderful gifts from God. What would we do without them?

One recent week we visited friends we'd known for a decade who had moved to Tucson. Later that day had lunch with other friends we've known for three decades. Then some friends we've known for four decades visited us the next weekend, and we also visited a couple we'd known for only a few weeks. It's great to have friends who care about you!

We all make a lot of casual friends in life, but only a few become true friends, ones who will be with us when we need them in times of joy or sadness, no matter what. A friend will talk with you and also listen. True friendship is marked by willingness to go to any length to help and be with others when they are needed.

1 Samuel 18-23 contains the story of David and Jonathan who were caring and loyal to each other, at times even going against family to help each other. When Jonathan was killed in battle, David lamented and wept over his death, for the Bible says, **"he loved Jonathan as he loved his own soul."** (1 Samuel 20:17)

Jesus loved His disciples the same way and was willing to give His life for them, even those who rejected Him. Jesus cares for us all, and so we say, *"What a friend we have in Jesus!"*

Help us, Jesus, to love others as You love us.

MAY 8

When friends visited us one winter, we took them to see sky jumpers near us. Due to heavy cloud cover there was little skydiving that day.

After lunch at the Bent Prop Café, we decided to check out "Sky Venture Arizona," near the airport with its wind tunnel to simulate skydiving and train people in how it's done.

We watched two to four people move into the wind-powered tunnel, floating up and down, left and right, even flipping over as they learned their moves.

We saw them arch their backs and keep their heads up, relying on small hand or leg movements to propel themselves this direction and that. Merely turning a hand, lifting a leg or arching their back sent them in a new direction.

Our everyday lives are often the same. We are buffeted by social currents and unfortunate events. Minor choices can result in major mistakes. Unexpected events, accidents, or the actions of others can alter our life.

Jesus helps us see what is most important in life, saying, **"This is the will of my Father, that everyone who looks on the Son and believes in Him should have eternal life, and I will raise him up on the last day."** (Matthew 5:16)

God's Word will help us follow the right directions with the right faith in our heart. Most of all, Jesus is ready, willing and able to forgive us our sins when we fail to do what's right.

Lord Jesus, help us follow Your will each day.

MAY 9

One spring after returning to Colorado from a winter in sunny, warm Arizona, we were greeted with a May snowstorm. Heavy flakes dropped for a full day and night, adding their significant weight to the tree branches, already heavy and soft from their new spring leaves.

During the storm two large branches fell onto the roof of our house, each time with a loud 'thud', driving me quickly outside to check for damage. Our roof survived, but one board on our deck fence split when a branch hit it. I might have repaired it with a new board, but chose rather to fix the old one. Using screws, wood filler and stain, I made it look very much like the other aged redwood. If I didn't point it out, no one would know how damaged it had been.

Some storms in life can damage us so badly that we need major repair, but people can be repaired only so far. We can't replace a broken heart or make a crushed dream whole again. We must rely on Jesus then to heal us.

A hymn says, *"How sweet the name of Jesus sounds in a believer's ear. It soothes our sorrows, heals our wounds and drives away our fears."* Jesus can heal us, whether we are paralyzed (Mark 2:1), deaf (Mark 7:31), or blind (Matthew 20:29).

Losing a spouse, a child or a beloved friend may damage us, but our Lord Jesus can put us back together again, for He is the Master Healer of all damaged people.

Thank You, Jesus, for healing all our sorrows.

MAY 10

(for Mother's Day)

Grandma met me at the door. *"Thanks for coming, Pastor, but I'm wondering, how can we baptize them here? I don't have a large dish that's nice enough."* I asked what she used to wash her dishes, and she showed me an old worn plastic dishpan. *"Surely you wouldn't want to use that old thing!"* she said.

It was 1973 and I had come to baptize her two small granddaughters (with their mother's permission, but she was not there). As I watched Grandma clean the pan, I realized she didn't have running water, just an old hand pump over the sink to draw water from a basement well.

Grandma scrubbed the dishpan while I talked to the little girls, telling them what God would do for them in baptism. When the pan was ready, Grandma poured in warm water from the teakettle and put it on the table.

After scripture reading and prayer, I held each little head over the old dishpan and spoke the words of St. Matthew, **"I baptize you in the name of the Father, and of the Son, and of the Holy Spirit."** (Matthew 28:19) Amid tears of joy, Grandma dried and hugged each washed little girl and said, *"I never thought that old dishpan could be used for something so wonderful."*

God's eternal blessings can come to us in humble ways. The forgiving waters of Baptism bless us, no matter how or when the water is applied. Jesus wants us to baptize all nations.

Lord, help us to follow all You want us to do.

MAY 11

A favorite spring flower of mine is the tulip. As it snowed lightly one October day, I thought of a bouquet of tulips my son gave His Mom on Mother's Day, and how the lovely blossoms lasted so long on the kitchen table, opening with the morning sun and closing when it set.

Some plants blossom only with sunlight, such as lilies and tulips. Others open only when the sun sets, such as some varieties of cactus. In one case it's open to receive the sun's life-giving rays, and in the other it's open to trap insects inside the cactus blossom to help pollinate it.

God has made all things on earth for a purpose. He has given us the sun to bring life to all the living, and He has given us His only Son to bring us eternal life.

After Jesus healed a paralyzed man, He said, **"I am the light of the world. Whoever follows Me will not walk in darkness, but will have the light of life."** (John 8:2)

What do you have in your life that needs God's special light of life? Are you struggling with a problem that is keeping you up at night? Are you praying about it? Is there anyone you can speak with about it?

There is no better way to deal with problems than through prayer, and, if possible, speaking to a Christian friend. Jesus will hear us at all hours. As I read on a plaque, *"Pray to Jesus any time because He's up all night!"*

Lord, help me with a special problem I have.

MAY 12

I always wanted to get married and have children, and I am so grateful God blessed us with two fine sons. Born seventeen months apart with personalities as different from each other as two boys could be, it was a challenge to be a new Dad, but as time went on, I learned a little.

Somewhere I found the money to buy a nice stereo with big speakers, a nice radio and a turntable for LPs. (Tape decks and CDs hadn't been invented yet) This new thing in the living room was interesting to two-year-old Chuck, so I set about teaching him not to grab the dials or that black turning thing.

When he reached out to touch it, I said, *"No"* and patted his hand down. He reached out again, and again I said, *"No"* and patted down his little fingers. After my doing this a few times, he left to find something else to play with.

After supper while I was helping with dishes, I heard little Chuck say, *"No"*. He was reaching out toward the stereo, then saying *"No"* and pull down his own little hand, just like I did. He did that several times, mimicking what I had done for him. How cute! But most parenting isn't that easy or cute.

God's Word says, **"Train up a child in the way that he should go, and he will not depart from it when he is old."** (Proverbs 22:6) That doesn't always work, but parents must try. How great to know God forgives parents and kids!

Dear Jesus, forgive us and show us a better way.

MAY 13

Losing a child is devastating. After coming to my first church, we were visiting friends at a small North Dakota lake on the Fourth of July. We'd heard a siren an hour or so before when someone knocked on the cabin door and asked for a pastor. An EMT came in and said, *"There's been a drowning. A couple lost their only son, and they're waiting for a priest to come. I hear that you are a Lutheran minister, but would you sit and maybe pray with them until a priest comes?"*

That was how I met Joe and Martha, a farming couple near our small town. They were in complete shock that their only son, a gentle and obedient teenager, had hit his head on a rock and drowned while diving in the lake.

What do you say in such a situation? I didn't say much, but prayed and shed tears with them, people I'd never met before who needed human care. In the weeks that followed we became friends and a year later, both of us couples became parents, we for the first time, they for the second. Martha knitted us a pink and blue baby afghan that I still have.

Jesus cried when He heard Lazarus had died, yet He didn't rush in with advice, only comfort. We can take a lesson from Him.

Apostle Paul wrote, **"We do not grieve as those who have no hope."** (1 Thessalonians 4:13) Our best words of hope at such a time come only through prayer to our loving and grieving God.

Dear Lord, help us always to share our hope in You.

MAY 14

Stephen Hawking died in 2018 at age 76. This famous Professor of Applied Mathematics and Theoretical Physics at the University of Cambridge, author of several works including <u>A Brief History of Time</u>, had spent over fifty years confined to a wheelchair due to ALS, also called Lou Gehrig's Disease.

The renown physicist was brilliant with his work on quantum gravity and black holes. But like many in his field, he stated he could not believe in a God or any Higher Power.

Despite failing to achieve his life goal, to find a mathematical formula that would explain the origin of life, he held fast to the idea of "chance." He believed that all the workings of the universe came through a process of evolution over massive time in endless space working on limited amounts of matter.

I was a fan of this amazing man, yet I grieved that he could come so close, yet miss the mark. In <u>A Brief History of Time</u> he said there could be only two explanations of the origin of life, either God or chance. *"I cannot believe in God,"* he said. I wonder now if he regrets his choice.

God has said, **"I am the Lord and there is no other. Besides Me there is no God."** (Isaiah 45:5) Mankind's brilliance is not greater than the faith of a child. All of our human wisdom and learning cannot explain life, especially eternal life.

Help us believe and trust in You, Lord Jesus.

MAY 15

Like most young men my age, during the 1960s I took up cigarette and pipe smoking while in college. All the "cool" people were doing it, so I had to join them. My Dad and brothers all smoked too, so it was a kind of rite of passage in our home.

After eight years of smoking, I was a new pastor, married, and expecting our first child. I knew I had to stop, so I went to my friend Roy, a member who'd quit years before, and I asked for his help. He told me to keep carrying an open pack of cigarettes with matches, and when I got the urge to smoke, I should go through the motions of lighting a cigarette, but not do it.

It was a successful plan. I carried that pack for two weeks, then put them in the cupboard, promising myself if I ever wanted to start again, I had to smoke one of those old ones first. Years later I threw the pack out, and have been smoke-free nearly five decades.

Bad habits need to be broken. I had been worried I couldn't write a sermon without a smoke, but Roy said, *"Quit anyway. It's worth a few bad sermons."* God helps us through caring people whom He places in our path.

Apostle Paul speaks to us, saying, **"As we have opportunity, let us do good to everyone, and especially to those of the household of faith."** (Galatians 6:10). Sometimes the best thing we can do for everyone is to break a bad habit.

Dear Lord, help us overcome all sinful acts.

MAY 16

It is very important in life to stand up for what is true, even if others object. It's especially true today when many Christians are told they should follow the world rather than God's holy Word.

In 1999, we visited the Holy Land with a group that included pastors of several denominations, and I was asked by the Jewish guide if I would lead the daily devotion for the group one day. My turn came when we were touring Mt. Carmel where Elijah challenged the prophets of Baal to a duel.

I explained briefly about Baal worship, the Old Testament paganism that required sacrifice of infants to insure they would have a good harvest and better life. I likened it to the practice of abortion which today is most often carried out to make life easier and even for economic reasons. Afterwards, a fellow angrily said, *"Keep your opinions to yourself!"*

It was an interesting response, since it came from another pastor. The world has crept into the church, and it's happening more each day. The Bible is God speaking His truth to us. His gift of life is sacred. To cave in to the world's standards is to risk His anger.

Christ came to forgive sins, no matter who, no matter what. **"Neither do I condemn you. Go and sin no more,"** He said (John 8:11). We know what Jesus wants, but will we do it? It takes courage and faith to follow His will, not our own.

Lord, help us follow ALL You tell us in the Bible.

MAY 17

Today it seems the whole world is on the move. People everywhere are moving to places less crowded with more safety, less strife, and even better weather. These reasons have made people move throughout history. This affects also those who just want to stay put. Immigration is a hot topic today.

In the 1970s and 1980s, American Christians were urged to help resettle refugees. At two Colorado congregations I served, we helped at least a dozen families from Bosnia, Ethiopia, Russia and the Czech Republic. We also became friends with Christians from India, some of whom joined my congregation.

God's chosen people, the Hebrews, were wanderers. God wants us to welcome refugees and offer home and food to those in need.

There can be problems helping refugees, but also blessings. Boaz told Ruth, a refugee from Moab, **"A full reward be given you by the Lord, the God of Israel, under whose wings you have come for refuge!"** (Ruth 2:12). Ruth was blessed, becoming an ancestor of Jesus.

Abraham, Jacob, Joseph and Moses all were wanderers in the land during their lives. It was part of God's plan to provide our salvation. Helping immigrants may show them the light of salvation as they are helped by those who follow the Savior of the Nations. May we never turn our backs on those in true need.

Lord, help us be welcoming to all who seek safely.

MAY 18

I've had so many experiences during my ministry that now bring a smile as I look back on them. Working with the church youth group holds memories of campouts, caroling at Christmas, Bible studies, swimming, meetings, sledding, and also hayrides.

Ah, hayrides! Who but country folk would know what those are today. At my internship church, St. Mark's in Minot, ND, I organized a hayride at a member's farm northwest of town. Two dozen laughing teenage youth loaded up on the hayrack, sitting on bales, being pulled by "Vicar Bob" who drove the tractor.

It was a lovely fall evening and the route was over a few miles of roads, all gravel except for a quarter mile of pavement I had to navigate so we could turn around. All was well until I saw flashing lights from a police car!

On that short section of highway, a police car came up behind us and one of the youth tossed some hay at it. A Justice of the Peace fined me twenty bucks which the youth paid. That's fifty years ago now, and it still brings a smile.

I often look back on life and pray, **"Oh give thanks unto the Lord for He is good! His mercy endures forever."** (Psalm 106:1) If I wrote a book about youth ministry memories, this one would stand above them all. I've had many interesting weddings and funerals, too, but those are for another time!

Lord God, You are so good to us. Thank You!

MAY 19

My first child was born in 1972 during deer hunting season, the time that I shot my one and only deer. My best High School friend Harley had come and said not to worry. He wouldn't get in the way. He didn't, but he did take my deer home with him when he left.

We lived 60 miles from the hospital and my wife went into labor on the opening day of deer season. Harley went hunting with friends, but we went to the hospital where chubby little Charles was born. The doctor told me it was a boy and then wanted to know what was going on in our Lutheran Church body. He'd heard this and that, so before even seeing my son, we discussed the news. First things first!

Next morning, I went out and shot my deer, then drove Harley to Bismarck to see my son and his Mom. On the way home we stopped at Pizza Hut and I wrote my sermon for the next day on napkins. Folks at the church said it was one of my best, but I have no idea what I said.

Harley become a Lutheran pastor, and we kept in close touch. Chuck is a career Lutheran School teacher, father of three, and his brother Brian is a Christian businessman and stepfather of two. I couldn't be prouder of them, their wives and their families.

"Children are a heritage from the Lord, the fruit of the womb a reward." (Psalm 127:3) God's blessings of family can be so wonderful.

Thank You, Jesus, for blessing us with families.

MAY 20

My father's father came from old Bohemia, an area today between Poland and the Czech Republic. Dad's and Mom's families were immigrant farmers who settled in Minnesota. When they married, Mom's Lutheranism eventually won out over Dad's Catholicism, so I was raised in a devout Lutheran home.

As the youngest, I was not the hardest worker, and Dad noticed it. One spring it rained so much he couldn't plant all the crop, so he and I worked whenever it was dry enough. One early May Saturday there were a few acres left to plant, and Dad said we had to finish planting that field no matter what.

I drove the digger and Dad followed with his old planter. We were nearly done when it started to sprinkle rain. Dad looked frantic as he drove those last few rounds, working to get that field done. Mud flew off our tractor tires as we drove the field, but we finished it. As we slid off the wet tractor seats, Dad shook my hand and said, *"We did it, son - Thanks!"*

I think that was my Dad's way of giving me his blessing. He knew I wouldn't become a farmer, but he was always proud I became a minister. Mom was proud, too.

Dad only made it through eighth grade and so he valued education. My parents taught me a lot by how they lived. Both of them were the best teachers I ever had!

Father, give the world Godly parents who care!

MAY 21

May 21st marks a turning point in the history of flying. On that day, Charles Lindbergh touched down at LeBourget Field in Paris, France, at the end of the first-ever solo, non-stop, trans-Atlantic airplane flight.

It was a historic day as "Lucky Lindy" stepped from his plane, "The Spirit of St. Louis" and was greeted by a throng of thousands of admirers. When he returned to America, he was further honored with parades and awards to celebrate his courageous achievement.

While his solo flight was dangerous, living in this sinful world can be far worse. Countless thousands of Jesus' followers have lost their lives for following the man they call Savior and Lord. The blood of martyrs has made the church grow.

On the night He was betrayed, Jesus promised us He would never abandon us. He said, **"I will ask the Father, and He will give you another Helper to be with you forever."** (John 14:16) Because of His promise, we will never have to "fly solo." He will always be there with His protection and guidance.

In our world today, there is much that can fill us with troubled hearts and despair. The Helper Jesus promised us gives us strength to trust in Him and follow Him rather than the attractions of the world. And if we should follow the world, He is always there with His forgiving heart, willing to take us back.

Thank You, Lord, that You pilot us in life.

MAY 22

Many people my age who grew up in rural areas know all about "Country School." For nearly two hundred years, one-room schools built by communities and staffed by one teacher, educated children in the fundamentals. These schools were often rustic, but what they taught was valuable to young and old.

Mine was "Great Bend District Two", a large white wooden structure that still stands northwest of Windom, Minnesota. It is very old, but no one seems brave enough to remove this reminder of older days. Miss Knudsen and Mrs. Fett taught me my first two years, and Mrs. Sylvester was my teacher the last four years.

Christians have always valued education, and many congregations, especially Lutheran ones, have built schools to teach children both the essentials of learning and the message of salvation in the Holy Bible.

Deuteronomy 6:7 says, **"You shall teach My Words diligently to your children and shall talk of them when you sit in your house, and when you walk by the way, and when you lie down, and when you rise."** The Psalmist says, **"Come, O children, listen to me; I will teach you the fear of the Lord."** (Psalm 34:11)

God blesses us with knowledge, especially knowledge of our Savior Jesus. He was the Master Teacher, the Rabbi of Nazareth and Son of God. Every age must learn of Him.

O Lord, help us teach our young about Your love.

MAY 23

Have you ever had a house that has been a "fixer-upper"? I bought one once and repaired it as best I could to make it livable. It had been tagged for destruction, but I convinced a local Savings and Loan to let me buy it and repair it well enough to live in.

I won't go into details about all the work involved, but the end result was good enough (and inexpensive enough) to sell to a young couple who'd just been married. I went back to that town many years later and saw that the old house was gone. I hope the years the couple spent there were happy.

Sometimes people need fixing up. Our bad choices, unexpected troubles or foolish sins can turn our lives into shambles. Dirt and neglect can wreck a person's life. Many years lived badly can wear a person down so that just making it from day to day becomes a chore.

That's when we need a divine "fix-up" from the Lord. It first requires us to make a decision. If our life is out of control, we need to admit it and get some help. This definitely requires God. No life can be changed for the better without help from the Almighty.

God says, **"Call on Me in the day of trouble. I will deliver you and you shall glorify Me."** (Psalm 50:15) No matter if it's a bad marriage, a controlling habit, or secret sins we hold onto, the Good Lord can fix us up.

Heavenly Father, help us come to You when in need.

MAY 24

Sharon decided to get in contact with John, an old friend she'd known since grade school. They'd often spoken by phone over the years, but not for a long time. Calling his phone, she found it was disconnected, and due to their age, she feared something may have happened to her old friend.

Sharon called John's church Diocese office, and though they had no information on him, they suggested she call someone in his hometown. She called the town bank there and spoke at length with its elderly president who'd lived there many years, but he didn't recall knowing John.

One evening a few weeks later Sharon got a phone call, and it was John himself. Hearing his voice she bombarded him with questions, *"Who told you I was looking for you? Who found you? When did you find out?"*

John quietly said, *"I just decided to call you. It's been a long time."* No one had told him of her search, but God knew about it and divinely reminded him to reach out to his childhood friend. It's nice to know that God cares enough to send us small reminders that He's watching over us and providing our every need.

Apostle Peter wrote, **"Cast all your cares on Him, for He cares for you."** (1 Peter 5:7) Do you have a story of God's caring for you? Have you shared it? God's love can bless those who hear it.

Lord Jesus, thank You for caring for us so well.

MAY 25

"She was standing not five feet from me, smiling, and then she was gone," the old man said through watery eyes. *"She collapsed and didn't take another breath. Married all those years and now she's gone. It just doesn't seem possible."*

People often talk of wanting to die quickly, with no suffering or lingering, but we probably won't have a choice in the matter. **"The Lord gave and the Lord has taken away; blessed be the name of the Lord,"** said Job (Job 1:21)

We all wonder what death will be like. Will it be like sleeping and suddenly waking up? Will we see things happening when we're dead? I wrote a Bible Study on Ecclesiastes called The Searching Disciple. Chapter 7:1 says, **"A good name is better than precious ointment, and the day of death better than the day of birth."** The writer, fabulously wealthy, looks back and decides it's better to die to be with the Lord than to struggle with life.

Death is probably like sleeping, then waking up again, all in an instant. Waiting for the end to come can be a struggle, like the weary old fellow who wants to go but knows it's not yet his time. Sleeplessly he prays for death and tries to imagine what it will be like. Then suddenly he's awake in the resurrection with its new heaven and new earth! He didn't even know he'd been gone. And all his questions are already answered!

Lord, give us eternal life through our Lord Jesus!

147

MAY 26

How much should we plan for the future? That question must weigh heavily on our nation if one relies the media. Articles and ads warn us that we must save money for that big event of the future – retirement. If we don't follow their advice, we're not wise, they say. It's as if the main reason we're alive now is to make sure we will be able to prosper in the future.

Planning for the future is important, but more important is the present. God has placed us on this earth to worship and honor Him, serve people and be good stewards of what we've been given. He seeks our faith in Him now, faith that will give us peace today and hope for tomorrow.

A man once came to Jesus asking Him to mediate an inheritance dispute with his brother. Jesus refused the man's request, warning him not to make possessions the main point of his life. He said, **"Watch out! Be on your guard against all kinds of greed, for life does not consist of an abundance of possessions."** (Like 12:15)

We are to use what God has given us wisely, but if planning for the future beclouds our living today in the present, we are being foolish. Like the man who worked his children so hard they missed school and didn't graduate. He said, *"But I did all this for their future!"* Faith in Jesus is most important, for it determines our future. Tomorrow is important, but today is, too.

Lord, keep us from living only for "things."

MAY 27

My wife and I visited the ruins of Qumran, a first-century Jewish community whose people were dedicated to pure living and the copying of God's Word. The people took great care, adhering to strict rules, ritual washings and holy living. They strived to live God's way.

However, they had a rule that cast a shadow on their faith. No one could enter who was lame, blind or disabled. They based this rule on the idea that anyone with a visible physical problem was unfit to serve God. During their meals, work or fellowship, no disabled people were present.

Ironically, this community existed at the same time as Jesus, Messiah and Savior of all people, was inviting everyone into the Kingdom of God. Rabbi Jesus of Nazareth welcomed all people into the Kingdom, even "sinners" and the disabled. He said, **"When you give a feast, invite the poor, the maimed, the lame and the blind. Then you will be blessed."** (Luke 14:13-14)

Who is on your guest list when you have a feast? Only those you've invited before? Or those who will invite you back? God's invitation is for all, especially those who may otherwise be excluded.

Only when people are in the presence of God and able to hear the Holy Gospel can they know of God's redeeming love and the forgiveness of their sins. It is left to us to share that Good News that God loves us, no matter what.

Jesus, help us be kind and loving to all.

149

MAY 28

Don't you just hate to wait? I excel at being impatient better than any adult I know. We wait in lines everywhere, Post Office, grocery store, bank, doctor's office, restaurant, Motor Vehicle Department and traffic light. Sometimes we give up and come back later. Waiting is just too much.

Waiting may be bothersome, but it can also be helpful. I've learned to wait before reacting to the foolish statement or an insulting remark. I've discovered it's better to wait until morning to write that letter of complaint. When someone you love says something hurtful, waiting rather than a quick response is a very sensible thing to do. Reacting too fast can be damaging.

Sometimes we wait so long that we forget what we're waiting for. Jesus told His disciples He would come back again to take them to His eternal home. It's been 2,000 years and we're still waiting for Him to come. But Jesus is true to His word, so we know He will keep it.

Psalm 40:1 tells us, **"I waited patiently for the Lord; He inclined His ear to me and heard my cry."** Proverbs 20:22 says, **"Wait on the Lord, and He will deliver you."** Patience is a virtue, and it will give us greater blessings than a quick thoughtless response.

What are you waiting for right now? Whatever it may be, give thanks that God has given you the time on earth to attain it. He cares for you whether you receive it soon or not.

Dear Jesus, help us wait with hope and peace.

MAY 29

Our English language contains names from many sources. It can be a location (Hill, Moore), vocation (Baker, Taylor), or color, skill, activity and most any other reason. In yesterday's devotion I mentioned "grocery store." This word comes from "groceries," a word for food. But what is the sources of "groceries"?

A thousand years ago, merchants organized caravans, loading beasts with precious goods and protected by armed men. The goods were taken by caravan to other places where people willingly paid for those items they could not provide for themselves.

Fairs and bazaars were held in towns and local merchants purchased large quantities for re-sale. A "gross" was a large number, so the one who had much was known as a "grocer." In time, a "gross" became twelve dozen.

The Christian faith is filled with such words. *"Redeem"* means to *"give in exchange for."* Jesus gave His life for ours as our *"Redeemer."* As *"Savior"* Jesus is, *"one who rescues."*

In Romans 11:26-27, Paul tells us the **"Deliverer will come from Zion,..."** and will **"...take away their sins."** Followers of our Lord Jesus have always used language to describe what God has done for us, and today we strive to translate the saving Gospel of Jesus into as many languages for people and tribes around the world as possible.

Lord, give us people willing to share the Gospel.

MAY 30

Throughout history there have been many people, inventions and movements which appeared to be unstoppable. Hitler's war machine was thought to be unstoppable, and for awhile it was. Communism was considered to be unstoppable, as well as diseases like the plague or polio. Yet today, Hitler, communism and many dreaded diseases are in the waste basket of history.

Numbers 22 tells us of Balaam, a man who thought himself to be unstoppable. He was offered a profitable assignment from a nearby king, so Balaam asked God if he could take the job. When God said no, the king's people increased their offer, so Balaam asked God again.

This time God said yes, but gave him strict conditions to follow. Balaam ignored them, so God has to cause his donkey to stop him from committing sin again. Balaam admitted he was wrong and said, **"I have sinned, for I did not know [an angel] stood in the road against me."** (Numbers 22:34) He was upset he got caught!

Not every obstacle that comes to us is meant to be overcome. Some are placed there by God to keep us depending on Him, such as Paul's "thorn in the flesh."(2 Corinthians 12:7) When our plans are hindered, it may not be from Satan. It may be that God is protecting us from harm. He wants to help us, and that often involves stopping us from doing what we want.

Lord, help me watch for Your direction in my life.

MAY 31

Moving to a new home can be difficult. It's not just selling the old place or finding a new one, or all the packing, tossing or giving away things, or even the dust. We also leave behind familiar places, schools, friends or neighbors, adults as well as children. We may welcome a needed move, but no matter the circumstances, moving is never easy.

This is especially true if we must move where we don't want to go, such as to an assisted living home. Even when we know it is needed, such a move can be painful.

Herman was an old man I worked for while attending college. He'd cared for his aged mother for years, then took in his brother who'd had a stroke for more years. Herman never married. *"Too busy for that,"* he said. One spring I painted Herman's house since his hands shook from Parkinson's. *"I need a new place now,"* he said sadly, *"and maybe someone to help me."*

That Christmas I got a card from Herman with a $20 bill. *"Never paid you enough for that paint job,"* he wrote. *"I sure got it nice now. They make my bed, do my wash, and feed me three squares. I got new friends. God is really good to me here. It's my last place, though. Thanks for being a friend."*

Herman said his "Rest Home" was the best place he'd ever lived. **"Be gracious to me, Lord, for I am lonely and afflicted."** (Psalm 25:16) God's blessings can include a good attitude!

Lord Jesus, give us gratitude for all we have.

EVERY DAY WITH JESUS
in June

✂

JUNE 1

How long have you gone without sinning? That's actually a trick question. Whether or not we think we have had a "perfect" day, seemingly doing all things correctly, we are still sinners because sin is embedded within our human nature. On a day, we may be able to look back and see no bad things, but we are still sinners in need of God's grace and mercy.

Sin is a condition, not a series of things done wrong. Sin came to us by our birth, our origin, and that's why it is called "original" sin. It came from our original parents who fell into sin, and sin has made the world a place of struggles, evil and death. Original sin shows itself in the actual sins we commit each day.

Sin separates us, from God, from the world and from each other. We can never escape the consequences of it, and that's why we are in constant need of Jesus our Savior. The Bible says, **"God made Jesus to be sin who knew no sin, so that in Him we might become the righteousness of God."** (2 Corinthians 5:21)

It may seem cruel or unusual for God to lay the sins of the world on His Son, but it was the only way we can be delivered from our sins.

Father, help us trust in our Savior Jesus always.

JUNE 2

What do you want out of life? What must you do to attain it? Teachers, parents and other adults often encourage children, saying, *"You can be whatever you want in life, even President."* But we know most of our dreams take ability, time, growth and other circumstances for us to accomplish them.

Born in 1972, Elizabeth Ann Carr grew to become a broadcaster, comedian and activist. In her thirties she became an actor and now has a regular role in the TV series, "Silent Witness." This might not be amazing, except that Liz is a very small woman confined to a wheelchair.

A rare illness, Arthrogryposis Multiplex Congenita, has deformed and stunted her body. Despite her startling appearance, she opposes assisted suicide saying, *"I don't think it's in their best interests to enshrine in law the right of doctors to kill certain people."* Those who know and see Ms. Carr perform are amazed and inspired at her strength, courage and capabilities.

Psalm 28:7 says, **"The Lord is my strength and my shield; in Him my heart trusts, and I am helped; my heart exults and with my song I give Him thanks."**

When trouble strikes, it is easy to give up and retreat into the shadows. But God has a reason for our life, and if we seek His guidance, we will find it. What we gain from life may not be what we hoped, but it cans still be good.

Dear Lord, help us see what You want for us in life.

JUNE 3

It is good we have so many English versions of the Bible. Not only do different translations allow for better understanding of the text, they also remove some of the older, more ancient expressions of earlier Bible translations.

One example is the word *"meek."* Some think the word to mean *"weak"* and one popular dictionary even offers a secondary definition of meek to be *"too submissive; easily imposed upon; spineless."* This word is important to me in a personal way since my wife's maiden name is Meek, and she is surely not weak or easily imposed upon.

This kind of definition causes us to question why Jesus would say, **"Blessed are the meek, for they shall inherit the earth."** (Matthew 5:5) Greek scholars state that the "meek" in the Bible is an attitude towards God *"in which we accept His dealings with us as good, and therefore without disputing or resisting."* We can see this in Jesus' dealings with His Father.

Jesus told His followers, **"Take My yoke upon you and learn from Me, for I am meek and lowly in heart, and you will find rest for your souls."** (Matthew 11:29) Jesus was meek because He had God's power at hand.

When we are tired and troubled, Jesus invites us discover the peace and comfort of trusting Him. He says, **"Ask and it will be given to you."** (Matthew 7:7)

Lord Jesus, help us follow You in being meek.

JUNE 4

How much should we plan for the future? That question must weigh heavily on the mind of our nation's people if one pays attention to the media. Countless articles and ads warn us to have enough money for that future big event most of us will face – retirement. It's almost as if the only reason we're living now is to make sure we can live well when we're old.

If planning for the future is the main reason for living, are we not missing the point of life? God has put us here to enjoy our time on earth and be good stewards of His gifts. He seeks our welfare by faith in Him. Trusting in Jesus gives us peace now and a bright hope for the future.

A man came to Jesus asking Him to judge a disputed inheritance. Jesus not only refused his request, He warned him not to make gaining possessions the point of life. He said, **"Watch out! Be on your guard against all kinds of greed; life does not consist of an abundance of possessions."** (Luke 12:15)

We are to use what God has given us wisely, including time to plan for our future. But if preparing for the future overwhelms the present, we're being foolish. Like the farmer who worked his children so hard on the farm that they didn't graduate from high school. *"I'm doing all this for their future,"* he said, assuming their future happiness depended on what they could earn, not what they could learn.

Lord, help us use what You've given us wisely.

JUNE 5

Have you ever been "conned," swindled by someone, and it cost you lots of money? I once sent funds through Western Union to buy a laptop. Money and laptop both disappeared!

George C. Parker was an American con man best known for his successful attempts to "sell" the Brooklyn Bridge. For awhile he illegally sold property he didn't own - Grant's Tomb, Madison Square Garden and the Statue of Liberty. Parker sold them to gullible people saying they could have control to collect entrance fees. Parker "sold" the Brooklyn Bridge several times until he was convicted of fraud and sentenced to spend the rest of his life in prison.

Some people have tried to prove that Jesus was a con man, fooling people for the past twenty centuries. But He had nothing to gain from it. For all He did, Jesus received nothing for Himself except crucifixion.

But we did. Isaiah says, **"He was wounded for our transgressions; He was crushed for our iniquities; His chastisement brought us peace, and with His stripes we are healed."** (Isaiah 53:5) Jesus' work on earth gave Him death, but we are so grateful that He gives eternal life to all who believe in Him.

God doesn't con people. He doesn't have to, because what He gives us can be gotten from no one else. Jesus' earned life with God for all who trust Him. That's a gift we can count on!

Lord Jesus, help us trust You for all that is good.

JUNE 6

There is a lot of mistrust in our world today. Despite a level of safety unmatched at any time in history, people don't feel safe. A question we all must ask is, *"Who is the enemy"?*

I don't think it is immigrants, even the ones who cross our borders illegally. People have been trying to improve their lot in life since before recorded history. Some think our enemy is the one who vehemently disagrees with our politics. But a disagreeable person rarely wants to harm us. Is our enemy the one who wants to kill us? Now we're getting closer.

Our greatest enemy is not human. Rather, it is death itself. Apostle Paul wrote to his friends at Corinth, **"The last enemy to be destroyed is death itself."** (1 Corinthians 15:26) Paul was writing to explain that Jesus had been raised from the dead, and because He had, death had no control over them. Jesus destroyed death's power.

God created the world because He wanted us to have life. His warning not to rebel against Him was to assure our own life. But Genesis 3 shows us mankind chose rebellion, thereby bringing death into the world.

Jesus came to bring us life. He brought back what sin and Satan had taken from us. He gave us life by exchanging His life for ours. That is what redemption means, to give His life so that we can have our life back again.

Lord Jesus, thank You for destroying our enemy.

JUNE 7

It is a custom in most Lutheran worship services to speak one of the three Creeds accepted all across Christianity: the Apostle's Creed, the Nicene Creed and the Athanasian Creed. More than two and a half billion people worldwide now accept the words of these creeds as being true expressions of faith in the Triune God, Father, Son and Holy Spirit. These statements are in agreement with God's Word.

One Sunday morning during a service we attended, the officiating pastor asked that the worshippers on the right side turn and face those on the left as we spoke the creed. I was near the aisle and could see many of those on the other side. It was fascinating!

At least a hundred faces looked my way - round and flat faces, young and old faces, smooth and wrinkled faces, light and shaded faces. Some were smiling and most all were speaking the words of the Apostle's Creed.

One of the first creeds was spoken by Jesus' friend Martha. He'd said, **"I am the resurrection and the life... everyone who lives and believes in me shall never die. Do you believe this?" Martha said, "Yes, Lord; I believe that You are the Christ, the Son of God, who is coming into the world."** (John 11:25, 26) That's a creed!

Seeing our Christian brothers and sisters share these words with us is a rare blessing, one which we might want to do more often.

Lord, help us trust You like Martha did.

JUNE 8

My wife Carol recently referred me to a quote she'd just read, *"Worry is like a rocking chair: it will keep you busy, but it won't get you anywhere."* I don't know if she thought this would make a good thought for a devotional, or if I had been worrying too much. Probably it was both. I do need to watch myself or I will get "needlessly" worried.

Is there ever a time to be "need fully" worried? If worry is used to keep us watchful of mistakes or bad habits, perhaps it is so. Worry is something we are usually told to avoid, but a little worry can be helpful if it will keep us on the right track. But, like guilt, worry rarely stays little; it grows.

Jesus spoke of worry as being anxious about life. In His Sermon the Mount, He said, **"Do not be anxious about your life, what you will eat or drink, nor about your body, what your will put on. Is not life more than food, and the body more than clothing?"** (Matthew 6:25)

"Rocking chair worry" doesn't do much for our problems. In our nighttime prayers, I often pray, *"Bless the hungry, homeless and unemployed"*, and though I've rarely been any of those, I can see reasons for worry by those who have.

Faith in Jesus will help us avoid worry. That is why He ended this part of His Sermon, **"Seek first the kingdom of God and His righteousness, and all these things shall be yours as well. Therefore, do not worry for tomorrow, for tomorrow will have its own worries."** (Matthew 6:33-34)

Lord Jesus, keep the wolf of worry away from our doors.

JUNE 9

I have always used Apple computers. No PCs for me, thank you! Steve Jobs, CEO of Apple, died in the fall of 2011 and he was a billionaire. Here are some of his last thoughts and words:

"I reached the pinnacle of success in the business world. In others' eyes, my life is the epitome of success. However, aside from work, I have little joy. In the end, wealth is only a fact of life that I have become accustomed to.

"At this moment, I am on my sick bed, and recalling my life. I realize now that all of the recognition and wealth in which I took so much pride, have become meaningless in the face of my impending death. You can employ someone to drive a car for you and to make money for you, but you cannot employ anyone to bear illness for you.

"Material things, when lost, can be found, but the one thing, that can never be found when it is lost, is your health and eventually your life itself. Whatever stage in life we are at currently, in time we all face that day when the curtain comes down."

Few have read his words, but it would be good if more did. I would add that health is not as important as our faith in Christ.

He said, **"Ask and it will be given to you, seek and you will find, knock and the door will be opened to you."**(Matthew 7:7) He was not urging us towards more things, but better things. Few people are billionaires, but all of us can be sons and daughters of the King by faith.

Lord, help us always seek what is needful in life.

JUNE 10

To live requires making choices. Every day we must choose what to wear, where to go, what to say, what to do, how to act and whom to trust. The biggest choice we face each day is in our relationship with God. Will we trust Him and follow His ways, or only our own?

During their lives, both Stephen Hawking and Clive Staples Lewis had the same choice we all have: Will I believe in God or deny He exists? Both Hawking and Lewis were born into Christian homes, and both rejected the notion of God in their youth. Hawking maintained his lifelong rejection of God, but Lewis did not.

Reading the Bible, Lewis realized Jesus could have been only one of three things: A Liar, a Lunatic, or the Lord. He said, *"You must make your choice. Either this man was, and is, the Son of God: or else He's a madman or something worse. You can shut Him up for a fool, you can spit at Him and kill Him as a demon. Or you can fall at His feet and call Him Lord and God."*

Lewis chose to believe Jesus was Lord. A blessing we all have from God is His personal encouragement to trust, given us by the Holy Spirit. Through Word and Sacrament, the Holy Spirit urges us to avoid rejecting Jesus and go His way through life, choosing Him.

May we say as Peter boldly did when asked by Jesus what he believed, **"You are the Christ, the son of the living God."** (Matthew 16:16)

Lord, I want to believe. Help when I am not sure.

JUNE 11

When my sons were small, I loved reading stories to them. They would sit on my lap and listen when I read from a book. It didn't matter if it was a new story or an old one, they'd listen as if it were the first time they'd heard it.

Sometimes I would make up stories to tell them, adding funny words and sounds. Then they'd giggle and ask if it were really true. Sometimes they'd ask if I could tell that funny story again.

Have you ever thought of your own life as a story? We all have our own personal story, our memories of growing up with parents, siblings, aunts and uncles or cousins. As you look at your life, where did God fit in? Was He present in your family? Was His name used in good ways, at least most of the time? Does your story include a time when you avoided Him?

Hopefully our story will have some chapters that show we lived our faith and mirrored Jesus to the people around us. Paul urges, **"Show that you are a letter from Christ delivered by us, written not with ink but with the Spirit of the living God, not on tablets of stone, but tablets of our hearts."** (2 Corinthians 3:3)

If you have experienced the joy of a grace-filled life that comes from faith in Jesus, you are truly blessed. If not, there is always time to call on Jesus to help you trust Him. He is always willing to help you write a new chapter.

Lord, help me know You each day of my life.

JUNE 12

What do you think about going to funerals? Do they affect you negatively or positively? All of us are affected in some way, since death reminds us of our mortality. Just as someone has passed into eternity, we know we will also, but we hope it will be a long ways away.

The growing trend of cremation today has changed some things. People are trying to put a more positive face on a funeral, usually calling it now a "Celebration of Life." But no matter what we may call it, it is still a reminder that one day we, too, shall pass.

A neighbor of mine told me of the funeral of her father. She and her mother were practicing Jews, but her father was a Methodist. *"You Christians really know how to do it,"* she said. She related how upbeat his funeral service was, a contrast to her tradition of covering mirrors and having week-long "Shiva" period of mourning. *"It was good to be there,"* she said.

Jesus said to Mary at His tomb, **"Why are you weeping?"** (John 20:15) We all may weep at a funeral, as Jesus did when Lazarus died. But all things change when Jesus comes into our life. When He is there, nothing is the same again. And that's very good!

The fallen state of our world brings us heartache and sadness, but our hope in Jesus is a source of peace and joy, no matter what our emotions may be at any given time.

Lord, help us find comfort when someone leaves us.

JUNE 13

A growing trend in modern literature is the proliferation of "superheroes." Movies, books and comics portray amazing men, women and youth, all trying to save the world. No longer are Batman, Superman and Wonder Woman enough. Now Spiderman, Captain America, Incredible Hulk and various X-Men (and Women) flash across the pages of fiction to solve the world's problems.

It'd be nice if even some of this were true, but it's all fantasy. Superheroes are mankind's invention to give us hope that someone out there will be able to save us from the evil that lurks in dark places nearby.

Some think the biblical Messiah is merely a divine superhero, one who will come to solve all the world's problems and usher in a new age of peace. But the Messiah from God is more than that. He's not just a spiritual Iron Man, He is the Son of God, and He will truly save us from ourselves and all the world's evil.

The Bible tells us we will know the Messiah when He comes. He will show Himself to all people of all times, and all people will see Him. Apostle John says, **"On His robe and on His thigh He has a name written, King of kings and Lord of lords."** (Revelation 19:16)

Jesus, the Messiah of God, will one day rule the new heavens and the new earth. He will reign over all things forever.

Oh Lord, we await Your coming again. Come soon!

167

JUNE 14

A clever young woman held a birthday party for herself and invited thirty of her friends. She requested they bring no gifts, and was very clear that if they promised to attend they'd actually show up. There would not be any "no-shows" at her party. She promised them good food and a good time, so all her guests did come.

When they were all together in a large room, she thanked them for coming and gave each of them a large cardboard puzzle piece with a colorful design and their own photo on it. She then told them to figure out how the puzzle pieces fit. Someone put down one piece on the floor and someone else put down another.

When the puzzle was all together, they could see the designs made a large picture of their birthday friend's face, and each of them was part of it. *"You all make up who I am,"* she said, *"and I want you all to know how important you are to me."*

Jesus gathered His twelve disciples many times, but the most memorable time was when they were all together in the upper room. He blessed them there with His Holy Supper. He said, **"I have earnestly desired to eat this Passover with you before I suffer."** (Luke 22:15)

Every time modern day disciples gather in worship for Holy Communion, they see Jesus in their midst and know they are part of why He came. His loving face sees each of us.

Lord, help us see You are with us in Holy Communion

JUNE 15

It's embarrassing to see the flashing red and blue lights in our rearview mirror, for we know we've been caught! This has happened to me a few times over the years, usually for speeding, but sometimes it has ended with a blessing.

Years ago I was pulled over just outside the small North Dakota town called Oakes, and a handsome police officer came to my window asking to see my driver's license. He took it back to his car and a few minutes later returned with a speeding citation in hand. *"Are you a minister?"* he asked. *"Yes,"* I said, hoping it might help avoid the ticket.

Instead he handed the citation to me and said, *"Better slow down. Say, where's your church and when is the Sunday service?"* I paid the fine, and later received that young man as a church member. I even officiated at his wedding. Sometimes God's sense of humor is easy to see.

Jesus once was caught up in a problem involving a woman accused of adultery. Some people dragged her to Him and asked Jesus what He would do. Instead of punishment, Jesus showed her mercy, and it disarmed all the people. He told her, **"I do not condemn you, but go and do not sin again."** (John 8:11)

Even our most embarrassing sins do not bring God's condemnation. He doesn't approve of sin, but neither does He condemn us. Jesus has already been condemned for our sins.

Thank You, Lord, for forgiving us, no matter what.

JUNE 16

I've usually bought used cars rather than new ones. It makes sense to pay less than the full price of a new one. This has served me well over the years, even though I've bought some new ones.

Buying used means I will need to pay for repairs. I recently bought a low mileage luxury car with a smooth, quiet ride. Its rattle didn't bother me until my trusted mechanic told me what it would cost to repair the exhaust system. I expect there will be repairs needed now and then for my used car, but this one was high.

But who will repair a sin-broken body or a rusted-out soul? Most people wouldn't want to drive a broken car, but they may live with a soul that's barely running. It is tempting to let pass those little sins of pleasure or rebellion. *"Who's getting hurt by what I do?"* we ask, not realizing what it's doing to us.

David thought he could get away with adultery and Peter thought his pride wasn't a big deal. Great people have been brought low when their sins of darkness were exposed to the light. With David we must pray, **"Create in me a clean heart, O God, and renew a right spirit within me."** (Psalm 51:10)

Jesus said, **"I have come that they might have life abundantly."** (John 10:10) His abundant life for us means sacrificing His own life. Our Lord willingly laid aside a perfect, joy-filled life on earth to suffer, that we might be saved.

Lord, thank You for exchanging Your life for ours.

JUNE 17

During the Civil War, Sgt. Richard Kirkland served in the Confederate Army. In December, 1862, at the Battle of Fredericksburg, hundreds of soldiers on both sides were killed, and dozens lay wounded and dying. Kirkland's unit was behind the stone wall next to Marye's Heights. Hearing the cries and groans of the wounded, Kirkland asked for and was given permission to help them.

He filled as many canteens as he could, leaped the wall and gave water to all he could as both sides watched. He also took blankets and warm clothing until he had helped each living person on the battlefield. During his brave actions, neither side fired a shot.

Kirkland showed his bravery at the battles of Chancellorsville, Gettysburg, Chickamauga. and was promoted to Lieutenant. In September, 1963, he was fatally wounded and his last words were, *"Please tell my Pa I died right."* Kirkland was a Quaker.

While few of us will face an enemy on a battlefield, we can still help those around us who suffer loneliness, loss, failing health and sin. Their cries for mercy can motivate us to "jump the wall" and minister to some who need our help. Jesus told us, **"Love your enemies and pray for those who persecute you, that you may be children of your Father who is in heaven."** (Matthew 5:44-45)

Lord Jesus, help us to do so whenever we can.

JUNE 18

It's natural that human beings want to pat themselves on the back for a job well done, but the events held for this purpose often go far beyond their intent. Every year the Academy Awards show (Oscars) is broadcast, it seems more of a spectacle of opulence, pride and politics than a celebration of good work.

Hollywood has changed. Gone are the days of the decent and innocent films, replaced by those with increasingly offensive themes, crude language and blatant, often twisted, sexuality. We're all somewhat to blame for this. Despite our finger-wagging at Hollywood, we still view their products or they wouldn't still be making them.

The words of Paul speak to this: **"Thus God gave them up in the lusts of their hearts to impurity, to the dishonoring of their bodies among themselves, because they exchanged the truth about God for a lie and worshiped and served the creature rather than the Creator."** (Romans 1:24-25)

Though from a past generation, I've tried to keep an open mind, hoping something positive will overcome the negative we see in this trend.

What can we do about this? We can pray and act! PRAY God will keep the devil, the world and our human frailties from overcoming and destroying us. ACT in ways that show our faith in God and resistance to dangerous, evil things. Our Lord will give us strength to do so.

Lord, help us resist what we know to be evil in life.

JUNE 19

Jesus often spoke unnerving words during His time on earth, but few are more so than these: **"Whoever desires to save his life will lose it, but whoever loses his life for My sake will find it."** (Luke 9:24)

I would like to have met Mother Teresa. She died in 1997, but her example of humility and service to society's unfortunate ones continues to inspire people everywhere.

British journalist Malcolm Muggeridge wrote of her: *"There is much talk today about discovering an identity, as though it were something to be looked for, like a winning lottery number. Once found, it is then hoarded or treasured. Actually, the more our life is spent, the richer it becomes. So with Mother Teresa. In effacing herself, she becomes herself. I have never met anyone more memorable."*

I wonder what Muggeridge would have thought if he'd met Jesus. The Bible describes Him as a magnet, either for admiration or condemnation. There was no central position when He said, *"If you want to keep your life, you'll lose it, but if you lose it for Me, you will find it."*

Jesus gave us His all. Some of His men and women may have given Him a lot, but He gave all He had. That is why He said from the cross, **"It is finished."** (John 19:30)

Few of us may be able to lose ourselves completely in His service, but doing as much as we can will become a blessing to all.

Lord, show us how we can give ourselves to You.

JUNE 20

There is no book of instructions on what to do when you suddenly lose someone you love.

The weeks that followed the sudden death of my 37 year-old wife in 1984 were a blur and a terror. Nothing I tried could fill even a little of the emptiness, and looking back now, I can see more clearly my many mistakes. Fortunately, God helped me get past them and accept His gracious forgiveness.

Of all the hundreds of cards, letters and gifts sent by friends and family, church members and neighbors, I remember clearly only one of them. It was a cassette tape of Great Christian Hymns sent to me by a man from our Lutheran District Office. I have since thanked him for his gift of music and told him how important it was. Over the years I've worn that tape out and replaced it with a similar CD which I still have.

Music has great power to move the human soul. It can rouse us to action, soothe our pain and remind us of enjoyable moments. That's why I've always enjoyed singing. God's people have known the power of music. The prophet Elisha once said, **"Bring me a musician; and when the musician played, the hand of the Lord came upon him."** (2 Kings 3:15)

David wrote, **"To You, O Lord, I will make music."** (Psalm 101:1) You and I are blessed when God's great music helps us look past the troubles of the world to His grace and see His mercy.

Lord, help us treasure the music You give us.

JUNE 21
(Part One)

We hear a lot about "unconditional love" these days, but I'm not sure most people realize what that term means. "Unconditional love" means loving or having affection for a person without any limits or conditions.

An example might be a parent's love for a child. No matter if the child's test score is disappointing, his decision is disagreeable, her argument is irrational, or his strong belief is dangerous, the amount of love from the parent is unchanging and thus unconditional.

Have you ever tried to love someone this way? Is there someone to whom you are so devoted? Is it not possible that our loved one can still do or say something that breaks the unconditional nature of our love?

Of course there is. Trust is not infinite. Human disappointment is not without limits. Only God in His divine and infinite power can have true unconditional love for a sinful human being. Only He can withstand the sadness and disappointment that can arise in a relationship.

Consider Jesus' love: **"He was wounded for our sins, He was bruised for our evil deeds. He endured the penalties we deserved, and with His punishment we are healed. We all like sheep have gone our own way, but God has placed on Him the sins of us all."** (Isaiah 53:5)

People will have their limits on love, but God doesn't. He cares for us, no matter what.

Jesus, how can You love sinful people? Thank You!

JUNE 22

(Part Two)

There is more to say about unconditional love. While actually having this love is very difficult, it is not impossible.

Consider the husband whose comatose wife lies unresponsive in her bed. While a stroke has rendered her helpless in mind and body, he has now become her mind and body. Daily he cares for her needs and makes all her decisions.

Or the wife whose barely responsive husband is in the nursing home, yet she comes every day to feed him, help clothe him and give him words of love and encouragement.

Or the parents whose child is born without a full brain and yet they watch over that child's every need, medically and personally, as if the child understands, although it cannot. We've all known of such people and perhaps have been part of the life of one who will never be able to live independently of us.

The Bible says, **"In this is love, not that we love God, but that He loved us and gave His Son as the means of our forgiveness."** (1 John 4:10) This is the source of any human capacity to show unconditional love. God loved us and gave us the powerful gift to love others.

The apostle continued in his letter, **"We love because He first loved us."** (1 John 4:19) Is not His love the source of any unconditional love? God showed us the way, and His Holy Spirit gives us the power. He will not fail us.

Lord, help us love unconditionally, as You love us.

JUNE 23
(Part Three)

There's third thing about unconditional love. What if you feel you can't do it?

What if you've been tested to your limits to show love and feel you've failed? What if you just can't visit that Nursing Home another time? What if you've run away from that loved one? What if you're too angry at God for giving you a love burden so big to bear?

Sometimes the straying spouse does the unforgiveable. Sometimes the rebellious teen goes too far. Sometimes the addict disappoints too much. Sometimes you just don't have it in your heart to give another chance. Sometimes you feel you're the failure. What then?

Just remember that you're not facing this alone. God will help you. Remember this verse? **"No temptation has overtaken you that is not common to all. God is faithful and He will not let you be tempted beyond your ability, but with the temptation He will also provide you the way to escape it."** (1 Corinthians 10:13)

Now change some words: **"No <u>problem</u> has overtaken you that is not common to all. God is faithful and He will not let <u>that problem</u> go beyond your ability, but with the <u>problem</u> He will also provide you a way to escape it."**

Lots of people have felt some task is too big to bear. God promises to give us strength to bear it or ways to deal with it. He stands behind His promises! He love us, and He forgives!

Jesus, help us bear our burdens with Your strength.

JUNE 24

On March 1, 1981, Rev. Martyn Lloyd-Jones lay on his deathbed. For the past twenty-nine years he had been pastor of Westminster Chapel in London. Though he'd been a dynamic preacher of the Gospel, now at the of his life he had lost the ability to speak.

People said they would pray for him, but he asked them not to. Wishing no further recovery, he wrote on a piece of paper, *"Do not hold me back from glory."* He just wanted to be with Jesus.

Life is precious, isn't it? It can be hard to let go of life, whether that of a loved one or our own. We live our years as though they will never end, but we know they will. God has set a time when He plans to call us home. The wise Psalmist says, **"Precious in the sight of the Lord is the death of His saints."** (Psalm 116:15)

What? Death is precious? I thought it was the final enemy! (read June 6 again) Which is it? Is death an enemy or can it be good?

When Paul saw that his death was hear, he was actually encouraged by what awaited him. He said, **"There is laid up for me the crown of righteousness which the Lord...will give to me on that day."** (2 Timothy 4:8)

Paul knew death was the beginning of his new life with God. No matter where we are on life's journey, our ultimate destination is **"to be with Christ, which is far better."** (Philippians 1:23) Does that make it more clear?

Thank You, Jesus, for giving us hope for a new life.

JUNE 25

During the Great Depression, millions of people needed work and income. One church sponsored a group to help the people cope. They gave out some small financial aid, but more than that, they offered helpful hints on how to find work. They discussed where to look and who to know. Especially they told them to pray, for themselves and for each other.

A problem came up, however. Whenever someone got a job, he or she never returned to the group with good news, or offered others the encouragement they'd received. Those who did not find work felt isolated and lonely.

We must take care not to make things worse by giving unwanted advise. The Apostle Peter wrote, **"Always be ready to tell anyone who asks you for a reason for the hope that you have. But do so with gentleness."** (1 Peter 3:15) Gentle encouragement is always welcome.

When things are going well for us, we may think we don't have troubles, or that we're better off because God is smiling on us. We may even think God loves us more than others!

But we are all loved by God, in good times or in bad. Our success or abundance are not indicators of more love from God, but they may be His way of moving us to help others. Sometimes our greatest encouragement is given not by our words, but by our actions. When we share of our bounty, God's love is also shared.

Lord Jesus, help us give as we have been given.

JUNE 26

It's human nature to want to blame someone else for our problems. If we're sick, we look for a cause, if we're hurt we want to know who did it, or if we're angry, sad or miserable, we want to know who is to blame.

But the fault may lie with ourselves. A little boy rides his bike on the sidewalk and runs into his house. He tries again a second and a third time, hitting the house each time. Amid scraped knees and a dirty face, he tearfully says, *"Why did you put the house there?"*

People often need pain and bruises to learn to follow God. Samson was born to be a Nazirite, dedicated to serving the Lord. He was warned not to drink alcohol, touch unclean things or cut his hair. But he fell to temptation, blaming his sins on seductive women.

When Samson was captured, he realized it was his own fault, and so he prayed, **"O Lord, please remember me and strengthen me, O God, only this once more."** (Judges 16:28) It cost Samson his life to learn not to disobey God.

Rationalizing bad behavior will not make it good, and blaming our sins on others will not remove our own guilt. We are responsible for what we do, so we must accept our part in what happens to us. It's a fact of life.

Jesus took His place on the cross that we might be forgiven. His forgiveness is a new start in life. He always give us another chance.

Lord, accept me always, especially when I sin.

JUNE 27

Ever since the Rockies Baseball Club came to Denver in 1993, I've been a fan. We were able to get two good infield seats for ten home games each year. It's always fun to go to Coors Field, even when they lose. If the game is close, I may get a bit nervous and get up and move around. If they win, it makes me happy. The tension is all part of the fun of baseball.

Recently, though, I watched a game we played in the 2007 World Series. I was surprised at how much calmer I was watching it. Why? Because I already knew the outcome. The Red Sox beat us in four straight games, so the suspense of the game didn't bother me. It was so relaxing that I fell asleep in my recliner watching it. But it was still fun to watch.

Life can be like this. There can be surprises and shocks, fears and frustration, high points and low points, mostly because we don't know what will happen yet. But when we remind ourselves we are safe from eternal danger because of Jesus, we can take comfort, even in the midst of our struggles.

Apostle John wrote, **"These things I have written to you who believe on the name of the Son of God, that you may know you have eternal life."** (1 John 5:13) Life may give us lots of surprises, but with faith in Jesus, we can have peace each day. Jesus has already shown us our eternal outcome in heaven.

Thank You, Jesus, for giving us Your peace.

JUNE 28

No matter how careful I am writing or how many times I have it proof-read, mistakes still show up. Seeing a forgotten, misplaced or incorrect word is irritating, especially if I have already published those words and know others may see them. But they're my words and my mistakes, so I take responsibility for them.

I've been told by experienced writers that no matter how many times you go over a manuscript, mistakes will be found, so don't lost sleep over it. Just do your best and hope others will enjoy what you've put into print.

After all, with seven billion people in the world, published writers are a tiny minority. With my Christian writings I follow the axiom, *"Do your best and let God take care of the rest."* That's actually good advice to follow in the rest of life, as well.

People love to think we can do something perfectly. But what is perfection? Is it not tomorrow's boredom? Didn't Rembrandt keep painting after finishing a masterpiece? Didn't Bach compose music till the day he died?

Jesus said, **"You are the salt of the earth... you are the light of the world... Let your light shine before others that they may see your good works and give glory to your Father in heaven."** (Matthew 5:13-16)

Our lights shine because God gives us His light. Hiding our light helps no one. Let it shine!

Lord, help me to live Your Gospel each day of my life.

JUNE 29

At one time I was an avid camper and enjoyed using (and fixing) our vintage 1964 Airstream trailer over twenty years. Before the "Silver Twinkie", I had a flip-up trailer and before that a tent. No matter what form my camping took, however, I always had along my Swiss Army Knife.

Karl Elsner, designer of surgical equipment, worked years perfecting a knife for the military. His Swiss Army Knife included a knife blade, saw, scissors, magnifying glass, can opener, screw driver, ruler, toothpick, writing pen and more. The Swiss Army Knife in itself can help the camper be equipped for survival.

We all need equipment to help us in life, especially our spiritual life. The Bible is God's true, inspired Word and contains all that is needed to take us through the world with its turmoil and trouble, joys and triumphs.

Paul wrote young pastor Timothy, **"All Scripture is given by inspiration of God, and is profitable for teaching, reproof, correction and instruction in righteousness, that God's people may be complete and thoroughly equipped for every good work."** (2 Timothy 3:16-17)

"Equipped" here means to *"furnish or fit."* The Bible teaches us, showing us our weaknesses, correcting and instructing us in righteous living. It is the most valuable tool a Christian can have to be equipped for spiritual survival.

Lord, help us seek Your inspired survival tool.

JUNE 30

One of my favorite restaurants is the buffet. For a single price, I can enjoy portions of 5 salads, 10 desserts or 15 main courses. There I can choose both what to eat and how much. If I want to try something else, I can always go back for more. Most are advertised as being, *"All You Can Eat."* Buffets have variety, speed, ease and informality. "Home Town Buffet." Doesn't that name sound inviting?

One buffet ad even said, *"Help Yourself to Happiness."* Wouldn't it be wonderful if their food would provide all we'd need to find happiness? A plate of meat, potatoes, veggies and dessert could drive away all our troubles.

Unfortunately, no restaurant could live up to that promise. Happiness is not a destination, but a by-product of life's journey. Finding happiness may involve food, but it will take lots of other things as well. We may find money, pleasure, beauty and accomplishments, but still not be happy in life.

The Psalmist defines happiness by our relationship with God. **"Happy are the people whose God is the Lord."** (Psalm 145:15) **"Happy is he whose hope is in the Lord."** (Psalm 146:5)

Life with God is like a spiritual buffet. God wants us to partake of the good things He has given us, so He says, "Help Yourself!" When we entrust ourselves to His care, we'll find His happiness. He knows best what we need.

Lord, thank You for blessing us with all we need.

EVERY DAY WITH JESUS
in July

✂

JULY 1

I have a sweet tooth. My doctor sees a high level of sugar in my blood test and has urged me to cut down on sugar. But a frosted pastry and a Cappuccino with whipped cream – Mmm good!

However, some good things must end. Lately my tummy has given me a "sugar ache" when I've had too much. Reader's Digest warns me of "25 Ways Sugar Is Making You Sick"(April, 2018). But I doubt I will ever stop enjoying it.

Nearly every good thing in life can become bad if we have too much of it. An exception is the goodness of God. The psalmist says, **"You are my Lord and apart from You I have no good thing."** (Psalm 16:2) We know God is good, but when was the last time you thought of Him as the highest good, the best thing in life, even better than Swiss chocolate?

In Psalm 16, David gives us a glimpse of just how good God is. He's our preserver (vs. 1), goodness-giver (vs. 2), chosen portion (vs 5), counselor and instructor (vs. 7), path of life and source of joy (vs. 11). **"Therefore my heart is glad, my whole being rejoices,"** David says.

Human nature seeks other good things, but nothing is better than God. He's the best!

Lord, thank You for all the blessings we enjoy.

JULY 2

I love most kinds of music, although I lean toward the classics more than the modern. I enjoy most kinds of musical instruments, except for loud, nasty, grating electric guitars. A good choir or well-sung hymn can stir my soul, but a hard rock metal band will drive me away. I'm not sure "Rap" is real music at all.

Some might say the same about one of my favorite instruments, the bagpipe. Someone said, *"Perfect pitch is when a banjo lands in the dumpster on top of a bagpipe."* That sounds a little harsh. A good pipe band is magnificent to hear. One of my favorite CDs is "Denver Brass and Pipes", and besides pipe and brass music, it includes flute, violin, Irish step dancers and a great Irish tenor. Luther often said, *"Next to the Gospel, music is God's greatest gift."*

I wonder how Jesus' singing voice sounded. He loved praising God, and the Bible is filled with praise songs, so our Lord was surely a singer. He would have sung David's hymns, such as, **"I will sing of steadfast love and justice. To You, O Lord, I will make music."** (Psalm 101:1)

We don't all have to agree on one kind of music, especially if it is offered to God. He accepts all our praises and finds joy when His children lift their voices, play their instruments or join together with songs of praise and thanks to Him, our Maker and Redeemer.

Help us, Jesus, to give You good and joyful praise.

JULY 3

It's summer, a time when couples might hold their wedding service. I've had the honor of presiding over several hundred weddings during my ministry. Now and then the couple will show me their wedding photos. The best ones usually feature the couple before the altar, and when a cross is shown above or between them, those are my favorites. Photographers are wise to remember this.

During the ceremony, most pastors will remind the couple that God has brought them together and Jesus will keep them together if they pray and remember Him in their home.

A pastor friend of mine makes the sign of the cross between them to remind them Jesus is their Lord in the home. *"When you see your wife, think of Jesus first. When you see your husband, see Jesus standing there between you."* Those are great words of wisdom at a wedding advice.

John reminds Christians, **"This is love, not that we have loved God but that He loved us and sent His Son to be the atoning sacrifice for our sins. Beloved, if God so loved us, we also ought to love one another."** (1 John 4:10-11)

Many of us may struggle in relationships with betrayal, rejection or abandonment. But in Jesus we are forgiven and given help to forgive others. God loves us, no matter what, and He will never leave us nor betray us. We have His promise on that, and God keeps His promises!

Lord Jesus, help us forgive those who have hurt us.

JULY 4

On July 4, 2017, the Colorado Rockies and the Cincinnati Reds began their baseball game with an announcement, *"There will be no soloist for the National Anthem. The audience is invited to sing along as it is played by Stewart Boone."*

Boone, in his wheelchair wearing his American Legion uniform, raised his trumpet to his lips and proudly played our beloved anthem with gusto. Not bad for being 92 years old.

Stewart Boone served in WWII in the 924th Field Artillery Battalion that fought in the 1944-45 Battle of the Bulge. It was Germany's last effort to defeat the Allies, and was one of the bloodiest battles of the war. Boone's 99th Infantry Division lost 59 of its 70 American soldiers, and whenever he plays his trumpet in public, it is in memory of the Army buddies he lost there.

"I play every opportunity I get," he said. Boone began playing the trumpet at age 5, and estimates he's played the National Anthem and "Taps" for public events over 1,200 times.

Colossians 3:17 says, **"Whatever you do, in word or deed, do everything in the name of the Lord Jesus, giving thanks to God the Father through Him."** Mr. Boone, part of the "Greatest Generation", has great faith in Jesus. He plays in thanks to God and to honor those who didn't make it home.

Help us give You thanks, Lord, for all our blessings.

JULY 5

A group can do a lot when people cooperate. Norman Jorgenson was a dairy farmer, and in the fall of 1972 he was a sick man. A weakened heart kept him bed-ridden for weeks, so he didn't yet have his hay gathered in for the winter. If the cows were to be milked and food kept on his table, the hay had to be gathered.

After visiting him in early September and learning of his predicament, I sat down with a few members and friends and asked what we could do. They suggested organizing a work day when people could come over and help. I and others spread the word that we'd all gather at his farm a week from the next Saturday. Thankfully, God gave us warm, dry days to make sure the hay would cure and store safely.

It was quite a day. Around seventy-five men, women and youth, descended on Norman's farm with tractors, balers, wagons and stackers. Women made lunch for all, and by four that afternoon we'd put up five thousand bales and thirty stacks of hay near the farmyard so feed could be brought in for the cows. His wife and kids would do most of the work, but Norman's cows would have enough feed.

Apostle Paul organized a fund drive to help starving Christians in Jerusalem. He said, **"On the first day of the week, each of you should put something aside as God has blessed him."** (1 Corinthians 16:2) So began our church offerings!

Dear Jesus, inspire us to give help to others in need.

189

JULY 6

The Smithsonian Channel has developed "Aerial America," a video series about all fifty states. The helicopter photography and narrative are well done, giving an impressive overview of places and events related to each state. This series is worth watching.

Nearly every video has one fact that is repeated, that Native Americans were poorly treated when our country was settled. Broken treaties and massacres bring up guilt of our past, and though necessary, it is hard to hear.

What can we do with guilt? We've all done things we wish we could forget. Is guilt a bad thing? It shows we have a conscience, but can it help us? Some therapists claim guilt over the past is always a destructive waste of time.

The Bible is filled with stories about God's people struggling with sin and guilt. The Psalmist says, **"Pardon my guilt, O Lord, for it is great."** (Psalm 25:11) Prophet Isaiah wrote that God told him, **"Your guilt is taken away, your sin is atoned for."** (Isaiah 6:7)

Guilt can torment us and be an enemy if it takes away hope. But in some cases, a reminder of a past failing can help us not repeat it. We need constant reminding that Jesus forgave us all our sins and guilt on the cross. Because He was punished for us, we need not fear the past. In Jesus, God remembers our sin no more.

Lord Jesus, thank You for removing our guilt.

JULY 7

When a bad thing happens, God can always turn it into something good. I believe this, because I've seen it happen many times.

An angry young man sent a threatening letter through the mail and was arrested by federal agents. Instead of jail, he was given probation and ordered to attend college. He complied and became a lifelong high school teacher, helping hundreds of students develop their skills and in some cases avoid a life of crime.

A young man born with cerebral palsy struggled with self-pity until his father told him to do something good for others. He became a pastor and organized a congregation that ministers to disabled people, bringing hope to those with his small but effective ministry.

A young man considered becoming a doctor, until he saw a child die. He then chose to become a chaplain in a children's hospital, serving the families and patients who suffer loss.

A Jewish Pharisee was stopped by God from killing Christians and began making new ones through preaching the Gospel of Jesus. He wrote, **"I persecuted this Way to the death, binding and delivering to prison both men and women."** (Acts 22:4) Paul's life was turned around by God.

When a bad thing happens, God can always turn it into something good. Whether through a bad illness, bad choice, bad accident or a bad relationship, God can make the outcome better.

Lord, when bad things happen, help me see the good.

JULY 8

Are you a gardener? If so, you're probably already pulling weeds around your vegetables or flowers. My son always has a nice garden with many types of vegetables and flowers, sometimes including pumpkins.

Dill's Atlantic Giant Seed Company has developed premium seeds that can result in record-sized pumpkins. In Atlantic, Quebec, during 2011, one of their pumpkins grew to a world record at 1,818 pounds, enough to yield a thousand pieces of pie. Wow!

The farmer who raised it said it came from the right seed being planted in the right kind of soil. Seeds are important, but the soil must also be right or the plant won't grow properly.

When Jesus told His story about the farmer who planted seeds in the field, He said, **"The seed is the Word of God."** (Luke 8:11) He wasn't talking about size of the seed, but the result of what it produced. He was saying the good seed of God's Word will grow in the good soil of a receptive heart and thus produce many believers.

Sinful, distracted or selfish hearts will choke or starve the Gospel so that people will resist it. God's Word can only change hearts if we stop resisting it.

We should ask ourselves, *"What kind of soil am I?"* Are we so busy we don't have time for God? Is our lifestyle toxic to the Gospel? Do we want the blessings God offers us?

Lord, help me be open to hearing Your Word.

JULY 9

All parents struggle with how best to raise their children. Some can become so obsessed with their child's happiness that they cause the opposite. As a parent, I had to guard myself against doing this.

I once helped my son too much. In the Sixth Grade he had a report due and was struggling. Instead of helping him write it, he told me what he wanted to write and I wrote the report for him. A Word Processor made it fun to do, but I should not have done his work.

His teacher gave him an A+ and also wrote *"WOW???"* after his grade. She knew it was too good. My son told me, *"I'll do it myself next time."* He told his teacher what he'd done and wrote all future reports in his own way.

In 1 Samuel 2, Eli the Priest helped his sons too much. When they did something wrong, he looked the other way. Instead of correcting them or letting them take the consequences for their actions, Eli made excuses. As a result, they were selfish, proud, rebellious men who disrespected God. Because he cared too much for his sons, he died and his sons were lost.

Parents have the great responsibility to love and discipline their children. God's Word says, **"Discipline your son and he will give you rest. He will be a delight to your heart."** (Proverbs 29:17) As we impart God's Word to children, we help them become God-fearing adults.

Lord, help parents to love their children wisely.

JULY 10

One of the best things about being a Christian is that no matter what problems today may bring, there is a better future tomorrow. No matter what evil may happen today, there is something better to come. God promises this.

The present is not all there is to life. We see the troubles of life each day, but we know God is with us every step of the way. God bids us to lean on Him saying, **"Call upon Me in the day of trouble. I will deliver you and you will glorify Me."** (Psalm 50:15)

We acknowledge sin in the world and in our personal lives, but we rejoice that Christ has overcome it. We look backward with gratitude but forward with joy. As Mrs. Ruth Graham said from her wheelchair before she died, *"So many wonderful memories, and so much to look forward to!"* Believers are able to see past the struggles of today, and look forward to the wonder and joy of what God has in store for us tomorrow.

Corrie Ten Boom, survivor of a WWII death camp, often said, *"When the Lord takes your hand, He holds you tight. When He holds you tight, He leads you through life, and when He leads you through life, He brings you safely home."*

Jesus holds our hand and brings us safely through critical times, even when we may feel we have lost hope. He holds our hand and doesn't let go. He promises that He never will, even if we try to go our own way.

Lord, help us always to hold Your hand in faith.

JULY 11

Once after a baseball game, I boarded the Denver Light Rail train and rode it twenty miles south to where I'd parked my car. The ride was an adventure! Union Station was a beehive with hundreds of people awaiting the trains or visiting shops and restaurants nearby.

The train car was noisy with laughter from the young adults who'd also attended the game. I found it a comfortable and safe experience, although I might have felt differently had it been late at night. The train car was humid and bouncy and interesting. A young man made sure I got off at the right station where I got into my car and drove home. On the freeway, I gave thanks for the peace and quiet of a smooth ride those last ten miles to my home.

The Apostles had no trains or cars. As they took the message of Jesus into the world, they had only their feet or perhaps a boat. Despite this, it was amazing how successful they were. Biblical history tells us that within only months of His resurrection, as many as ten thousand people had already become followers of Jesus.

The Holy Spirit inspired the early witnesses who saw Jesus alive again, and their witness spread the faith like wildfire. Peter and John said to all, **"We cannot but speak of what we have seen and heard."** (Acts 4:20)

May we also be witnesses to Jesus, the God-Man who brings salvation to all who believe.

Lord, help us to share the joy and hope we have.

JULY 12

Life is short. I once asked my aged father about his life, and he said it sure went by fast. Born in 1898 and dying in 1995, he was alive from the Wright Brothers to the moon landing, from electricity to computers, from telegraph to cell phones. He also lived through a century almost constantly at war.

Yes, life is short. There is little that is constant, but in these ever-changing times, God's Word gives us something solid to hold onto. Jesus said, **"Never will I leave you, never will I forsake you."** (Hebrews 113:5) His Word of hope gives us something lasting!

God cares for us and has given us this fascinating world where we live. His presence and mercy are always there for us and His love is solid as a Rock.

In the time we have left here, we need to treasure our loved ones. Carol and I took our family of twelve on a short cruise one year and enjoyed seeing them get to know each other better. My Dad and Mom held several family reunions for the same reason. Family members can even become good friends.

My Dad's home-going was a blessing after his long life. We know Jesus is our Lord, and with faith in Him life never really ends. It enters a new stage where we will live with Him in eternity. Of this we can be certain. We have His unfailing promise on it.

Lord, thanks for staying with us all through life.

JULY 13

There's a saying: *"What goes around comes around."* It could mean what we do now may come back to haunt us. It might also mean that something old-fashioned done long ago returns again, this time as being fashionable.

When second son Brian was born, his older brother Charles wanted to play with his Mommy on the way home, so I picked up a cardboard grocery box for baby Brian to sleep in on the way home. It was a crude but effective bed.

A recent article told that it has now become fashionable for Scandinavian hospitals to give new parents baby items in a cardboard box that can serve as its first bed. Some American states are starting their own baby box programs, with lots of goodies, complete with instructions and warnings on usage. Perhaps there will soon be rules drawn up to regulate baby box use. *"What goes around comes around."*

The Old Testament book of Ecclesiastes begins with the words, **"There is nothing new under the sun."** (Ecclesiastes 1:9) The writer says history repeats itself, so don't expect things to change. His cynicism is evidence He must have forgotten that a Messiah had been promised who would deliver us from our sins.

Give thanks today that we see our Savior Jesus in our rear view mirror, forgiving our sins of yesterday, and giving us hope for today, and offering help for future days.

Help us, Jesus, to see You with us every day.

JULY 14

My Arizona cactus garden contains an ocotillo (oh-koh-TEE-yoh). Most cacti varieties have green pads, barrel heads or arms growing skyward, but the ocotillo is an ugly bunch of prickly sticks usually barren of foliage.

Surprisingly, it can be started by planting a piece in the ground that takes root and eventually starts to grow. I planted a one-foot ocotillo stick at the edge of my garden and it has grown several inches each year.

The stick is usually dried up, making it look dead, but a desert rain will bring it back to life. Tiny new green leaves appear quickly to adorn the thorny branch with a glob of red-orange flowers growing on the tip which will lengthen it another inch or two.

Only rain water can bring an ocotillo back to life, and only nutrients from the air can make it leaf and blossom. It will never look as pretty as other varieties, but its spiny sticks contain life. Its tiny flowers bloom only a day or so, but by God's grace they will give the plant life.

The Bible says of our Lord, **"He grew up before Him like a young plant, and like a root out of dry ground; He had no form or majesty that we should look at Him, and no beauty that we should desire Him."** (Isaiah 53:2)

Jesus bloomed awhile, died, then came back to life in glory everlasting. All who trust in Him also shall rise from the dead to be with Him forever.

Lord, help us also rise to new life with You.

JULY 15

In our ever-changing world, we are often surprised when something once considered good is now considered bad. Take the loaf of bread, for example. For centuries it was a needed part of our diet, but now it is supposed to be bad for us, and not just due to refined flour. One popular diet tells us to avoid the "whites" – bread, rice, potatoes, sugar. If we want be thin and healthy, avoid those!

In Jesus' day, a diet without bread would be strange. I think it is still good food, however. And if nutritious food is needed, the other "whites" are okay too, if taken in moderation.

Imagine if today Jesus would feed crowds a meal of only bread and fish. Critics would say it needed more variety, less starch and no salt. Someone might report Him to the FDA!

But what Jesus gave the crowd was life-giving. As God provided manna and quail in the desert, so Jesus fed His people true bread from heaven. They just wanted food, of course, but Jesus told them they needed the spiritual bread that only He could give them. He said if they took what He offered, they would feed more than just their bodies on earth.

He said, **"I am the bread of life; whoever comes to Me shall not hunger, and whoever believes in Me shall never thirst."** (John 6:35) A first century follower would not go without bread. May we never try to live without Jesus.

Lord Jesus, thank You for feeding us Your bread.

JULY 16

One of my wife's favorite aunts lived through the Great Depression and the Dirty Thirties when field dust was blowing due to a long and severe drought. Carol once asked Aunt Hildegard what the most amazing invention she'd seen during her lifetime. She said, *"Indoor hot and cold running water."* She told Carol how much time and effort was spent in those days bringing water into the house, especially good drinking water from the farm well.

At our farm home we didn't have indoor running water until I was ten. In Arizona our tap water is good for washing, but I get our drinking water from a machine. It tastes better.

There is a spring next to Israel's Dead Sea called Ein Gedi. Its clear waters literally gush out of the desert rocks creating an oasis of life and shade with trees, bushes, flowers and plants. People and animals alike seek its clear water.

Running water in the Bible is often called "living water" because it is purified in the earth and gives life. When Jesus met the woman at the well, He offered her living water.

He said, **"Everyone who drinks of this [well] water will be thirsty again, but whoever drinks of the water that I will give him will never be thirsty again."** (John 4:13-14)

Jesus purified us by giving His life on the cross. His blood was shed that we might have eternal life. May we seek His forgiveness.

Lord, help us find eternal life in You.

JULY 17

My father had a team of horses to help him farm the land. Horses require much food, care and equipment, and harnesses require repair. As a boy I found an old bridle hanging on the barn wall and asked Dad what those large flaps were near the top. *"Blinders,"* he said. *"They help keep a horse looking straight ahead so it won't get distracted by things on each side."* *"Do they blind the horse?"* I asked. *"No,"* Dad said. *"The horse gets accustomed to them and works better when it looks straight ahead."*

"Blinders" might be good for people, too. There is much in the world to distract us from important tasks. If we're serious about following Jesus and His Word in life, we will take steps to avoid those distractions. Daily devotions and Bible reading, regular prayer and worship will help keep our eyes fixed on Jesus.

Christian "blinders" are not meant to take joy out of life or to blind us from doing good. Following Jesus need not be a somber task. Even Jesus danced, sang and ate hearty meals with His people. God wants us to be blessed and enjoy the world around us.

The Psalmist says, **"Make a joyful noise unto the Lord, all the earth. Serve the Lord with gladness."** (Psalm 100:1-2) Our Lord brings us joy as well as forgiveness. We follow Him and are blessed as we work our jobs, live our lives, and love those around us.

Lord, keep us from being distracted by the world.

JULY 18

On what do you base your life? Is there one thing that is most important to you? If all else fails, what do you want to have left?

Near Boise, Idaho, there's a volcanic butte that rises high above the plains. In 1866, three years after Idaho Territory was established, Lafayette Cartee was appointed Surveyor General of the Territory. The next year he hired Peter Bell to survey the new land. Bell began by hammering a brass post into a point at the very top of that volcanic butte.

That stake is the "Idaho Baseline." From that point, Bell surveyed the rest of the territory. Townships were designated north and south of that initial point, and Ranges were designated east and west. Using that system, Bell not only described the territory, he helped people living there always to know exactly where they were.

The Bible gives Christians a baseline for life. Its Old Testament tells us that God would send the world a Savior from sin, and its New Testament tells us that Savior is Jesus. No matter where life takes us, we know where we are if we keep our eyes on Jesus.

In the Bible, He says, **"I am the Way, the Truth and the Life, and no one comes to the Father but except through Me."** (John 14:6) The Bible also says, **"Jesus is the same yesterday, today and forever."** (Hebrews 13:8) If we have the Bible, we will never need to be lost in life.

Lord, thank You for giving us Your Holy Word.

JULY 19

Living in Colorado this time of year, the aspens are all leafed out. I have several of them growing in front of our home, and they all share a common trait: Their bright green, round leaves seem to be in constant motion. Their technical name is "populous tremuloides" or, "trembling aspen." Due to how the leaves are attached to the branch, even the slightest breath of wind will make the tender leaves shake ever so gently.

Some people feel they are shaking like a quaking aspen. When life is filled with concerns or dramatic events, even a little action or slight comment can make them feel unsteady and insecure. Some may be calm, even when the storms of life rage around them, but others are unnerved by the smallest of things.

Gratefully, the Bible gives us calm amid the turbulence. Apostle Paul wrote, **"May the God of peace Himself give you peace always in every way."** (2 Thessalonians 3:16) Not only does God offer us peace, He is the God of peace. Hearing and trusting His voice in His Word, we can rest assured we will have His strength to give us calm and peace.

A contest was held for artists to paint a scene that best depicted peace. The winner was a mother bird calmly sitting in its nest on a branch that stretched out over a raging waterfall. When life is unsettling, the God of peace calms us.

Father God, help us through our times of trouble.

JULY 20

During a hospital visit to an elderly member, a pastor touched on the probability of the man's death and asked him if there was anything he could do for him. He said, *"Pray God will give me courage. I'm not afraid of death, but I do fear dying. I don't want it to be painful."*

Christians believe God gives His children eternal life, and that thought is comforting. But being fearful that the way there is filled with pain or suffering is not something we want. Going into **"the valley of the shadow of death"** (Psalm 23:4) can be daunting or even terrifying, unless we remember that Jesus is with us as we go. He's been there and He's already come back, so we couldn't have a better companion along the way.

Apostle Paul knew his death would come soon when he wrote, **"The sting of death is sin, and the strength of sin is the Law. But thanks be to God who gives us the victory through our Lord Jesus Christ."** (1 Corinthians 15:56-57)

The process of dying is like being escorted into the presence of God for eternity. Few have been given a glimpse what this will be like, but there's a person we can talk to who has been there and returned, and that's Jesus.

When it is our turn to walk that path, He will walk beside us with His strength and comfort, holding our hand. **"Your rod and your staff they comfort me."** (Psalm 23:4)

Lord, hold our hand all through life and forever.

JULY 21

Sometimes a day just doesn't go well. Our son is a Christian School teacher who rarely plays golf. But one year he was part of a charity "best ball" tournament in Florida. Each member of his four-person team played from the best shot made on any given hole. Chuck's poor playing seemed redeemed with his last Tee-shot, a mighty blast. Alas! His best ball all day landed right next to an alligator! Needless to say, his team members played from another ball.

Paul had a bad day at Philippi. He healed a demon-possessed slave girl, but was arrested because her owner could no longer charge money for her divinations. Paul and Silas both landed in jail, but were later freed when a midnight earthquake crumbled the gates.

But they didn't leave. Knowing the jailor would be punished for losing his prisoners, they stayed, and the jailor was so amazed that he asked to hear the Gospel. **"Believe on the Lord Jesus Christ and you will be saved, you and your household,"** Paul told him. (Acts 16:31)

God can give us joy in the midst of our sorrow, and He can make sense out of senseless, evil events around us. As Corrie ten Boom said, *"There is no pit so deep that God's love is not deeper still."* We need not fear when days seem to go bad. God has given us every moment of every day, and all day long He will show us His grace and mercy.

On our bad days help us, Jesus, to see Your goodness.

JULY 22

We heard that a house down our street had termites, so I called for a termite inspection. Fortunately the news was good. We had no termites because we don't have dampness or wood in piles next to the house.

Termites are tiny and very destructive. They chew whatever wood they like and are able to weaken even large timbers. Their damage isn't evident at first, but given time it will be seen. The deck on the neighbor's house started to sag, and when the repairman was called, he said they needed to eradicate the bugs before he could repair and strengthen their deck.

People can get bugs in their lives also, not real insects, but little things that eat away and damage a peaceful life. Constant worry, or irrational fears, or bad little habits, or neglect of God can damage a life. Small unrepentant sins can grow into big problems.

When God let Israel conquer Jericho, He told people to kill all living things and not keep anything from the city. Achan thought no one would miss a few coins or a few jewels. When his theft was discovered, God caused the Israelites to lose a battle. Achan said, **"I truly have sinned against the Lord God of Israel."** His little sin caused a great defeat.

Our little sins can do the same. The Bible says, **"If we confess our sins, God is faithful and just and will forgive us our sins."** (1 John 1:9)

Lord, forgive us our sins and help us follow You.

JULY 23

One morning a friend stopped by and caught me at the ironing board. Yes, I told him, I do the ironing here, and also vacuuming and washing windows. Carol does other more important things around the house.

I enjoy taking wrinkles out of shirts and pants, and it started when I went away to college. Mom helped me pack a suitcase and taught me how to use an iron. *"You'll need to know this,"* she said, as she imparted the basics of the ironing board.

Ironing helped my wardrobe, and it also became a source of spending money. Seven shirts took about an hour, so I charged fifteen cents a shirt or seven for a dollar, which seemed a good wage. College men those days wore dress shirts to class. Word went out and soon I got some business. It wasn't hard work, and they were glad I made their clothes look better.

Taking out wrinkles fits well with God's forgiveness. Like John said, **"If we say we have no sins, we deceive ourselves and the truth is not in us."** (1 John 1:8) Forgiveness removes the wrinkles we make each day.

When we regularly come to God with our dirty life, He cleans it for us through Jesus. The Holy Spirit helps us iron out the wrinkles each day so we can live more like Jesus, and maybe not mess things up so much up the next time. Makes sense, doesn't it?

Dear Jesus, thank You for straightening us out!

JULY 24

It's often said, *"You get what you pay for."* But Ernie didn't think it was true. He'd always bought cheap stuff because he was sure "expensive" was a term someone made up. *"There's no difference between the most expensive and the cheapest."* Ernie said.

One day, as he was getting ready to join his wife who'd gone ahead to her sister's, Ernie saw she'd taken their only suitcase, so he went to town to buy a new one. At a crossroads along the way, he saw a pickup loaded with items for sale. Ernie stopped, and there it was - a zippered suitcase, like new. And only $4.98!

He gave the guy five dollars and proudly told him to keep the change. He packed it tight, and the next morning went to the bus station. Ernie proudly handed his new suitcase to the bus driver who tagged it and tossed it by the storage door where it exploded! All the zippers on his new suitcase ripped open and Ernie's private things went flying. He heard someone say, *"You get what you pay for!"*

But there's a time when this is not true, when it's about forgiveness. Forgiveness from God comes to us free, with no price attached, because Jesus has already paid the highest price of all, His life. And Jesus didn't quibble about the expense, He just paid it. Because He did, we're blessed forever. **"The blood of Jesus, His Son, cleanses us from all sin."** (1 John 1:7)

Thanks, Lord, for paying the high price for us.

JULY 25

Travel today is amazingly easy. I wonder how Moses would deal with travel if he were alive today. He led his people through the wilderness for forty years, but he never had to deal with Denver International Airport.

He'd have found water wasn't from a rock but a metal fountain. Or when night came, he'd bed down behind a plastic tree, not in a cave. Instead of manna and quail, he'd eat little bags of peanuts and pretzels, but only during the flight.

Rather than fight hostile tribes, he'd have to deal with TSA and their growing list of airport security measures. Requiring removal of certain clothing might have moved him to draw his sword in protest, but that would already have been taken after going through the X-Ray.

Moses couldn't herd camels down the interstate, as they'd get run over by trucks or speeding drivers. Highway Patrol would cite him for parking his caravan at the Rest Stop too long or entering construction zones without "Slow-Moving Vehicle" signs on his animals. But enough this metaphor!

We are all travelers in life, and praise be to God He promises to go with us each day we travel, no matter where we may be. Jesus is our constant companion, reminding us, **"Lo, I am with you to the end of your journey."** (Matthew 28:20) He gives us a divine roadmap and even helps us follow it when we get lost.

Stay with us Lord, Jesus, wherever we go in life.

JULY 26

When the Arizona winter season ends, our park offers free golf all summer to the residents who remain. One year they offered free golf beginning April 16. We stayed nine more days, so for nine straight days I played nine holes of free golf. I began on the Fourth Tee and ended on the Third Green, next to our home. I wished it could have been that way all year.

I'm not sure I was a better golfer after those nine days, but I did learn what clubs to use on each hole. I had a few pars and birdies, but no hole-in-one. Maybe next time!

Just as more days golfing may not mean better golf, so also more days of trying to live right may not mean a better life. Sinful people still struggle with the same temptations, same weaknesses and even the same sins. Gratefully, we all have the same Lord and Savior who forgives us when we confess to Him.

Jesus is the source of hope in our life. When Paul addressed the Athenian people in the Areopagus (the marketplace), He told them, **"In Him [Jesus] we live and move and have our being."** (Acts 17:28) No matter what we are like, or no matter what we've done, He accepts, loves and forgives us.

I guess we could say Jesus gives us a hole-in-one for life. He is our winner, no matter what the contest. In Him, we're all we can be, and for that we thank Him!

Lord, how can we thank You enough for all You do?

JULY 27

When gathering with friends, new and old, a question is often asked, *"Where are you from?"* Knowing a person's place of origin or former residence is a good way to begin a conversation and learn about that person.

Sometimes the answer is vague. The person may have just moved, or may have lived in many places. They may be a "full timer", living in a Motor Coach or Fifth Wheel rather than a house.

In the book of Judges, Jephthah of Gilead had a hard time telling others of his origin. His half-brothers didn't respect him, because his mother was a prostitute. One day they even chased him out of town in derision.

But Jephthah was a born leader, and when an enemy clan came to fight against their clan, his brothers asked him to return. He said, **"Did you not hate me and drive me out of my father's house? Why have you come to me now when you are in distress?"** (Judges 11:7) But Jephthah did go back and with the Spirit's power, he led his brothers to victory.

God sometimes uses the most unlikely persons to do His work, including ourselves. It doesn't matter where we are from or what has brought us to this moment, God gives direction to work for Him and strength to get it done. What matters is how we respond in faith to follow His will for the good of others. He always has a plan for our lives.

Lord Jesus, show us Your will and help us to live it.

JULY 28

God loves us, but it's not always easy to love each other. Differing opinions, personalities and even appearances can make us think less of others. We must learn to look past our pride to see all of God's people.

I was recently in the Wal-Mart store on a Friday afternoon. Being the end of the week and the end of the month, the normally busy store was packed. Checkout lines were long, children were fussing and tempers were short. Knowing checkout would be awhile, I took my place in line and spent some time looking at the people around me in the store.

They were all different, those in front of me, on the sides, and those behind. Whether old or young, tall or short, heavy or thin, well dressed or sloppy, pretty or plain, no one looked the same. All were different.

I thought how God loves all these people, including myself. No matter who they are or where, God loves all people of the world, all seven billion of us! How can He do it? How can He keep track of us or put up with so many who don't care about Him?

"God so loved the world that He gave His only Son, that whoever believes in Him shall not perish, but shall have eternal life." (John 3:16)

It takes the greatest love imaginable to love all these people, all because of His amazing grace! I couldn't do it, but God can. Praise God!

Lord, help us love people with Your love.

JULY 29

While today we rely on satellites and GPS technology to map the world and our location, there was a time when lighthouses were most important to ships. One would think the state with the most lighthouses would be on the east or west coast, but the winner with 120 lighthouses is Michigan. But few lighthouses today are guiding points as they did in former years.

In the 1670s, explorer Jesuit Father Joseph Marquette tried to map that Michigan coastline, hoping to find a waterway to the Pacific Ocean and make Christian converts among the natives along the way. He died in 1675 at the age of 37, having mapped 2,000 miles of that coastline and also baptizing a few new souls.

Michigan today has changed so much that none of those pioneers would recognize even the curve of its lakeshores. But the Christians there today number in the thousands. The seeds of the Gospel Marquette planted have taken root.

Jesus told His followers, **"Go and make disciples of all nations, baptizing them in the name of the Father and of the Son and of the Holy Spirit, teaching them to observe all that I have commanded you. And I will be with you always, to the end of the age."** (Matthew 28:19-20)

Jesus is still with us, in Word and Sacrament and in the hearts of all who believe He is our Lord and Savior. Jesus is God's Lighthouse to the world, showing us the way to the Father.

Lord, show all the world the way to God the Father.

JULY 30

Bridges are very important for travelers, especially if they must cross deep rivers. One of the great bridges in America that connects the Upper and Lower Peninsulas of the state of Michigan is the Mackinac Bridge. Completed in 1957, its five-mile span crosses parts of Lake Michigan and Lake Huron, along a scenic part of Interstate 75. It connects Mackinac City on the south with St. Ignace in the north.

Every year since 1958, the "Mackinac Bridge Walk" has been held on Labor Day, bringing thousands of people to make the five-mile hike, often led by the Michigan Governor. Although pedestrians are normally not allowed on the bridge, that day thousands cross it together.

What bridges must we cross in life? Some liken marriage to a bridge between people, or baptism to a bridge between God and people. Bridges are needed for safe travel, and God has provided the ones we need.

When God's people of old needed to cross a river, God parted the waters. The Jordan River was parted at least three times, once to bring the Israelites into the Promised Land, and twice during the ministries of Elijah and Elisha.

The Psalmist says, **"God struck the rock so that water gushed out and streams overflowed. Can He not also give bread and meat for His people?"** (Psalm 78:20) Our Lord Jesus is God's bridge between God and mankind.

O God, thank You for bridging the gap with Jesus.

JULY 31

On clear, moonless nights in the Colorado Rockies, one can only marvel at the sky. The Milky Way shows its thousands of points of light from stars, planets and faraway galaxies. Our universe was created by God and is held together by His almighty hand, using laws, elements and formulas to give light and life to us here on planet earth.

Apostle Paul tells us, **"For by Him [Jesus] all things were created, in heaven and on earth, visible and invisible, whether thrones or dominions, rulers or authorities. All things were created through Him and for Him. He is before all things, and in Him all things hold together."** (Colossians 1:16-17)

People in the north are dazzled by the aurora borealis ("northern lights") created by particles from the sun's energy colliding with the earth's atmosphere. Incredibly colorful movements in the sky have captivated mankind since God created life on the earth.

But nightly displays of grandeur can't be compared with the glory of God when He sent His Son to earth. When the angels sang, **"Glory to God in the highest!"** the sky was ablaze with angelic beings praising our Creator God.

"The heavens declare the glory of God and the sky proclaims the work of His hands." (Psalm 19:1) What can give us more evidence of God's power and mercy in our world today?

Lord, show us Your power and glory always.

EVERY DAY WITH JESUS
in August

❧

AUGUST 1

When Dr. Billy Graham died in 2018, he was buried in a casket made by three convicts. Inmates Liggett and Bowman were serving life sentences for murder, and Krolowitz thirty years for armed robbery.

The Louisiana State Penitentiary, also called "Angola", was built on a slave plantation where thousands of people from Angola in Africa were forcibly taken. Warden Burl Cain saw a casket holding remains of a deceased prisoner break apart during burial, so he ordered that better caskets be made for all who died there.

When Dr. Graham could not make his scheduled visit there, son Franklin Graham and his sister Ruth came with the message of salvation in Jesus. Dozens of prisoners and also Warden Cain, received Jesus as their Savior.

Dr. Graham then asked that his own casket be made there. Thus, a casket made by convicts containing the body of one of the world's great evangelists, lay in state in the U.S. Capital, a tribute to what the Gospel can do for sinners.

Jesus died for our sins between two convicts, and before He died told one of them, **"Today you will be with Me in paradise."** (Luke 23:43)

Lord, thank You for forgiving us our sins.

AUGUST 2

There is an old saying, *"When you always do what you've always done, you'll always get what you've always got."* It basically means that if you want to change your life in some way, you need to change what you do.

Years ago a woman told me that she was frustrated because she chose men so poorly. She said, *"Each time I think I've found 'Mr. Right', I find out he's just like the last 'Mr. Wrong'."* She revealed her past relationships centered on men she met at a western dance hall. *"I love drinking a beer and dancing, but I don't like the guys who do that."* I was amazed she didn't see the solution.

What would you tell her? If I recall correctly, I just looked at her without saying anything, and she eventually said, *"I know what I should do, but I just don't know how to do it."*

Apostle Paul knew that to be true in his own life. He said, **"I do not do the good I want, but the evil I do not want is what I keep on doing."** (Romans 7:19) It isn't enough just to know what is right, God must help us do what is right.

A young pastor told me, *"If you give people the right information, they'll probably do it."* That pastor later learned a hard lesson that it didn't work. Information alone does not make good works. It takes the Holy Spirit's help.

Jesus had trouble with sin, but not His own. It is our sin that took Him to the cross, and it's His love that forgives us each day.

Holy Spirit, show us the right way and help us do it.

218

AUGUST 3

Ernie Johnson, former Major League pitcher for the Milwaukee Braves, played alongside Warren Spahn and Hank Aaron, and pitched against the likes of Stan Musial, Ted Williams and Jackie Robinson. He later went into the broadcast booth and shared some amazing moments with his listeners.

His favorite story, however, wasn't about the giants of baseball, but about his son Ernie Jr. when the boy was in Pee Wee baseball. During a game the ball had bounced over the fence into the lot next door. Coach and players were having a conference on the mound when someone noticed the outfielders were missing.

Ernie Jr. and two others had climbed the fence to retrieve the baseball and ended up picking ripe blackberries from a patch nearby. The delay became known to the Johnsons as the "blackberry moment," a time of briefly stepping away from the game (or job, meeting, task) to follow something more interesting and better. Those moments are to be cherished.

Have you ever had a "blackberry moment"? God gives us special times that may never come again, such as lending a helpful hand, speaking a kind word to a stranger, watching children at play, or giving a needed gift.

Moses told his people to help others in need, **"And the Lord your God will bless you, as He promised."** (Deuteronomy 15:6)

Thanks, Lord, for special moments that we can share.

AUGUST 4

Friends of ours lost a loved one and heard the pastor say, **"The Lord has given, the Lord has taken away; blessed be the name of the Lord,"** (Job 1:21) Those are true words, but they weigh heavily on the heart when a loved one dies.

We went to visit them one evening after a slow rain. As we drove, the setting sun broke out brightly in the west. As rain sprinkled on us, a lovely complete rainbow appeared behind us in the eastern sky. It was beautiful and peaceful.

After the rain comes the rainbow, God's promise of salvation. Most daytime showers produce rainbows, yet we don't always see them because we aren't looking for them. But after the rain, there are always rainbows. If there was no rain, there would be no rainbow.

Every good thing in life has a rainbow, a blessing from God, but we don't always recognize it. Sometimes we can only see the bad side of every blessing (i.e., "polluted air," or "cancer-causing sun.") But rainbows are still rainbows and they remind us of God's promise.

Whether we suffer storms of illness, frailty, conflict or anything that causes grief, rainbows are there, reminders God still cares for us. Even if we don't see them, they are there.

Jesus endured suffering and death for us on the cross, and He promises strength for every burden. His love helps us to enjoy rainbows here and unending heavenly joys there.

Lord help us look past our sorrow to see Your rainbow.

AUGUST 5

A few years ago a solar eclipse occurred when the moon passed perfectly between the sun and earth so that its shadow blocked all direct sunlight. The sun and moon were in correct alignment, and the moon's orbit brought it to an exact distance from the earth. Without these divinely ordained alignments, there couldn't be a total solar eclipse.

I saw most of it from my Colorado deck, and pondered again the words, **"When I look at Your heavens, the work of Your fingers, the moon and the stars, which You have set in place, what is man that You are mindful of him, and the son of man that You care for him?"** (Psalm 8:3-4)

That solar event momentarily took our minds off all the political intrigue in our world. Journalists and politicians relinquished their bully pulpits for a moment, looking up to see something breath-taking, three celestial orbs all in agreement, proof of God's handiwork.

God has made humans the highest of His creation. People are blessed to learn and explain many things. How did this eclipse come about so perfectly? Mankind has advanced, but that event reminded us we still have a lot to learn.

God's entering human history through Jesus is the event that defines everything else. In His Son, God offers us a look at His power, beauty and mercy, and He offers us our place in His family for eternity. Nothing else tops that.

Lord, help us give You honor as we see Your world.

AUGUST 6

Have you ever heard a knock at your door and wonder who it is? One evening we heard a loud knock on our door, a salesman wanting to know if we would be interested in his product. After his rapid exit, Carol asked if there was a better way to see who's on the other side of our door. So I installed a new door viewer.

These days more than ever we need to know who's at our door. Shady characters, politicians, and the noises of the world can unnerve us. We fervently pray the sounds outside will not come from evil, and we ask that God will give us leaders with wisdom and common sense.

When David was attacked by son Absalom, he pleaded, **"Arise, Lord! Deliver me! Strike all my enemies on the jaw; break the teeth of the wicked, for from the Lord comes deliverance. May Your blessings be on us."** (Psalm 3:7-8) Such fear and faith coming from a king!

Despite our technology and ever-expanding knowledge, we still do not have peace between nations. Nuclear threatens rapid destruction to so many, so fast. We pray God will protect us.

Mankind's sinful condition keeps us fighting each other. It propels us selfishly to seek our own way and take unwise risks to get it.

God gave us His only Son so that we may take refuge in His sacrifice on the cross. Without Jesus, life would be hopeless. But with Him, we have strength for each day.

Dear God, protect us from the world's troubles.

AUGUST 7

We've recently heard about government "leaks", secrets revealed because the leakers think we need to know them. Knowledge is power, and some of us want power over others.

There are other leaks that are also irksome, and also dangerous, such as when water leaks out of a pipe and into our house. If undetected, that leak becomes very damaging. We've probably all had leaks like that in the past.

I once had a water supply tube break behind a toilet tank and spray a few gallons onto the bathroom floor and down into the basement. Another time a ceiling pipe sprung a little leak and dripped water into the basement. Damage was extensive and included mold. Another time rain dripped into my office window and onto my desk. Some quality caulking stopped that.

Our sins resemble water leaks. Some things we do are easily seen, but secret sins are harder to stop. No matter what we may think, sin will show itself, and we dare not forget that **"The wages of sin is death."** (Romans 6:23). No matter how successful we are in hiding, ignoring or denying our sin, it will show itself and hurt us.

Thanks be to God that Paul didn't stop with the above six words! He continued, "**But the free gift of God is eternal life through Christ Jesus our Lord.**" When we see our sins and ask Christ for forgiveness, He will remove them. Trusting in Him, our sins will not become fatal.

Lord Jesus, help us see our sins and stop doing them.

AUGUST 8

Although not a fan of boxing, I became interested for a time when Muhammad Ali was world champion. He was an athlete you either liked or hated. Some didn't like that he changed his name from Cassius Clay, and others disliked his tactic of taunting his opponents.

In his 1974 fight with George Foreman, Ali taunted him to hit harder and fight better. His snippy jabs made Foreman angry, resulting in wasted punches and weakened confidence. *"Show me what you got, George, that don't hurt."* Ali said, *"I thought you were supposed to be good!"* Ali laughed. Infuriated, Foreman lost the fight.

This tactic has been used for centuries. Tobiah tried to weaken Nehemiah with it and Goliath tried to discourage David. Neither worked, since God's people depended on God's power, not on themselves.

A discouraging remark can be a powerful weapon. Jesus' half-brother James wrote, **"The tongue is a small member, yet it boasts of great things. How great a forest is set ablaze by such a small fire!"** (James 3:5)

Taunting or disparaging remarks can come from many sources, including those close to us. Our Heavenly Father encourages us through His promises that He will never leave us nor forsake us (Hebrews 13:5). He says we can rely on Him for His help (Hebrews 4:16), and that He will renew our strength (Isaiah 40:31).

Lord, help us use our voices to praise and serve You.

AUGUST 9

Batteries! What would we do without them? They start our motors, power our hearing aids and make our electronics work. How often have we read on the box, *"Batteries not included"*? Indeed, Walgreens and similar stores are open Christmas Day in case batteries are needed for our child's new toys.

Batteries come in all sizes, from the tiny silver watch battery to the heavy, black auto or truck battery. Some are rechargeable, but most small ones are tossed or recycled when they've run out of their one-time electrical charge.

Batteries supply power to make things work due to their chemicals, but what gives us spiritual power? What makes our faith, peace or patience run smoothly?

The Bible says the Holy Spirit is God's power. The Spirit was there in the beginning at creation (Genesis 1:2), and it was with Gideon and the Old Testament prophets (Judges 3:10, 1 Samuel 10:6). It was present when Jesus was baptized (Matthew 3:16) and when the Church began at Pentecost (Acts 2:1). The Spirit displays the power of God in the lives of God's people, and even tells people where they can go to serve Him (Acts 8:29).

The Bible says, **"The disciples were filled with joy and with the Holy Spirit."** (Acts 13:52) The Spirit is God's gift to empower people in His service. The Holy Spirit is God's power and is also GOD Himself.

Holy Spirit, show Yourself in our lives each day.

AUGUST 10

When my boys were young, someone gave them a "Rock Em-Sock Em" toy. It was made of inflated plastic, and stood about two feet high. The challenge was to punch it and knock it over, but no matter how hard you hit it, it would pop back upright again.

The toy's secret? It had a weight in the bottom that always kept it standing up. I am told sailboats operate under the same principle. The heavy weight below (ballast) in their keel provides a counter weight to balance the ship above the water during strong winds.

The life of a believer in Christ needs the same principle. Our ability to survive the struggles and challenges of life resides not in our human strength, but in the strength of God within us. We have His power to hold us up and sustain us when the winds of life blow hard and threaten to capsize us.

Apostle Paul wrote: **"We are hard-pressed on every side, yet not crushed; we are perplexed but not in despair; persecuted but not forsaken; struck down but not destroyed."** (2 Corinthians 4:8-9)

Paul had no instruction manual for his work of sharing Christ to people in the early church. He had only the new message of God's love that Jesus told him to share. That alone was enough to hold him upright when he felt he was tipping over. We have that power as well!

Lord, if we should fall today, help us stay upright.

AUGUST 11

Everyone wants his or her name to reflect something good. Some names, however, are perceived as negative. If someone were to say, *"Your name is Mud!"* you would probably not appreciate it. The negative connotation is from Dr. Samuel Mudd who was imprisoned for treating the broken leg of John Wilkes Booth who had just killed President Lincoln.

Another name is Ponzi, associated with the financial fraud of Charles Ponzi. Since 1920, "Ponzi scheme" has referred to money taken from new investors and given back to former investors. Ponzi lost 20 million dollars of his investors money and caused several banks to fail. After serving 3 years in jail, he was deported to Italy where he died penniless.

Proverbs often contrast wise and foolish people. **"The memory of the righteous is blessed, but the name of the wicked will rot."** (Proverbs 10:7) **"A good name is to be chosen rather than great riches, loving favor rather than silver and gold."** (Proverbs 22:1)

Christians wish to have a good name, not to honor themselves, but to give glory to our Lord Jesus. He gives us a name in Holy Baptism and blesses us with it. Poet Nelle Williams wrote,

"You got it from your father,
It was all he had to give.
So it's yours to use and cherish
For as along as you may live."

Thanks, Lord, for giving us Your name: CHRISTian.

AUGUST 12

Many years ago, a church member offered us his cabin in the mountains for a youth "overnight." The youth counselors welcomed the chance to enjoy the mountain air, quiet scenery and a little fun on a weekend, and without tents!

It was a nice, large log cabin with an open living area and big loft for sleeping. We enjoyed games, food and singing, and we spread our sleeping bags everywhere.

All went well until bedtime when we had unwelcome guests. Just before lights went out, a boy yelled, *"What's that flying up there?"* and the girls squealed! We had real, live bats flying up near the ceiling peak! What should we do?

We made several unsuccessful attempts at shooing the flying rodents outside. Then we found a pole and opened the high cabin windows that had no screens. We all made lots of racket until the bats flew out, or so we hoped they had. We didn't see them any more, but some of us didn't sleep well that night. That event was remembered for years.

One of the counselors had a great devotion the next morning. He read from James: **"My brothers, count it all joy when you fall into various trials, knowing that the testing of your faith produces patience."** (James 1:2-4)

You and I are not expected to enjoy trials or celebrate suffering. But when unwelcome events come, God will help us deal with them.

Thank You, Jesus, that You are with us in our trials.

AUGUST 13

I read an article about a powerful typhoon that almost ruined the city of Tacloban, Philippines, in 2013. An estimated ten thousand people there died and thousands more were left homeless and without work.

Three months later, a rainstorm struck while the town was still struggling to dig itself out of destruction. During that storm, a baby was born along a roadside near that town. Although the weather brought back painful memories, residents worked together to find a midwife for the mother and child, and to transport her to a clinic. Mother and baby survived and became a symbol of hope during their days of despair.

In the Old Testament times, before there were kings, God raised up judges, both men and women, to direct the affairs of His people. At one time the people had to endure forty years of oppression by the cruel Philistines. An angel appeared and told a woman God would send her a child who would deliver her people from their troubles. **"He shall begin to deliver Israel out of the hand of the Philistines,"** said the Lord (Judges 13:5). That baby was named Samson.

Trouble in life is unavoidable. However, we do not face it alone. Jesus, God's Son, was born to rescue us from the despair of our sins. He was born to give light to a world in darkness and in the shadow of death. (Luke 1:79) He would also guide us into the way of peace.

Lord Jesus, thank You for coming to be our Savior.

AUGUST 14

Times have surely changed. A few days after coming to serve my congregation in 1975, I got the a bad cold and went to a local doctor for help. He was glad to meet me, and after writing a prescription, he said I could pay the bill out in front. The window lady said, *"An office visit is $4, but for pastors it is half price, $2."* Wow! I'd never paid a doctor so little. I pulled out my wallet and she said, *"Paying cash? That's a 10% discount. You owe $1.80."*

It was a big difference from the Emergency Room visit thirty years later when I had a similar problem. With insurance it still cost me $380. Yes, times have surely changed.

One thing that's unchanged in my years of ministry is my schedule of fees for services – I've never had one. Sometimes after days of work, *"Thank you, Pastor"* is all that's offered. But that's okay. I'm there to serve and God will provide.

And well He has provided. Since leaving home and earning my first paycheck, God has always given us enough. Prophet Jeremiah had a good attitude. He prayed, **"But as for me, behold, I am in Your hands. Do with me as seems good and right to You."** (Jeremiah 26:14)

His attitude required a huge faith. We'd like to have a little input into what God does with us, wouldn't we? Thanks be to God He does with us according to His will, not ours.

Lord, help me be grateful for all You do for me.

AUGUST 15

Few people living in North America know there is a massive network of ancient roads and trails across the land, mostly in the central and eastern areas. A unique feature along some of these trails are "Trail Trees," oaks and maples that have been intentionally shaped for hunting purposes and giving directions.

Trail Trees have a horizontal bend in their trunk a few feet off the ground and several feet long, with remaining trunk growing vertically. Their L-Shape makes them visible at distances, even in the snow. Experts believe these were intentionally shaped by ancient people who disappeared from the continent long ago.

Even today, modern hunters in certain areas look for Trail Trees while hunting large game animals. Although it's unknown how many of these trees are still alive, one Trail Tree known as "Grandfather" is still alive in White County, Indiana.

The Old Testament writings give similar directions to us. The Ten Commandments show us the right way to live, and the prophets show us how to relate to God. The Old Testament says a Messiah will come to redeem us from our sins, and the New Testament says He is Jesus.

The Psalmist wrote, **"They pierced my hands and feet, they divided my garments, casting lots for them."** (Psalm 22:16-18) What greater "Trail Tree" than Jesus can we have?

Lord Jesus, help us believe You are our Savior.

AUGUST 16

Evangelist Billy Graham said, *"In dialogues with young people, many say that more than wanting things, they want to know how to find meaning and purpose. I suggest they can achieve these desires only when they find three things: A moral code to follow, a cause to serve, and a creed to believe in."* Let's look at what Dr. Graham said:

A moral code to follow: Each of us needs a moral compass, a point from which our acts and decisions can be made. Without it, life will be empty and confusing. At the least we need someone who can model that code for us.

A cause to serve: Our life's purpose is for more than just making money. It's to use our talents and interests to provide for ourselves, our loved ones and those in need.

A creed to believe in: Every person has beliefs, but only by faith in Jesus as the Son of God can we have direction for this life and hope for the life to come. Jesus fills the void created by sin, and He helps us fulfill a life's purpose through faith and living as He wants us to live.

Apostle Paul wrote, **"I have learned in whatever situation I am to be content."** (Philippians 4:11) Being a Christian does not guarantee us an ever-content, trouble-free life, but it does give us godly joy on earth and a bright future in heaven. Morality, purpose and a creed are blessings God can give us. May we seek His will every day.

Lord, help us find our compass of life in You.

AUGUST 17

A successful entertainer was driving her car too fast on a highway and was pulled over by a patrolman. When he asked for her license, proof of insurance and registration, she screamed, *"I don't have those things with me. Do you have any idea who I am?"* The patrolman said, *"Yes I do, ma'am. Right now you are under arrest."*

An old saying goes, *"If you have to tell people who you are, you probably really aren't who you think you are."* God's Word says, **"When pride comes, then comes disgrace, but with the humble there is wisdom."** (Proverbs 11:2)

When Jesus came to Jerusalem for the last time, it caused quite a stir among those who saw Him. Some asked, **"Who is this?"** and others replied, **"This is Jesus, the prophet from Nazareth of Galilee."** (Matthew 21:10)

Jesus didn't come demanding special treatment, but in humility, riding a donkey. He came in obedience to His Father's will. The words He spoke and things He did were usually greeted with respect, but often He came at times that showed weakness and failure. The people then saw a sad religious man, but with time the world realized He was the Son of God.

Jesus comes into our hearts in meekness, and transforms us into God's children. He is worthy of our love and devotion, whether we recognize Him or not. May we always grant Him the honor He deserves.

Lord, help us know You as our Savior and Lord.

AUGUST 18

An elderly woman joined my congregation years ago, and I learned she was a direct descendant of C. F. W. Walther, one of the leaders of the group of Saxon Lutherans who came from Germany in the 1840s seeking religious freedom. Margaret was a remarkable woman who served our church until into her 90s.

During a visit, she said she needed both knees replaced and decided to get them done as close together as the doctor allowed. *"He said I'd have a lot of pain no matter when it was done, so I decided to get the pain over with as soon as possible."* And she was in her 80s!

Some might call this "pain with a purpose." Whether it's pain of childbirth, surgery or loss of a loved one, it is necessary to bear because it serves a larger purpose.

Before Jesus' suffering and death, He told His disciples, **"You will have sorrow now, but I will see you again, and your hearts will rejoice, and no one will take your joy from you."** (John 16:22)

Sorrow comes to us all on our journey in life. Jesus is our best example of getting through pain to the joy on the other side. **"For the joy that was set before Him, Jesus endured the cross, despising the shame."** (Hebrews 12:2) His suffering did what we needed, opening the way of salvation to God. Because He suffered pain with a purpose, you and I are blessed.

Lord, thank You for doing what needed to be done.

AUGUST 19

The news came of houses sliding down a hillside after a long rain and an earthquake. I said a brief prayer of thanks that I wasn't there, although I once had lived near there while serving a congregation in southern California.

California sits on the Pacific Rim area called the "Ring of Fire." Ninety percent of the world's largest earthquakes happen in the Ring of Fire. Some of the buildings along it are anchored on bedrock, but even that doesn't insure they can't be shaken. Foundations need to be very solid in areas where earthquakes occur.

Jesus told His followers they needed a solid foundation in life. His story of the two houses, one built on sand and the other on the rock, makes this clear. **"Everyone then who hears these words of mine and does them will be like a wise man who built his house on the rock."** (Matthew 7:24)

If our life is built on the changing sands of wealth, power or pleasure, we are living on shifting, unstable soil. When we base our lives on Jesus, He gives us stability and strength to hold firm in life now, with the promise of life to come with Him in the future.

It's always best to seek God's wisdom and direction each day. Whether in work or family, daily decisions or choosing priorities, He will provide us a firm and trustworthy foundation on which we can build our lives.

Father God, show us how to live and help us live it.

AUGUST 20

One of the most memorable messages I ever delivered occurred early in my ministry. I was hosting a small Pastoral Conference which began with a communion service for ten pastors and their wives. We were all sitting around a large square of tables, and I was speaking on the words of 1 Peter 2:2, **"Like newborn infants, long for the pure spiritual milk, that by it you may grow up into salvation."** When I looked up, I realized one of the young wives was nursing her baby right in front of me.

Needless to say, I was flustered and babbled something until I got back on track of my message. Afterwards the young wife quietly said to me, *"Sorry about that. It was the only way I knew for sure he'd stop fussing."*

The 2010 documentary film called "Babies" follows four infants born in Namibia, Mongolia, Tokyo and America. There was very little narration, only scenes and sounds of the little babies as they began to discover their world. On thing was certain - they all liked milk!

Followers of Jesus should crave the milk of God's Word, for it leads to spiritual growth. Peter urged the people to set aside their feelings of anger and jealousy toward each other, and seek what is needful to grow in their faith.

God loves to see His children grow. He gives us to drink of His spiritual food and helps us increase in our faith each day.

Lord, help us grow in faith by seeking Your Word.

AUGUST 21

I took up snow skiing when I was 30 years old. Friends at my church had talked about it, and both my wife and boys were interested in learning a winter sport. That was back in the 1970s when a lift ticket on a big mountain cost only $15-20. Today that same mountain lift ticket can cost $150, just for one day of skiing.

I enjoyed the sport each winter until costs became too great, both monetary and health. Not that my old body couldn't have continued longer, but I was run over a time or two by young skiers, and I decided to play it safe and let them have the mountain. My ski equipment needed replacing, too, so I gave it up.

I learned a few things about life from skiing. When you're going down a hill, know 1) Where is the bottom? 2) Which run should you take? 3) What's right in front of you on the trail?

It's much like life: 1) Where do you want to end up? 2) What path will you take to get there? 3) How will you live each day to do so?

Our Lord's words help us: **"For which of you, desiring to build a tower, does not first sit down and count the cost, whether he has enough to build it?"** (Luke 14:28), **"Watch, for you do not know the day nor the hour."** (Matthew 25:13), **"Seek first the Kingdom of God, and all these things will be yours as well"** (Matthew 6:33)

God's blessings include sports! But watch where you are and see where you're going.

Lord, show us Your path to take in life each day.

AUGUST 22

Health specialists tell us we need to walk more. Walking is easy, inexpensive and helps us live healthier and live longer. A recent study showed that walking 2.5 hours per week can result in a person living 3.5 years longer.

I know all that stuff, but still don't walk enough. When I do get off the couch and go for a walk, I have several paths I can take, and since I get bored while walking, I try to vary my route, often walking the route the opposite way. It makes walking more interesting.

Its amazing what you see when you go the other way. Houses, plants, lawns, trees and even the cars in traffic look different. It's easy to get caught in a rut, so it's good to get out of it by varying where you walk.

Jesus once told his disciples to try another way. After His resurrection, they went fishing all night and caught nothing (maybe to discourage them from going back to being fishermen). He told them, **"Cast the net on the other side of the boat and you will find some."** (John 21:6) They did and were overwhelmed with their huge catch.

God has plans for us all. Somehow by His almighty power He is able to keep track of us and point us in the right direction. He gives us other routes and shows us a new way of seeing things. When we take the chance of following Jesus, our life's path can be new, interesting and even challenging.

Lord, show us Your ways and teach us Your paths.

AUGUST 23

A young man was engaged to be married that summer and had been accepted into college that fall, but he decided to have one last fling. Late in the spring one night he drank a few beers and pulled a prank that landed him in jail and in front of a judge.

The judge knew the young man and his family, so he listened to the evidence, declared the man guilty and gave him a sound tongue-lashing. He also sentenced him to two years of probation, and ended by saying, *"You will get married, you will go to college, and don't ever let me hear of you doing something like this again."*

The young man did as he was told. He married and became father of two fine sons and taught High School classes for 35 years. Some of his former students attended his funeral and stated that he had helped change their lives.

God can turn a bad life into something good. He made a fanatical youth named Saul become Apostle Paul. He made a hedonistic young Augustine to become a Bishop in the early Church. He also made Rahab, a prostitute, to become great-grandmother of King David.

It's the same David who later wrote, **"O Lord our Lord, how majestic is Your name in all the earth."** (Psalm 8:9) God can do wonders in the world, turning bad into good, and He does it, as one Bible scholar states, *"With or without our approval."*

Thanks, Lord, for forgiveness that makes us all good.

AUGUST 24

A few years ago my son gave me a copy of John Wooden's autobiography, <u>They Call Me Coach.</u> During his 27 years as coach at UCLA, Wooden's NCAA basketball teams won an unprecedented 10 National Championships. Yet when Wooden died in 2010, he was remembered not just for what he accomplished in basketball, but for the kind of person he was.

The reason was simple: John Wooden lived his Christian faith. His genuine concern for others, especially his players, shined as a bright light in the world of sports obsessed with winning. In his book he wrote, *"I always tried to make it clear that basketball is not the ultimate. It is of small importance in comparison to the total life we live. There is only one kind of life that truly wins, and that is the one that places faith in the hands of the Savior. Until that is done, we are on an aimless course that runs in circles and goes nowhere."*

At only 5 feet 10 inches tall, John was a giant of faith among giants in a sport. He honored God in all he did, and by his words and example, he challenged others to do the same.

Jesus said, **"Let your light so shine before men that they may see your good works, and glorify your Father in heaven."** (Matthew 5:15) To honor His Lord and Savior, John Wooden let his light shine, and is often still mentioned during the America's annual NCAA "March Madness" tournament. His faith still shines today.

Father God, let our faith shine in all we do and say.

AUGUST 25

A woman wanted her son to take violin lessons from the great Isaac Stern. After one of his performances, she made her way backstage holding a tape recorder. *"Mr. Stern."* she said, *"You must hear my son play. He plays just like Jascha Heifetz."* Stern decided to stop and listen to her tape and said, *"My goodness he does sound just like Heifetz."* The woman said, *"Well, the tape is by Heifetz, but my son, he plays just like him."*

Albert Einstein once said, *"Only two things are infinite, the universe and human stupidity, and I'm not sure about the former."* Sadly, it is true that people say and do foolish things that cause us to shake our heads.

King David did many foolish things and often poured out his heart to God about them. He wrote, **"There is no soundness in my flesh... no health in my bones... my iniquities have gone over my head, like a heavy burden, they are too great... I am feeble and crushed."** (Psalm 38:3,4,8)

David does not give us details why he wrote those words, but we can almost imagine the reasons. His own foolishness usually caused his troubles. All people, kings included, are sinful and need God's grace and mercy in Jesus.

But David knew what was needed, so he later also wrote, **"The fear of the Lord is the beginning of wisdom; those who practice it have a good understanding."** (Psalm 111:10)

Lord Jesus, help us find our wisdom in You.

AUGUST 26

I wonder if God will give us "replays" in heaven. Our baseball team, the Rockies, had an unusually bad record one April, but on May 2, they hammered the Cubs 11-2. It was a great game, but we were gone and forgot to record it. However, we were able to see the highlights replayed that evening, not the whole game, but the great plays. Replays made it possible.

Maybe God will give us replays of the great moments of our lives. Wouldn't that be great? Because of Jesus, we need not fear replays of our sins. But in His mercy, maybe we'll see the good times again. But heaven will be so great that we won't have the need to see them.

Just before entering the promised land, Moses prayed that God would overlook their sins. He said, **"Remember Your servants, Abraham, Isaac and Jacob, but do not regard the stubbornness of this people or the wickedness of their sin.** (Deuteronomy 9:27) Moses, a giant of faith, wanted God to forget the bad times but remember the good ones.

We may often pray the same way, asking God to overlook our sins while highlighting the good we've done. But due to what Jesus has done, God will forgive all our sins and not count any of them against us. That's His Gospel: In Jesus, we'll only see the good!

What replays in your life would you like to see? Marriage? Children? Success? Final Four?

Lord, thank You for giving us good times to recall.

AUGUST 27

I am always amazed at the accuracy of today's weather forecasts. As a young man I used to joke that the only weather report I could depend on was the one I could see outside my window.

But now the "App" on my "Smart Phone" gives me a very accurate forecast of what the weather will be. High or low temperatures, cloudy, rainy, snowy or sunny skies – I can see them each hour of today, tomorrow or next week. This helps me know what to wear, how to drive, and many other details of my day.

The Bible is also filled with forecasts, not about the weather, but about one's life. If we follow sinful ways, we'll suffer consequences. But if we follow God's will, we will see His abundant blessings for us.

Paul sums it up: **"Whatever one sows, that will he also reap. The one who sows to his own flesh will from the flesh reap corruption, but the one who sows to the Spirit, will from the Spirit, reap eternal life."** (Galatians 6:8)

That's Paul's forecast of what will happen when we live our Christian life of faith. If we sow a life of sin, we shall reap a life of sadness, but if we sow a life of faith in the Son of God, we will reap His gift of eternal life.

God's forecast is given to us all, and He is does not make inaccurate promises. Thanks be to God, then, that we have forgiveness in Jesus.

Jesus, help us follow Your ways in all our doings.

AUGUST 28

My home state of Colorado attracts thousands of visitors each year, many of whom do not realize the dangers of living here. For example, people can become dehydrated in our dry climate with its intense sun at higher elevations. Our home on the eastern edge of the Front Range is 6,200 feet high, and we have low average rainfall. Thus, tourist maps, signs and other information urge people to drink lots of water.

But despite many warnings, many people ignore it. Every year dozens of dehydrated visitors get sick. I know this because it happened to me. One Sunday morning I passed out in the pulpit. I'd been trying to lose a few pounds and hadn't drank enough water. How embarrassing it was to be carried to the Emergency Room and there be scolded for not drinking enough water.

Jesus is our Living Water, and He told the Samaritan woman at the well, **"Whoever drinks of this well water will thirst again. But whoever drinks of the water I give him will never thirst again."** (John 4:13)

Hearing Jesus' words, the woman went back to her village and said, **"Come, see a man who told me all that I ever did. Can this be the Christ?"** (John 4:29) She became His follower and invited others to do the same. That's what Jesus wants us to do as well.

We can't live without water, nor without Jesus. He is our Lord - Come see Him often!

Lord, give us Your living water every day.

244

AUGUST 29

People around the world are fascinated by royalty. Queen Elizabeth II has reigned over the British Empire since 1952, and each royal birth or wedding in her family draws attention from all over. Video series like "The Queen" or "Downton Abbey" attracts millions of viewers. Everyone seems interested in royalty.

But not everyone likes royalty. When Prince Harry and Meghan Markle decided to get married, her half-brother Thomas told the Prince to call off the wedding because she was unworthy of him. No reason given, just advice.

Many people, however, seek the status of royalty. When Crown Prince Albert, son of Queen Victoria, visited America at the end of the 19th century, wealthy heiresses descended on each of his royal balls, hoping to become his royal bride. "Berty" was quite a lady's man.

Christians are already assured of being in God's royal, heavenly family. Apostle John tells us this: **"Let us exalt and give Him glory, for the marriage of the Lamb has come, and His bride has made herself ready. She clothes herself in fine linen, bright and pure."** (Revelation 19:7-8)

In John's book, Christ is the Bridegroom and believers are His bride. As the bride of Christ, we are to make ourselves "ready" by trusting Him and striving to be like Him. We look forward to the day we will be with Him forever.

Lord Jesus, help us be ready to live with You forever.

AUGUST 30

While most new homes today are built on tiny lots, we are blessed with 1/5 acre, and it's loaded with many shrubs and big trees, some 35-40 feet high. When the high winds blow, I pray the big branches won't break.

We have animals and some of them are a nuisance. Tiny voles (field mice) chewed up our big juniper hedge one winter. Rabbits make gardening impossible and squirrels chewed holes our neighbor's roof. Large deer may walk silently through our yard, but noisy squirrels can wake up the neighborhood.

These two animals represent two ways of living. Squirrels prepare for winter, hiding the acorns of our oak brush, but deer store nothing. Winter or summer, they eat whatever they can find, including shrubs and garden plants. Squirrels would starve if they lived like deer, and deer can starve if they can't find enough of what God and His people plant.

The deer and squirrel show us how God cares for us. He enables us to work and save for the future, but He also meets our needs when resources are scarce. The Bible says, **"Whoever works his land will have plenty of bread, but he who follows worthless pursuits lacks sense."** (Proverbs 12:11)

God's good message for us is to work while we can, save what we can, share what we can and trust God for all the rest.

Lord, thanks for all our blessings. Help us share them.

AUGUST 31

Have you ever had plans shattered? Have you felt huge disappointment because what you hoped for never came true?

A writer named Julie told me of her friend Linda who wished to become a medical missionary. She wanted to serve God as a doctor who could take the gospel to sick people in other parts of the world. Linda did become a missionary, just not the way she planned, because God had other plans.

At age 14, Linda developed a chronic health problem requiring her to be hospitalized for surgery several times a year. Meningitis put her in a coma 2 weeks and left her blind 6 months. Several times Linda was not expected to live, but God had other plans.

Instead of serving God as a doctor, Linda served Him as a patient. No matter how sick she was, the light of her faith shone through her days of hospitalization. She was a joy to be around.

Her attitude evoked words of Peter, **"In this you rejoice, though now for a little while, if necessary, you have been grieved by various trials, so that the tested genuineness of your faith, more precious than gold and perishes though tested by fire, may be found to result in praise and glory and honor at the revelation of Jesus Christ."** (1 Peter 1:6-7)

Linda lives yet on earth, but Julie is now with the Lord. Praise God for all His servants.

Lord, help me be joyful in the midst of any troubles.

247

EVERY DAY WITH JESUS
in September

❧

SEPTEMBER 1

Labor day will soon be here. Some people believe work is bad, a curse due to sin that must be endured as punishment. This mistaken belief leads people to think their jobs aren't important, or aren't as important as the work someone else does.

But no matter what we may think of it, work is good. For much of my ministry I looked forward to a time when I would not be hemmed in by a daily schedule. Now that I am retired, I see every day the need for things to do, and the benefits found in physical and mental activity.

Time hangs heavily on our hands when there is no work. True, it's a pleasure to have time off to rest. Even Jesus did that and urged His disciples to do the same. But we need activities, labor to shape life and time to share our life with others.

The one who prefers to remain idle, who lives off the labor of others, expecting them to provide all needs, becomes more than lazy. He becomes a parasite, taking from others and giving nothing back. That person thinks others "owe him a living", so he creates reasons not to work.

Good work helps everyone, but evil or neglected work destroys people and society. Approaching each day's labor is best done with an awareness of the dignity of the work God gave us in the world. **"God saw everything that He had made and behold, it was very good."** (Genesis 1:31)

Lord, help us enjoy our work and helping others.

SEPTEMBER 2

Syndicated artist Stephan Pastis drew a Sunday cartoon that caught my attention. It went something like this:

"Burt had a realization: 'I am unhappy.' So he played the lottery every day for ten years until one day he said, 'I won, I won!' So he went out and bought a fleet of cars, and a giant boat, and a huge house. But then he had a realization, 'I'm still unhappy.' Burt spent the rest of his life yelling at his money, 'MAKE ME HAPPY!' In the final panel a pig said, 'There's a lesson here somewhere.'" ("Pearls Before Swine", Denver Post, 5/6/18)

What would you say the lesson is? I wonder how many people work hard to make lots of money, and get an even a bigger house, but still feel unhappy like Burt.

Happiness should not be our quest. It is a by-product of life, a gift from achievement or from the love of a good person. "Happy" is rarely found in the Bible. More often God's Word speaks of "contented", "peaceful" or "blessed."

Paul speaks of the Holy Spirit giving us **"The fruit of the Spirit: love, joy, peace, patience, kindness, goodness, faithfulness, gentleness, self-control."** (Galatians 5:22-23)

Knowing Jesus as our Savior beings us such wonderful happiness. In Him we know God loves us and seeks our welfare. In Jesus, we know we can be happy.

Lord Jesus, help us find our true happiness in You.

SEPTEMBER 3

Many people have a hard time waiting. Whether youth, working adult or senior citizen, we struggle if we have to wait a long time.

One year I filed an Amended Tax Return that promised a large refund. I tried not to think of it, yet every day I expected it would be in the mailbox. The check came four months later, but by then I'd become so accustomed to the wait, it was days before I stopped looking for the mail to come. Waiting can leave its mark on us.

But what if we don't know whether or not what we're hoping for will happen? How does a hostage deal with waiting for release? How does a cancer patient deal with waiting for remission?

How does a young lover wait when Mr. Right or Miss Perfect fails to come along? How do Christians deal with waiting for Christ's return when centuries pass after His promise?

A goal can make our waiting easier, but without one, our wait can drag us down and lead us to feel abandoned.

The Psalms give us encouragement: **"We wait in hope for the Lord."** (Psalm 33:20), **"I wait for the Lord, my whole being waits."** (Psalm 130:5) **"Hope in the Lord and keep His way."** (Psalm 37:34) These are but a few of God's encouraging verses.

Waiting for the Lord with trust can give us confidence, courage, and strength for each day. The almighty God will not let us down. He will give us what He has promised.

Lord Jesus, help us place our hope in You.

SEPTEMBER 4

"Why do people rebuild after disasters?" asked Greg Hobbs, Denver Post columnist. Hurricanes destroy homes, wildfires burn businesses and floods ruin towns, but disaster survivors nearly always say, *"We will rebuild again."*

Dobbs asked this of a survivor who'd lost homes in three hurricanes. The man retorted, *"And where are you from?"* Dobbs said, *"San Francisco,"* *"Don't they have earthquakes there?"* *"Yes, but I live in Colorado now,"* Dobbs said. *"Don't they have fires there?"* said the man.

Communities along the Mississippi are flooded, but they rebuild. In Oklahoma and Kansas, people have homes torn apart by tornadoes, but they, too, rebuild. Dobbs concluded his article, *"If one doesn't get you, another might."* My father used to say, *"Everyone has to be somewhere."* So simple, yet so true. And there's no place without some danger.

The bad news is that it's all our fault. People are responsible for these disasters. The perfect world is messed up by sin. God cursed the ground because of our rebellion, so we'll have pain and suffering, thorns and thistles, work and sweat, as long as we live.

The good news is God's love will provide us a new heaven and a new earth. **"God will dwell among the people... He will wipe away all tears... There will be no more death or mourning or crying or pain."** (Revelation 21:3-4)

And all because of God's love. Thank You, Jesus!

Jesus' crucifixion for the sins of the world is the "great reversal." In Him, almighty God became human, that we might be set free.

In the movie "Spartacus", a Roman officer demands to know which of the captured slaves is Spartacus. As Spartacus arises, a slave next to him stands, saying, "I'm Spartacus!" Another slave says, "I'm Spartacus!" And so do they all, confusing the soldiers and sacrificing themselves for their leader. Historians say the body of Spartacus was never found, and all the slaves in his army were crucified.

The movie is a reversal of Jesus' parable of the rich man and Lazarus. Our Lord Jesus was willing to sacrifice Himself to free all people who are enslaved to sin. He became like Lazarus, poor and despised, while being God's Son on earth to bear the punishment of our sins.

Paul wrote, **"You know the grace of our Lord Jesus Christ. Though He was rich, yet for your sake He became poor, that by His poverty you might become rich."** (2 Corinthians 8:9).

Again, **"For our sake He made Him to be sin who knew no sin, that in Him we might become God's righteousness."** (2 Corinthians 5:21) Jesus actually became sin in order to forgive us.

"Lazarus" means, *"The one God helps."* At the Judgment Day, Jesus shall say, *"I took the place of those sinners."* The Divine Helper was crucified for us, and so we are all set free from slavery of sin to live eternally.

Lord Jesus, help us understand Your love for us.

SEPTEMBER 6

While it is sad to see the devastation of storms, it is a joy to see people cooperate in the aftermath. Sometimes more people step up to help than those whose lives were torn apart.

We hear much today of a divided America, so it is good when people put feelings aside to help each other. One year, two hurricanes, Irma and Harvey, hit the eastern seacoast, one after the other. They came at the time when Congress was returning from its summer recess, and we saw elected officials lending helping hands in the cleanup efforts.

What will it take to bring us together? Storm and devastation can do it if people cooperate. Prayer certainly helps. Asaph, David's worship leader, prayed when the Ark was brought to the tabernacle, **"Save us, God our Savior; gather and deliver us from the nations, that we may give thanks to Your holy name, and glory in Your praise."** (1 Chronicles 16:35)

Celebrations can unite us. Many a church that struggled in the past can find joy in a joint service of celebration, anniversary or other community event. God can use many ways to bring His people together. We show Him our thanks when our efforts are successful.

Jesus prayed that His people may be one, just as He and the Father are one (John 17:21). May we seek this among ourselves also. If we do, we will be truly blessed.

Thanks, Jesus, for bringing us together in any way.

SEPTEMBER 7

People have doubts, because we like proof. To experience doubt about God is part of being human. Doubt is feeling uncertain about the supposed truth or reality of something. We can't see God, so we wonder if He's really there. We see creation, and wonder if it came from chance.

We want proof, yet we live every day without it. We turn on the light and expect it will work because it did yesterday. We believe our loved ones will act or feel about us today as they did yesterday. Hearing or seeing something different may cause us to wonder, but wondering is not sinful. Nor is doubt in itself.

Doubts are like temptations coming through images, thoughts or words. Apostle Paul said, **"There is no temptation that is not common to all people... but with the temptation God will provide us a way out."** (1 Corinthians 10:13)

Jesus prayed to His Father in the Garden to show Him another way to save the world. He prayed for a less painful way. Was that doubt? We know His Father didn't condemn Him for it.

Here are three principles: *1) Don't run from your doubts or think having them makes you less Christian. 2) Deal with them through God's Word. 3) Doubts are overcome by a person, not a situation.*

Jesus is that Person. He helps us deal with our doubts. They won't disappear just because things change. Jesus' brother Jude once wrote, **"Lord have mercy on those who doubt."** (Jude 1:22)

Lord, help us trust that You are the Creator.

◆ Despite attempts by those who would force us into their way of life, we are still free.

◆ Despite the laws from governments that restrict speech and actions, we are still free.

◆ Despite endless edicts from non-elected regulators to "protect us," we are still free.

◆ Despite those who say the world will fall unless we follow them, we are still free.

◆ Despite legalization of acts humanity has considered unwise for ages, we are still free.

◆ Despite being swamped by useless bits of information, we are still free.

◆ Despite all those who claim believing in God is dangerous, we are still free.

☆ We are free to worship God as we choose, despite what others may threaten.

☆ We are free to defend ourselves and loved ones, even with force, for it is a God-given right.

☆ We are free to think whatever thoughts we may have, for no one can police our mind.

☆ We are free to pursue happiness so long as we do not harm others in our quest.

☆ We are free to cherish our loved ones and keep marriage commitments until death parts us.

☆ We are free to give thanks to God and mankind for the right to live without fear.

"If you abide in My word, you are truly My disciples, and you will know the truth, and the *truth will set you free."* (John 8:31-32)

Lord, keep us free to follow You and Your will.

SEPTEMBER 9

Over the years I have written several dozen hymns, some completely new, some to support a sermon, and others to add verses to published hymns during worship. When I mentioned this in a Bible Class, a woman said I should publish them. I thanked her and declined. There are so many better hymns.

Charles Wesley (1707-1788) wrote more than 9,000 hymns and sacred poems! Many of them are well-known, such as, *"O For a Thousand Tongues to Sing," "Christ the Lord Is Risen Today," "Hark! The Herald Angels Sing," "Jesus, Lover of My Soul,"* and *"Love Divine, All Loves Excelling."* A favorite of mine is this:

> *"Gentle Jesus, meek and mild,*
> *Look upon a little child.*
> *Bless me and remember me,*
> *Savior, let me come to Thee."*

The hymn brings to mind children coming to Jesus and His disciples trying to stop them. He said, **"Let the little children come to me and do not hinder them, for to such belongs the kingdom of heaven."** (Matthew 19:14)

Children rarely seek position or power, but rather love, acceptance and security. Jesus never turned children away. Wesley wrote in one of his 14 verses to this hymn:

"Loving Jesus, gentle Lamb / In Thy gracious hands I am / Make me, Savior, what Thou art / Live Thyself within my heart."

Lord, help us always have the faith of a child.

257

SEPTEMBER 10

When a marriage breaks up, there are so many emotional struggles to confront. Christine was bitter and vowed never to meet Fred's new wife, but eventually she knew their children would make this impossible. After much prayer, she realized it would be best for their children if she and their father's new wife, Mary, could at least be cordial to each other.

With God's help and prayer, Christine and Mary became friends. As time passed, their friendship took a crucial turn when Fred died in an auto accident. God used their friendship to help them all deal with his loss.

Genesis 16-21 is the story of Abraham and Sarah dealing with being childless. When Sarah suggested Abram have a child with her servant Hagar, their home situation became worse. When the baby Ishmael was born, Hagar and Sarah became bitter rivals.

Sarah blamed Abraham and Hagar for her sadness. Even when God gave them Isaac 14 years later, his birth celebration was spoiled by Sarah's attitude. Dealing with disappointment in family troubles is rarely easy. Shattered hopes and dreams can last a lifetime.

"Blessed is everyone who fears the Lord, who walks in His ways." (Psalm 128:1) Family healing requires faith, prayer, commitment and forgiveness. It is loving and honoring all those who God puts in our lives.

Lord, help us honor marriage and love all people.

SEPTEMBER 11

If you've had to go on a liquid diet, you may understand a little about suffering. Whenever I've had a certain medical procedure, not being able to eat the day before is worse than the test. A body can only take so much broth or Jello.

Felix Hoffmann was a chemist in the 1890s who was given the task of finding something to alleviate pain. Many of his new compounds caused other problems, like nausea and gastric pain. Hoffmann's father suffered from arthritis, so he agreed to let Felix try out different compounds on him to see which worked best.

The result was the discovery of "acetylsalicylic acid," commonly known as aspirin. While the new drug provided wonderful pain relief, old Mr. Hoffmann went through more pain and suffering from the various compounds until the right formula was found.

As we read God's Word in the Bible, we discover restrictions on what we'd like to do, such as drinking too much alcohol or having sex outside marriage, actions which may seem natural but carry negative consequences. When God's Word tell us to avoid these acts, we may not like it, but it's for our good.

The Psalmist wrote, **"I am afflicted and in pain; let Your salvation, O God, set me on high!"** (Psalm 69:29) Struggles and pain may make us cry out to God in troubled times, but the end result of faith and peace is worth it.

O God, heal me, that I may serve and praise You.

SEPTEMBER 12

This time of year we are reminded that things of the world don't last forever. Leaves, alive and fresh during the summer, fade and die in the autumn. Decorative bushes change from green to deep red, and aspen leaves turn gold. All will soon fall off, leaving barren branches at the mercy of winter's snow and cold.

The Bible says, **"All flesh is like grass and all its glory like the flower of grass. The grass withers, and the flower falls, but the Word of the Lord remains forever."** (1 Peter 1:24-25)

If we only see what ages and dies, we would have little or no hope for life. However, the Word of the Lord remains, giving us lasting hope amid the cycle of life and death. That Word from God lasts forever.

Nothing in creation lasts forever, but God's eternal mercy and grace do. Despite death being ever present, mankind has tried to find a way to live forever. People have always sought a "fountain of youth" that gives eternal life. Happily, in Jesus there is such a life with God in eternity, and it is ours by faith in Jesus.

We live between the eternities, the one that was before us and the one that is to come. Life may seem short, but God's mercy gives us purpose. We can share our hope and love with others. Yet we cannot share what we do not have. We must seek God's blessings in His Holy Word, for that lasts forever.

Lord, help us to share Your love and hope today.

SEPTEMBER 13

A mother was belting her two little ones into their airplane seats as the flight attendant was giving instructions. Mom whispered something to the little ones, and when the flight attendant finished with, *"Thank you,"* the little girl said, *"Amen!"* She thought her mother had said the flight attendant was praying. How nice the little girl had respect for God in prayer.

I wonder how many of the flight crew really pray to God, before, during or after a flight. I've always been fascinated with flight and had once considered getting my pilot's license. But these days I appreciate having both my feet on the ground, and usually give a prayer of thanks when my flight is over. Modern travel is amazing. It's fast, comfortable, economical and it surely beats walking or riding a horse.

Two men were walking the first Easter Day when Jesus joined them, although they did not know Him. He explained to them the Scriptures about the Messiah, and when they reached their home, they said, **"'Stay with us, for it is toward evening and the day is now far spent."** (Luke 24:29) So He stayed, and as they ate together, they recognized who He was.

We, too, will recognize Jesus when we listen to Him in His Word. He shows us that He is the Promised One who forgives our sins and grants us peace and contentment. In Jesus, all our crucial needs are fully met.

Thank You, Savior, for being with us in life.

261

SEPTEMBER 14

Bill and Joann had been happily married many years and enjoyed each other's love and companionship. As the years went by they laughed at how similar to each other they had become, thinking or saying the same things.

Bill learned that whenever Joann said, *"Bill I've been thinking…"* that meant she had some work for him. And even if he first said "No", he eventually went and did what she wanted. When she said she'd lost something, he just waited for her to say, *"I found it!"* They'd learned to know each other well.

God knows us well, too. We may grumble at life and even wonder if there really is a God who cares about us, but we know He is there. We may not like the way things are going, but we know He is in control and we trust Him.

"Lord, You have been our dwelling place in all generations. Before the mountains were brought forth, or ever You had formed the earth and the world, from everlasting to everlasting You are God." (Psalm 90:1-2) So writes the Psalmist. It is good to know we can trust God for all that is to come.

What better can we do than to trust Him? Trust ourselves? We are selfish and fickle. Trust knowledge? It changes and contradicts itself. But this much we know: **"The Lord is good; His steadfast love endures forever, and His faithfulness to all generations."** (Psalm 100:5)

Lord, how can we thank You enough for Your love?

SEPTEMBER 15

The Bible is filled with examples of evil men, but only a few evil women. We may think of Delilah who tricked Samson by cutting off his hair, or Jezebel who got Ahab to murder poor Naboth, but most Bible women were good.

But have you ever heard of Athaliah? She appeared a gentle grandmother in public, but in secret she was evil. When her son. King Ahaziah, was killed, she ordered his entire royal family be put to death so she could take over the throne. Athaliah had a good teacher, for she was a descendent of King Ahab and Jezebel!

But Athaliah's hired killers missed one of her grandsons. Baby Joash was hidden and raised by those loyal to the royal family. When he was grown, Joash was made king and evil Athaliah was executed. Under King Joash, Judah served the Lord. The Bible says, **"So all the people of the land rejoiced, and the city was quiet after Athaliah had been put to death with the sword."** (2 Chronicles 23:21)

Many the Bible stories are very harsh and bloody, but the Bible is based on true history, however sinful it seems. Through the prophets, God directed His people to follow His will, so that they would not fall from His grace.

God has no grandchildren. Others may teach us the faith, but each of us must believe in Jesus personally. People of each generation must follow Christ and be rooted in faith.

Lord Jesus, give us faithful teachers and leaders.

SEPTEMBER 16

Have you ever sent an e-mail and wished you hadn't? Maybe you've received a hurtful one and you're not sure why. Our age of instant messaging can work for good, but it can also give rise to words better left unspoken.

In 49 BC, Roman General Julius Caesar and his armies crossed a river. He'd done this countless times before, but this time it was an act of treason. By law, no Roman General was allowed to bring his troops into the city of Rome. So crossing the Rubicon was irreversible, and it started a bloody civil war. *"Crossing the Rubicon"* today is a phrase meaning passing the point of no return.

Sometimes people speak hard and spiteful words, and they can't be taken back. Words may bring hope and comfort, but hateful words can do lasting damage. James says the tongue can be like a fire that destroys, thus we must take care what we say. (James 3:6)

Realizing this, Paul says, **"Let your speech always be gracious, seasoned with salt, so that you may know how you ought to answer each person."** (Colossians 4:6) Take care what you say!

How blessed we are that Jesus forgives. He who was derided and scorned, knows how easy it is for people to do the same. When we repent, He offers us a second chance to make amends and to encourage, show love and lift up instead of spreading rancor and hatred.

Lord, when unsure what to say, help me first to pray.

SEPTEMBER 17

This time of year thousands of young sons and daughters have left home for college, many of them for the first time. Most parents want their children to "cut the cord," some even insisting their children not call them unless it is a serious matter for many days or weeks. One father told his daughter they'd not accept any phone calls from her until six weeks had passed. He later said she did as he said, but it was hard on them both.

Today kids with cell phones may call home often, and parents may worry if they don't. God gives parents a great task of raising young ones, giving them, *"roots to stand and wings to fly."* A parent bird will push its young out of the nest, forcing it to fly on its own. Kids can't stay in their parents' comfort zone forever.

God told Moses to take His people out of Egypt. Despite centuries of slavery, they didn't all want to leave. In the hot, dry desert they complained, **"We remember the fish we ate in Egypt that cost nothing, the cucumbers, melons, leeks, onions, and garlic."**(Numbers 11:5) Like homesick teens, they missed home cooking!

Moses didn't want to lead the grumbling people, but he did anyway. When he heard their complaints, he was fearful of becoming a bad leader. God scolded him and gave him the courage he needed. When we must leave our comfort zone, as Moses learned, God will go with us. We won't face the wilderness alone.

Lord, stay with us today and give us courage.

SEPTEMBER 18

While I have no wish to go surfing, countless people of all ages get thrills from riding the big ocean waves. If injured, the accidents and healing do not deter them from going back. Whether bitten by sharks, broken by waves or struck on the head and nearly drowned, most surfers keep going back.

Pascale Honore knows this. Left a paraplegic from an auto accident, for years she dreamed of going back to the surf where she had been thrilled as a young woman. When she turned 50, she decided to try again.

Duct-taped to the back of a professional surfer, the pair was towed out to sea by jet ski and carefully balanced on a surf board. Then they rode a big wave back in. She said, *"Having been down the past 18 years, I feel like I'm moving again."*

It takes a lot of trust to place our lives into the hands of someone else. We live in a dangerous world filled with many perils. God gives us joy when someone lends us strength to ride the churning waves of life. Jesus does that.

The Psalmist says, **"Let those rejoice who put their trust in You."** (Psalm 5:11) No matter what life may bring us, no matter how large the danger or challenge, we have a Lord who will lend us His strength and guidance.

Jesus is strong enough to help carry us through. There's no wave so big or wind so strong that He cannot safely bring us through it.

Jesus, You are the wind in our sails. Thank You.

SEPTEMBER 19

Technology has surely changed our lives. Not only do we have more information faster, we are able to see and even participate in what goes on across the world, participating in events which formerly would not have been possible.

A man living thousands of miles away loses his wife, so he sets up her memorial service on computer so that his scattered family and friends can see it as if they were there.

When a couple's wedding plans are interrupted by spring floods, and their pastor can't attend, the wedding goes on as planned, but their pastor officiates over the ceremony as seen through Skype on computer monitors.

When the sole medical doctor serving in Antarctica requires immediate surgery, doctors in the States set up a live video feed, instructing others there what to do to save the doctor's life.

I wonder what the apostle Paul would have done with today's technology. Some suggest the church wouldn't have grown as much as it has, because Christianity is based on love and relationships, not laws and information.

Jesus said, **"By this all people will know that you are my disciples, if you have love for one another."** (John 13:35) Christianity does not require electronics, but relationships. We have a vertical relationship with God, and horizontal relationships with each other. These two – up to God and sideways to each other - form a cross!

Jesus, thanks for showing us Your love on the cross.

SEPTEMBER 20

Health laws in nearly every American city prohibit the re-sale of old mattresses. Landfills will take them, but Tim Keenan of Colorado Springs wanted to give these a better use. His business employs people to extract the components of metal, fabric, and foam for recycling. This old stuff makes him money.

But that's not the best part. A local journalist wrote, *"Of all the items Keenan recycles, it's the people that may be his biggest success."* Keenan hires people from halfway houses and homeless shelters, giving them a job and a second chance. *"He takes guys nobody else wants."*

Perhaps Keenan takes his ideas from Jesus. Luke 5 tells us of Jesus healing a paralyzed man let down by others through a hole in the roof. (Luke 5:17-26) Then Jesus ate a meal at the home of Levi, a tax collector, considered a wicked man. (Luke 5:27-29). When accused of associating with "sinners", Jesus said that's why He came. **"I have not come to call the righteous, but sinners to repentance."** (Luke 5:32)

Our culture creates all kinds of "throw-aways", some of them even people. Many people feel they are in the landfill of life, wasting away - until they meet Jesus. He offers His hand to bring them out and give them a new beginning. He said, **"I came that they might have life in all its abundance."** (John 10:10)

Lord, give me a new in life, that I might serve You.

SEPTEMBER 21

I enjoy classical music and sometimes think people my age are the only ones who do. I was surprised then to find my youngest son also enjoyed some of the classics. He gave me a number of CDs for Christmas one year and when I thanked him for them, he said some of them were his favorites.

My 40+ son likes Strauss and Handel? How about that! When I asked how long he'd enjoyed them, he said for the past decade or so. He said he didn't talk about it to others, he just enjoyed the music when he listened to it.

An orchestral conductor was having a great rehearsal. The strings were in tune, the brass wasn't too loud and the drums were providing just the right amount of rhythm, but he rapped his baton on the stand and said, *"Where's the piccolo?"* The piccolo player raised his hand and said, *"Sorry, sir. One of my keys wasn't working right, so I quit playing."* The conductor said, *"Stay with me everyone. On this piece, each one of us is essential."*

It's the same with the Church. Christ has given us His Body, and every person has an important part in it. Paul said Spiritual Gifts were vital since all came from the same Spirit, **"For the body does not consist of one member, but of many."** (1 Corinthians 12:14)

Jesus has given each of us a part to play in His heavenly orchestra to make music together.

Lord, help me always know I am important to You.

SEPTEMBER 22

During a worship service the church youth leader was giving the Children's Message on the First Commandment, **"You shall have no other gods before me",** and she suggested some ways for the kids to keep it *"Nothing should come before God with you, not candy, not school, not video games, not even ice cream."* She ended by saying God wants us all to follow all of His rules. *"Any questions?"* she asked. A little voice answered, *"Will God love me even if I don't?"*

Sometimes when trying to teach children or adults to obey God we make the Christian Faith a matter of obedience rather than faith and trust. That's not good to do. True, God wants us to follow Him, just like the parent wants the child to obey. But even though the Law says, *"Obey the rules, and if you don't, you're in trouble!"* the Gospel says, *"Jesus has obeyed the rules for you. He will forgive you, so trust in Him."*

The Law doesn't really give us any hope. It doesn't save us. Rather, it condemns us for any small sin, any little infraction of the rules.

In answer to the child's question, yes, God will love us even when we don't obey Him. Both Law and Gospel are wrapped up in this verse: **"The wages of sin is death, but the free gift of God is eternal life through Christ Jesus our Lord."** (Romans 6:23) It is God's mercy that we have Jesus to forgive us. He did not come to condemn the world, but to save it!

Lord Jesus, how wonderful You are to us every day.

SEPTEMBER 23

An exciting movie was made in 2010 called "Unstoppable" which tells the story of a runaway freight train, and the people who work to stop it.

Sure that he had set the brakes, an engineer steps off the train and too late sees it move. He runs to catch it, but it speeds up and he can't get back on. The unmanned speeding train carrying toxic chemicals it is headed towards a city. Can it be stopped or will it crash and kill people?

The remainder of the movie is how a veteran engineer and a young conductor are able to board and stop the train. The movie is filled with increasing suspense as each attempt at a solution fails. A friend of mine who spent his career working with railroads told me the movie was quite authentic, and their solution, however fantastic, was possible.

Many things in this world seem unstoppable. When Adam and Eve rebelled against God's rule in the Garden, they set in motion the runaway affects of sin which have been unstoppable in history. Wars, selfishness, pride, evil and avarice have never left us, until God sent His Son Jesus into the world. He said, **"I have not come to abolish the Law, but to fulfill it."** (Matthew 5:17)

Jesus' purpose for His birth, life, suffering, death and resurrection, was to stop the runaway train of sin. With His entrance into the pathway of life, He has given hope to us all.

Lord, help us follow Your guidance on all our paths.

SEPTEMBER 24

Do you wish you'd know the Bible more than you do? Do you feel you should read it more, but rarely do? If you're struggling with this, don't berate yourself, but don't stop trying to read God's Word more, either.

Historians say human beings developed written language only about 5,000 years ago. Spoken language is far older than that, but archaeological findings indicate people began recording stories and agreements on clay tablets only about 3,000 years before Jesus. Considering all the stories and information people had to pass on to their young, this is surprising.

Cave figures and some of the ancient rock pictures tell a few things, but clay tablets seem to be the earliest writings. Paint and clay gave way to pen and ink and eventually modern printing. Today we have incredible ease and low cost in recording our stories and thoughts.

The Bible has many uses, but above all, it is instructive. It tells us of God and how He wants us to live. When the Psalmist says, **"Your Word is a lamp for my feet and a light for my path"** (Psalm 119:105), he is telling us he trusts the Word God passed on to him by others.

God's Word tells us how God loves us and wants us to be with Him. No other religion has a God who wants to help people. Only Christians do. 1 Peter 5:7 says, **"Cast all your cares on Him, because He cares for you."**

Thank You for caring, Jesus. Help us to care, also.

SEPTEMBER 25

One year my son asked me to find a nice restaurant where we could take our family and have our Mother's Day meal. I should have gotten reservations earlier, but I waited too long. We ended up at a smaller café, several economic steps down from the one we'd hoped for. But it was actually a very nice place, so we enjoyed our family fellowship there.

Every year when we return from our winter home, new restaurants have opened in our hometown. We've tried going out each Friday to a different one, but new ones spring up too fast.

How easy life is for people today! Only a hundred years ago people spent half their time providing and preparing food. The other half was paying for fuel and making clothes. Life today is convenient, but people still gather for meals.

Abraham met three men in the wilderness and ordered that a lamb be prepared for supper. Someone had to kill and skin the animal, cook it over a fire, prepare other items, draw water or wine to drink. Then they all sat to eat on dry, rocky ground. Compared to that, our Macaroni Grill meal was a feast in paradise!

When I was young, at church and home we rarely missed praying, **"Oh give thanks to the Lord, for He is good; His mercy endures forever."** (Psalm 118:1) God's food helps both body and soul as we gather. That's why many have found it hard to eat alone.

Thank You, Lord, for food and drink, amen!

SEPTEMBER 26

I was recently crossing a parking lot with a young store clerk (he carried a heavy item to my car) when he said, *"People sure are stopping today. Some days I almost get run over, but today they're all stopping."* I turned to him with a smile and said, *"I think they're stopping for me. Grey hair gets me a lot of courtesy these days."*

Some may disagree, but I have found there to be a lot of respect for older people, both in public and private. A sign in a large bank chain lobby says, *"Our philosophy of service is summed up in one word: Courtesy."* Wouldn't it be nice if that were true throughout our society?

Courtesy is defined as, *"The showing of politeness in one's attitude and behavior toward others."* Good manners, civility and respect are never out of style. If they should disappear, society will be in danger of chaos.

Paul echoed these sentiments when he said, **"Be kind to one another, tender-hearted, forgiving one another as God in Christ forgave you."** (Ephesians 4:32). Wise old King Solomon said, **"Whoever pursues righteousness and kindness will find life, righteousness and honor."** (Proverbs 21:21)

It's easy to be impatient with those who move slower, forget more easily or hear poorly. Even living in a retirement community, I find myself wishing those old guys would hurry up! But God values patience, no matter how old we are.

Father God, grant us mercy and patience as we age.

274

SEPTEMBER 27

A middle-aged man was attending a High School reunion when someone spoke his name. Turning, he knew the face immediately and felt his throat tighten. The woman there greeted him far more warmly than the last time they had spoken. Twenty years before, she had rejected him and his feelings towards her, and it was at their Spring Prom.

He heard her words now, but was thinking back to the cruel note she had shoved into his locker door, words that had crushed his young spirit. But despite having forgotten so much of that night and that person, he smiled at her. Inwardly, he was thinking someone ought to teach her a lesson in how to treat people.

Some negative things are hard to let go. It's almost as if Satan wants us to dredge up the ugly past and get some kind of vengeance. But that would only give birth to hurt all over again.

Apostle Paul, no stranger to cruelty, told the Christians at Rome not to seek vengeance, for that belongs to the Lord. He further wrote, **"Do not be overcome by evil, but overcome evil with good."** (Romans 12:21)

Bitterness hurts the bearer more than the one it to whom it is pointed. As the two classmates spoke, a sad story unfolded of a failed marriage. Although there was no attempt at re-kindling an old romance, the two parted with kindness rather than acrimony.

Lord, help us let go of hard feelings towards others.

SEPTEMBER 28

Have you ever felt like you were second-best? Leah must have. Jacob had worked for her father Laban seven years with the promise he could then marry Leah's sister Rachel.

But Laban wanted Leah, his eldest, married first, so he tricked Jacob by covering Leah's face while she was dressing, a time when the groom was not allowed to see his bride. When the deception was discovered, Jacob agreed to work for Laban seven more years to gain Rachel as his wife also. But Leah knew she was never Jacob's favorite. She'd always be second-best. (Details of this story are found in Genesis 29).

This is why in Jewish weddings today the groom may always be allowed to see his bride veiled. He doesn't want to be tricked like old Jacob was. It's a true fact!

But in the end Leah was blessed with more children than Rachel. Although her Hebrew name meant "weak", Leah was the strong wife, out-living Rachel by many years.

Sometimes we may wonder if God loves us as much as He loves someone else. Then we must remember Paul's words, **"While we were still sinners, Christ died for us."** (Romans 5:8) No one can earn God's love. In His eyes, each of us are worth the price of sending Jesus to earth to earn forgiveness by His perfect obedience, death and resurrection. God sent His greatest gift for us, and He loves us, no matter what.

Lord, help us look past our sadness to Your gladness.

SEPTEMBER 29

How will people be led if their leaders goes bad? Studies have shown that most people by nature want someone to lead them, rather than take total responsibility for their own lives. From this fact have come kings, Dukes, and Dictators, the good and the bad. And when it is bad, people ask, *"How did this ever happen?"*

After gaining the Promised Land, Joshua told the people to choose their own leaders who'd work out problems and keep the peace. But many tribes soon followed after other gods and went to war against each other. God then raised up Judges to help people solve problems, keep the peace and fight the enemy. But the people wanted what their neighboring tribes had. They wanted a king and kept insisting to have one.

God warned them that a king would take their sons to be soldiers and their daughters to do his work. A king would take their land and animals, their servants and money. They would be the king's slaves, and they will cry out to God. But the people refused to heed God's warnings, so He gave them King Saul, a man who looked good on the outside, but was weak and did more harm than good. (1 Samuel 8:11-22)

A country suffers when its leaders are selfish, quarrelsome, godless or inept. We must hope God will listen to our prayers today, as He has in the past. **"Blessed is the nation whose God is the Lord."** (Psalm 33:12)

Lord, hear the cry of Your people. Have mercy on us!

SEPTEMBER 30

(I begin this with an apology to all good and responsible people who own a Porsche. Today's thoughts are based on my experiences with them. Safe driving!)

I read an article about an impatient man in San Francisco who tried to beat the traffic which had come to a standstill. After sitting there a short time, he swerved onto a shoulder, gunned his engine and promptly slammed his red Porsche 911 Carrera right into fresh cement. His car was never the same after that incident.

When I was pastor in California, I was asked to officiate at the wedding of a member whose fiancée made it plain he was wasting his time being in church. To help, I speeded up their prep meetings, and they were married, driving away in his white 911 Carrera. It was promptly stolen that night from their hotel parking lot, and pieces of it were found in a "chop shop."

Both of these men suffered mightily from their haste. The Bible tells us King Saul did also. Eager to show his prowess as a king, Saul passed up giving God the sacrifice he'd promised, and promptly lost his kingdom in a poorly fought battle. Saul was never the same.

The Bible says, **"Blessed is the man who makes the Lord his trust, who does not turn to the proud, to those who go astray after a lie."** (Psalm 40:4) When a person becomes successful, it is tempting to assume he or she has no need of humility. But God will show them otherwise!

May we be humble, Lord Jesus, just as You were.

EVERY DAY WITH JESUS
in October

OCTOBER 1

When there's been damage, do you repair or replace? It depends on what the damage is. Our lovely juniper hedge was nearly all dead after one winter, the result of field mice using it for their winter residence and food pantry. One guy said to remove and replace would cost $1,000, but another guy (myself) said cut out the dead stuff, water it often and see if it would come back. I was sure they'd grow back, and my price was much better. I eventually came to my senses and replaced the hedge with new plants.

Things can be replaced, but people can't, unless God is involved. When the world's first people went bad, God decided to replace them in the flood, but it was a one-time thing. After that, God promised a Savior who would repair people, not replace them. He said, **"I am the way, the truth and the life."** (John 14:1) His rainbow was the symbol of his promise.

Jesus Himself is our replacement for sin. Because He lived a perfect life in our stead, we are given a new relationship with God. Instead of deserving God's wrath for our sins, we are given a new life. Jesus didn't just forgive us, He recreated us!

Thank You, Lord Jesus, for giving us a new life!

OCTOBER 2

Have you ever said, *"Too much red tape!"* The phrase refers to customs or rules that prevent things from getting done in a timely fashion.

Originally the phrase referred to the practice of official documents being bound with red ribbon. Historian Thomas Carlyle used the term to protest his government's policies that took too long to engage. After the Civil War, *"Ted Tape"* came to mean all the time-consuming policies that resulted in veterans struggling to receive their benefits.

Governments, courts and even hospitals may be noted for their bureaucratic Red Tape, but there is one place where it does not apply, in our prayer life with God. In his letter to the Romans, Paul speaks of Jesus, **"through whom we have access by faith into this grace in which we stand."** (Romans 5:2)

God hears and answers our prayers. When we feel beaten down or our hearts are broken because of trouble, there is no *"Red Tape"* involved with God. We need not stand in line for Him to hear us. He is as close, and as helpful, as any prayer we offer Him.

The writer of Hebrews (perhaps Barnabas) wrote, **"Let us then with confidence draw near to the throne of grace, that we may receive mercy and find grace to help in time of need."** (Hebrews 4:16) God's throne is never closed to us due to Red Tape.

Thank You, Jesus, that we can pray to You any time.

OCTOBER 3

An American farmer was traveling on a road through a lovely countryside in Scotland when he saw something that made him laugh. On a hillside was a small flock of pink sheep. The shepherd was near the road, so the traveler stopped and commented about his colored flock. The shepherd said, *"Some put a few splashes of color on their flock, but I paint them all. It comes off, but everyone knows my sheep when they see them."*

"Sheep" is a term the Bible calls followers of our Lord. **"The Lord is my shepherd, I shall not want"** (Psalm 23:1) is written from the view point of sheep. We also have a unique mark of identification. Our "pink mark" is two-fold: Baptism and love for God and people.

Jesus said, **"Love one another as I have loved you. By this all will know that you are my disciples, if you have love for one another."** (John 13:34-35)

In word and deed, Christian people are to show they are sheep of the Good Shepherd. A Christian's attitude towards others should be as obvious as the painted wool of those Scottish sheep. Conversely, if believers do not display God's love in their lives, one wonders if they really are a part of the Shepherd's flock.

As you consider your everyday actions of life, is there any proof that Jesus is your Good Shepherd? Are there ways you might change to make it more obvious to others?

Dear Shepherd, help me show my faith to others.

OCTOBER 4

A class of college freshmen was asked by a speaker on Orientation Day, *"What do you expect from life? Do you hope for a life that is happy and free of pain, or one that helps you face daily challenges?"* The speaker went on to give several realistic expectations the new students should have. Afterwards one student said, *"Wow, that wasn't what I expected!"*

In the C. S. Lewis book, <u>God In The Dock</u>, he wrote, *"Imagine a set of people all living in the same building. Half of them think it is a hotel, the other half think it is a prison. Those who think it a hotel might regard it as quite intolerable, and those who thought it was a prison that it was really surprisingly comfortable."*

Lewis uses this contrast to show how people might view life based on their expectations. He continues, *"If you think of this world as a place intended simply for our happiness, you will find it quite intolerable. Think of it as a place of training and correction, and it's not so bad."*

Jesus is the source of Lewis' thoughts here. He told His disciples, **"In the world you will have tribulation; but be of good cheer, I have overcome the world."** (John 16:33) When we face life's troubles or blessings, Jesus can give us an inner peace that our life is happening in the best way, according to God's plans.

Some people scoff that God has a plan for our lives. Jesus Himself is God's plan for us.

Lord, help me always to seek Your path in my life.

OCTOBER 5

Howard Levitt is a well-known and successful lawyer in Toronto. His work in labor and employment law is legendary in Canada. It has led him to become a wealthy man.

But even the most successful person can make a big mistake. One day after a big rainfall, he was driving home in his $200,000 Ferrari and entered what looked like a big puddle. It was, however, an enormous hole, and his beautiful car with its 450 horsepower engine nearly floated away with Howard inside it.

When I hear of the wealthy losing riches, I think of Solomon's enormous wealth and how he came to regard it as more of a problem than a blessing. In Ecclesiastes 5:14 he wrote, **"Riches perish through misfortune."** In the next verse he said, **"We came into this world with nothing, and we'll take nothing with us."** The next verse says, **"What gain is there if a person toils with the wind?"** He means life is futile if all we work for is wealth.

Reading this we might think, *"That's easy for you to say. You had it all. I'd like to know what it's like, too!"* But there's something lasting that won't spoil, be stolen or disappear. It's our faith in Jesus. No one can take it from us.

Paul wrote, **"Seek those things above where Christ is sitting at the right hand of God."** (Colossians 3:1) Jesus can't be taken from us. Only we can let Him go or push Him away.

Father God, help us hold on to Jesus in all our life.

283

OCTOBER 6

One of my wife's friends fell while playing Pickleball and broke both her wrists. For several weeks she lost the use of her arms and hands as a metal cast held them in a certain position so the bones could heal the right way. She tried to joke about the problems this caused, but we all knew it was very hard.

Our arms and especially our hands are used for everything. Simple tasks such as brushing our teeth or eating with a spoon are impossible without them. If both arms are in a steel cast, we can't even hug someone.

The Psalmist helps us cope. He writes, **"Be still and know that I am God."** (Psalm 46:10) "Being still" means putting our hands at our sides and not using them. It means letting God do the work, something risky for people to do. It's like the saying: *"Let Go and Let God."*

We all want to be in control of our life. We believe that's what we must do always, but God wants us to do otherwise. Faith means letting Him do what we no longer can. Faith means letting Him be our hands.

Parents often struggle to keep their hands off their children's lives. We want the best for them, and we believe we know what that is. But this isn't always true. At times we must realize our hands are tied. We must *"Let Go and Let God"* take over. When we trust Him to help those we love, life will happen in a better way.

Lord, help me stay out of the way so You can work.

Does God care about us? Does He always know what we're doing in life? Are there times He just lets us wander wherever we want?

George Lacy was a missionary in the early 1900s, during which time he and his wife lost all five of their children to scarlet fever. Lacy wrote a letter to his mission board about their deep grief and loneliness, saying, *"Sometimes it seems more than we can bear. But the Lord is with us, and He is wonderfully helping us."*

As I read his prayer, I wondered how in the world those two parents had enough faith to bear up under such loss! After losing all their children, how could they still say the Lord was wonderfully helping them? In that dark hour, how did he know Jesus was there?

He knew by faith. One of my favorite Psalms says, **"To You, O Lord, I cry, and to the Lord I plead mercy. What profit is there in my death if I go down into the pit? Will the dust praise You? Will it tell of Your faithfulness? Hear, O Lord, and be merciful to me. Lord, be my helper."** (Psalm 30:8-10) Then it says, **"You have turned my mourning into dancing. You have removed my sackcloth and clothed me with gladness."** (Psalm 30:11)

May we never forget, **"His anger is for a moment, but his favor for a lifetime. Weeping may come for a night, but joy comes in the morning."** (Psalm 30:5)

Father God, help us ever to know You are with us.

OCTOBER 8

The end of World War Two was the start of the Cold War. As countries jockeyed for power and influence, two blocks of nations developed, West and East. In 1961, Eastern nations built the Berlin Wall which stood for nearly three decades as a symbol of the lingering animosity.

On November 9, 1989, an agreement was reached and citizens could again cross freely from East to West Berlin. A year later the wall was all torn down. I have a small piece of that concrete wall in my office.

When Jacob's biblical family (Genesis 37-50) was split by politics and hatred, Joseph refused to put up a wall between himself and his brothers who had sold him into slavery. When a famine came, Joseph treated his brothers with kindness, saying, **"You meant evil against me, but God meant it for good."** (Genesis 50:20)

When we are faced with anger or hatred, we must choose how to react. A kind attitude can help restore an old grudge and build a bridge between people. Unity is an admirable goal and tears down walls of manmade separation.

Our Savior Jesus is God's bridge between Himself and sinners. If we have built any walls of separation or anger with others, Jesus is ready and willing to help us break them down. The only wall God wants us to have today is between us and Satan. When we refuse to bend to Satan's ways, God will bless us with His peace.

Lord Jesus, help us follow You in every way possible.

OCTOBER 9

In a popular travel series, viewers can see marvelous parts of the earth from a helicopter high above. An artist's project on an 11-acre field near Belfast, Ireland, started small, but ended up being the largest land portrait in the British Isles. Jorge Gerada used 30,000 wooden pegs, 2,000 tons of soil and 2,000 tons of sand, plus grass and stones, to create his artistic work.

At first only he knew what he wanted. The workers, both hired and volunteer, had no idea what the project would become. They just saw a lot of stuff hauled in and shaped here and there, bit by bit. When it was all done, it didn't look like much on the ground, but from the air it's a portrait: the face of a smiling little girl.

God has done something far grander in the world. The Divine Artist knows what His final work will be. Paul says to new Christians, **"We are God's fellow workers and you God's field, God's building."** (1 Corinthians 3:9) We are the workers God is using to make His **"royal priesthood, and holy nation."** (1 Peter 2:9)

God, who sits above in the Heavens, knows what the final picture will look like. We cannot see it from here, but one day we too will see His wondrous and holy artwork, made here on earth, but best seen from heaven.

God knows the Big Picture each of our lives will make. We see a glimpse, a shadow, part of the puzzle, but Jesus sees it in full and loves it.

Lord, one day let us see Your handiwork on earth.

OCTOBER 10

I love to learn about the countries of the world. One day I met two people from Singapore, so I looked it up. It is a tiny island just south of the Malaysian peninsula, so small that few people could point it out on a world globe. It is very densely populated.

A man wrote to his fiancé' who was coming to Singapore for the first time: *"Space is limited. You must always have a sense of space around you. You should always step aside to ensure you are not blocking anyone. The key is to be considerate."*

That sounds like good advice to follow no matter where we are. Apostle Paul wrote to young pastor Titus similar words: **"Remind the people to be obedient, ready to do whatever is good, to slander no one, to be peaceable and considerate, always gentle towards everyone."** (Titus 3:1-2) We show our faith by what we do.

In countries abroad, many people there expect Christians to be different. They must not be selfish, rude or greedy. If others see Christians acting like this, they will wonder if this is what Christ is also like.

In college, when there was a scuffle between the guys, I once said, *"Be nice, guys!"* A class mate laughed and said, *"What do you expect? We're guys!"* Consideration is good to have at all ages and among all genders. Jesus is our best example. He laughed, but didn't mock. He had a good time, but didn't get carried away.

Lord, help us follow Your example in all we do.

OCTOBER 11

When Biddy Mason died in 1891, it wasn't remarkable that she was laid to rest in an unmarked grave, nor that she was born into slavery and granted her freedom in an 1856 court decision. What made Biddy Mason remarkable was the extent to which she had become an accomplished businesswoman.

After winning her freedom, Bridget Biddy Mason became a nurse and through many wise business decisions, made a small fortune. She saw the plight of immigrants and prisoners, and reached out to them, giving so much to charity that people frequently lined up outside her house for help. In 1872, just 16 years out of slavery, she and her son-in-law financed the founding of the First African Methodist Episcopal Church in Los Angeles.

Biddy embodied the words of Paul who said, **"In all things I have shown you that by working hard in this way we must help the weak and remember the words of the Lord Jesus, how He Himself said, 'It is more blessed to give than to receive.'"** (Acts 20:35)

In 1988, in a ceremony attended by the Mayor of Los Angeles and 3,000 members of the little church she started over 100 years before, a tombstone was unveiled for Biddy Mason. She had once said, *"The open hand is blessed, for it gives an abundance even as it receives."* May many more Christians show such gratitude to Jesus.

Lord, may we follow Biddy's example of charity.

OCTOBER 12

There are a number of things in life that are seriously under-rated. Today I'm thinking of three: A good night's sleep, a good day's work and retirement. The last two may seem to conflict with each other, so I will let them alone. It's the first one that deserves some thought: a good night's sleep. Here are some reasons why:

◆ Good sleep improves productivity.
   Poor sleep weakens the heart.
◆ Good sleep improves social interaction.
   Poor sleep is linked to depression.
◆ Good sleep keeps you healthier.
   Poor sleep can cause weight gain.

There are more reasons, but I will leave that to a <u>Reader's Digest</u> article.

In college, working a night shift or two shifts in a row was a sign of determination, and I did it many times. Today I realize it wasn't the smartest thing I could have done, although it paid the bills. Gratefully I graduated with no debt, but college costs were far less back then.

God has made people with a need to get rest. The body wears down and needs sleep to rejuvenate. The Bible says, **"On the seventh day God finished His work that He had been doing, and He rested on the seventh day from all his work that He had done."** (Genesis 2:2)

Jesus is our best example. After preaching and healing, He prayed and rested. Look at your schedule and see if you can do the same.

Lord, help us take care of both our bodies and souls.

OCTOBER 13

I spent one October morning getting our two cars serviced. Both of them are well used but in good condition and enjoyable to drive, partly because I make sure they are serviced regularly, usually every 3,000 miles.

Recent mechanical innovations, however, have made it possible for new cars to be serviced every 30,000 miles, and some advertise going even longer. But that doesn't mean drivers should avoid checking fluid levels more often. I once bought a two-year old Buick with only 20,000 miles on it. But checking the engine, I found the oil so thick it was doubtful it had ever been replaced since the car was new.

In the same way, our faith also needs regular servicing. Regular worship is very helpful, *(Is that why it's called a worship service?)* and so is regular prayer and Bible reading. Prayer and Holy Scripture are available to us at any time. So is worship, although worshipping with others has special blessings, such as Holy Communion and Holy Baptism.

Our Lord Jesus recited the Psalms during worship, saying, **"Come, let us worship and bow down; let us kneel before the Lord, our Maker."** (Psalm 95:6) It was a reminder of the blessings God gives us in worshipping Him.

How is your faith doing? Does it need the fuel of God's Word or the cleansing of confession and absolution?

Lord, help me to see my need for regular worship.

OCTOBER 14

In the 1970s my congregation decided to sponsor a refugee family from Laos. I will always remember meeting them as they got off the airplane one cold winter day at the Fargo, ND, airport. Most of their children were under age 12, and the first thing they noticed was the snow under foot. *"What is that?"* they asked their father who could speak English.

Their father said he had tried to explain it to the children, but snow needs to be experienced, not explained. I told them it was very cold water covering the ground so the earth could sleep and rest. *"Will it warm up soon?"* they asked anxiously. Those children went most of the winter without shoes inside whenever they could, but learned quickly that bare feet were not made for snow.

The Bible gives us an important purpose for snow: **"For as the rain and the snow come down from heaven and do not return there but water the earth, making it bring forth and sprout, giving seed to the sower and bread to the eater, so shall my word be that goes out from my mouth; it shall not return to me empty, but it shall accomplish that which I purpose, and shall succeed in the thing for which I sent it."** (Isaiah 55:10-11)

An elderly woman asked, *"Is it true the Bible never talks about snow?"* I quoted her Psalm 51:7. **"Wash me and I shall be whiter than snow."**

Dear Savior, thank You for washing away our sins.

OCTOBER 15

There is great interest today about ancestry. The internet has sites where one can find not only names of ancestors, but in some cases where they lived, what they did and how they came here.

Imagine if you found this description of an ancestor? *"Widowed, had an affair with her father-in-law."* Would that embarrass you or make your curious? Meet Tamar, whose son Perez led a clan of the Israelites. (Genesis 38)

How about this? *"Prostitute, harbored enemies of the government in her house, and lied about it."* Meet Rahab, who helped the Israelites conquer Jericho. She married an Israelite and became great-grandmother of King David. (Joshua 2)

How about this woman? *"She had an affair with a King and saw her husband murdered."* Meet Bathsheba, whose son by David became another king named Solomon. (2 Samuel 11)

The Bible is filled with stories about God's imperfect people. Yet God was always merciful, forgiving the repentant and granting them blessings even when they had sinned greatly.

God's love is amazing. He can take people with a bad reputation, transform their lives and make them examples of faith. He can even take an over-zealous man who killed Christians and make him a powerful witness. Meet Paul!

If we think we're too bad to be forgiven, remember those people. **"Gracious is the Lord and righteous. God is merciful."** (Psalm 116:5)

Father God, thank You for being merciful to us.

OCTOBER 16

This time of year on Midwestern farms, the harvest is underway. Some fields of soy beans are already in the bin while other fields await their turn. Soon the corn harvest will take place and millions of tons of grain will be stored up to feed people and animals in the world and produce materials used every day.

Massive machines will move quickly up and down the fields reaping what has been sown months ago. Reaping and sowing are the Bible's word pictures that help us realize the cause and effect of our actions. Paul said, **"Do not be deceived, for whatever a man sows, that he will also reap."** (Galatians 6:7)

God gives us the right to make choices in life, including things that may be bad for us. We are not created as robots that must follow God. He wants us to choose what is good, especially to follow Him as willing and faithful sheep who follow their shepherd.

Our sins are caused by our inability to make good choices. God knows this and offers us His Holy Spirit to help us choose what is good. We can certainly refuse His goodness, but to make sure we don't miss out eternally, the Spirit gives us His "holy nudge" to trust Jesus.

One day God will call in His heavenly harvesters to gather up His people into His presence. When that time comes, will we have stored up any heavenly treasures?

Lord Jesus, help us follow You all through life.

OCTOBER 17

Many years ago while attending the seminary, one of my classmates called and asked if we could come over. They needed help moving because their home was falling down. We quickly went there and saw it was really true. Their apartment building was literally breaking apart.

It started in the basement decades before when the builders hadn't built it on a strong foundation. Rather than digging and pouring concrete footings, the builders had poured the concrete floors, then laid brick walls on top of it. Now, decades later, when the basement floor had been dug out to be replaced, the walls were falling. Their side was starting to look like a huge doll house.

I have used this example many times to illustrate what Jesus meant by His story of the two houses, one built on sand and the other on rock. We know for sure that if you don't build something correctly at the start, that building won't last.

Jesus said, **"Everyone then who hears these words of mine and does them will be like a wise man who built his house on the rock."** (Matthew 7:24) Whether building a house, or building a life, the right foundation makes all the difference.

Jesus knows the people listening to Him. We are all tempted to take shortcuts, make excuses or find an easier way to follow Him. He urges us to trust Him, the Builder of our Faith.

Lord, keep us from trying to take easier paths in life.

OCTOBER 18

One morning after working a double shift at a St. Louis hospital, I went outside to the parking lot and found my car had been stolen! I knew exactly which door I'd taken into the hospital and where I'd parked my car in that lot. Now it was gone. Somebody stole my car!

I quickly found a security guard and frantically told him my problem. He took me to the center of the hospital at ground level and asked, *"When you parked it, which door did you come in?"* *"That one, I think,"* I muttered. He said, *"Okay let's try the other side."* And there just outside the door was my car!

Some unwise architect had designed two nearly identical parking lots, one on each side. The guard patted me on the shoulder and said, *"I'd like to give that guy a piece of my mind!"*

Life is filled with opportunities to get turned around and take the wrong road. Things that look so good can be so wrong. Satan seems like an architect who wants to confuse us.

Jesus was also tempted by Satan. Nearly starving, He was walking in the wilderness when Satan said, *"Are you hungry? Make those stones into bread. Go ahead – You can do it!"* Jesus said, *"We need more than bread to live."* Satan said, *"Hey, forget the cross and do what I say. It'll be a lot less painful."* Jesus said, *"Leave, scram, beat it!"* The Lord knows what life can do to us, and He wants to help. That's good enough for me!

Lord, when we're afraid, give us Your courage.

OCTOBER 19

Some periods of my life are filled with dreams, and they're not always good. When I don't feel well I often dream of being out of control, lost or having missed an appointment. After watching a disturbing movie, I may dream that I am being chased. If I've read a murder mystery, I may dream that someone's trying to murder me.

Some dreams come from what I've read and watched, but I've also developed the ability to know if I'm dreaming or not while I'm still asleep. If something terrible is happening, I know it's a dream, so I wait until I wake up.

<u>The Curate's Awakening</u> is by 19th century novelist George McDonald. It's the story of a minister who is called to the bedside of a dying man who is haunted by a murder he committed. The minister's realizes he no longer believes in God, but then is relieved when he wakes up and realizes it's all been a dream.

The relief of waking up from a bad dream is nothing compared to waking up to the reality of God's forgiveness. When a guilt-ridden sinner comes to believe that he is forgiven by Jesus, it's like something too good to be true.

Apostle John said, **"I am writing to you, little children, because your sins are forgiven for His name's sake."** (1 John 2:12) There is nothing any of us can do to take away our guilt. But there's no worry because Jesus has removed it forever.

How can we thank You, Lord, for forgiving us?

OCTOBER 20

Although I live in a desert climate half the year, it's hard for me to realize there are places in the world that have no rain at all. Of the 10 driest places on earth, 8 are in Africa and 2 in South America. Arica, Chile, receives less than 1/10 of an inch of rain per year and some places in the Atacoma Desert have not had rain in 500 years! Think of that the next time you complain about having to water your lawn.

In 2012, villagers living in China's Yunnan Province had a terrible drought. Their corn and rice required much water, but it wouldn't rain. The locals tried superstitious acts, and when nothing worked, they blamed the five known Christians living there for offending ancestral spirits. So those five gathered to pray, and soon a heavy downpour began that lasted all night. While most of the village did not believe it came from the Christian God, some did, and asked to know more about Jesus.

Long ago, God brought a severe drought to King Ahab's realm as judgment for his pagan ways. Elijah told people Almighty God would show them His power by lighting the sacrificial fire. When God ignited Elijah's altar the people cried, **"The Lord, He is God!"** God then sent a great rain for their crops. (1 Kings 17-18)

God wants to hear all our prayers, for they show we trust Him. Although we may not understand His timing, He hears and helps us.

Lord, help us trust You for all our daily needs.

OCTOBER 21

60 year-old Robert Boardman once wrote, *"If the seventy years of a normal life span were squeezed into a single 24-hour day, it would now be 8:30 PM in the evening of my life. Time is slipping by so rapidly."* Very pensive words! Maybe he wasn't not feeling well that day.

It can be hard to admit that life is short. We're usually so busy doing things that we don't take time to see where we're going with our life. So it is good to reflect that our life is short and thus value our remaining days.

But we can take this too far. Someone has invented a watch called a "Tikker." Instead of telling you what time it is right now, it calculates the approximate time you have left to live. It's a countdown of your life right at your fingertips! Who dreamed that up? I am not sure I want that for my next birthday!

The Psalmist, ever the realist, hints at our time left. **"The years of our life are seventy, or even by reason of strength they be eighty, yet their span is but toil and trouble. They are soon gone and we fly away."** (Psalm 90:10) He sounds like he'd had a bad day.

Does God want us to think of life as a countdown or as a count-up? Rather than brooding about long we have left till zero, why not think of how many days are left until we are in the presence of God? Each day gets us closer to His love, each moment to His peace. That's better!

Lord, rather than backward, help us look forward.

OCTOBER 22

When I was young, October was a time of excitement due to pheasant hunting. Living in southern Minnesota, the first weekend of the season was a big event. Hunters would come from all over with dogs and guns, ready to walk the fields, groves and ditches, hoping to bag a few birds to take home and roast.

People prepared for it. Hunters came to the early church service and sat in the balcony dressed in their tan and brown gear so they could leave early and go directly to their 10:00 starting place. Some even kept their dogs in their cars. You could hear guns boom at starting time, even in town.

As the hunter wants to be ready for the hunt, so we want to be ready for the time God comes to take His people to heaven. But we must be prepared. Jesus said, **"Watch, for you do not know when the Master returns, at midnight, dawn or in the morning."** (Mark 13:35) A hunter would not dream of waiting until season started to buy his license or ammunition. He will be ready ahead of time!

We ready ourselves for Christ's return by reading His Word, helping others and praying for His guidance. A hunter will practice before the hunt. Christians can practice by discovering interests and skills to be able to serve people.

As the day of Christ approaches, may we be found in readiness, glad the day is coming soon.

Lord, help us be ready for Your joyful coming.

OCTOBER 23

Some kids liked to play with fire. I liked to play with firecrackers. A neighbor boy would bring my older brother a sack full of fireworks purchased off the back of a truck or in another state since they weren't legal where we lived. Then we'd plan some fun, hoping not to get into trouble with anyone, and also praying not to hurt ourselves or each other.

Sparklers were for the little kids. We made a cannon from a piece of metal pipe that could shoot a marble and hit the barn. A small can inside a larger one that held water could blow "sky high" with a small firecracker. We were usually very careful. Only once do I remember Dad threatening us with some serious words: *"If you ever try that again…!"* I won't go into details what he said or what we did, but it was memorable. I never let my boys do that.

It's a blessing God watches over us when we do foolish things. It's a sign of His grace that we are not hurt more as we grow up. The words of Psalm 41:2 seem written for some people: **"The Lord protects him and keeps him alive."** While I was more careful not to engage in youthful foolishness, some of my friends were not.

The boy Jesus must have seen His share of pranks, and He may even have taken part. But He always remained faithful to His heavenly Father, staying away from things hurtful and wrong. He knows why we need forgiveness.

Lord, show us Your way in life and keep us safe.

OCTOBER 24

Parents today are generally more protective of their children than in days past. Forty or fifty years ago there was more trust, perhaps because we knew our neighbors better or trusted family and friends more.

Doran and Hazel were a blessing to us in our first congregation when our boys were small. Living 500 miles from our closest parents, we were glad they could fill in so admirably as "adopted grandparents," sitting with our little boys during worship services, playing with them, sometimes even taking them home after church so we could participate in another event.

Raising a family well requires more than just parents. Today Carol and I visit neighbors or church members who are new parents. We try to encourage them in word and deed. Being grandparents and has been a great joy God has given us. The Bible says, **"God sets the lonely into families."**(Psalm 68:6) Grandparents living near their family are rarely lonely.

Families are where God's people can instill God's teachings in other loved ones. While we rightly expect Sunday School or other church agencies to teach the Bible, we can teach each other in word and deed as well.

Jesus and His disciples were like a family. The Gospels are filled with His teachings about the Kingdom. He taught them, not only as a Rabbi, but as a brother who loved them.

Lord, help us be examples of Your love to others.

OCTOBER 25

Dr. Mark Zehnder tells the story of his seven-year-old girl whose older brother signed her up for a "Kiddie Slam Dunk" contest during the halftime of a basketball game. When she was announced as a participant, she asked *"Daddy, what's a Slam Dunk?"* Realizing what happened, Mark and her brother took the little girl out to the entry where there were small plastic hoops and balls and tried to show her what to do. When it came time for her to show off her skill, the little girl ran past the hoop, turned around and dunked it backwards! She won the prize.

"Slam Dunk" is a term for a certainty in life. It's something that will help us win or come in first most every time. There are not many such life events or skills that are a Slam Dunk, because humans are imperfect. We sin and mess up in life. As much as society wants us to tell our kids they are perfect just the way they are, it's better they learn the truth while young so they will know why their life has problems.

Christians know there's only one true Slam Dunk, and that's the forgiveness of sins Jesus earned for us on the cross. When we firmly trust Him to help us deal with whatever comes in life, our future is a Slam Dunk.

Apostle John wrote, **"This is love, not that we loved God but that He loved us and sent His Son to be the means by which our sins are forgiven."** (1 John 4:10) Jesus is our Slam Dunk!

Lord, thank You for loving us, no matter what.

OCTOBER 26

I recently read a shocking statistic. In a study of the major branches of Christianity, it was found that one pastor leaves the pastoral ministry every hour. That equates to 24 pastors leaving each day, over 8,700 per year. Wow!

Dave Anderson has spent his entire life sharing the Gospel of Jesus through music. The more he worked with churches, the more he saw the stress pastors were under, and the more pastors he saw leave the ministry. He learned that 35-40% of trained pastors actually leave the ministry, most after only five years.

This moved Dave and his wife Barb to establish "Shepherd's Canyon Retreat", an intense program to help pastors, church workers, and spouses, take time to reflect and re-direct their lives so they might be able to stay in church ministry. At "Standing Stones" retreat center in Wickenberg, Arizona, Dave and Barb have organized over a hundred retreats and helped minister to more than a thousand people. Www.shepherdscanyonretreat.org gives all the details. Check it out.

God brings people into our lives when we need them. Fine, gifted workers are struggling, and it's sad when they have nowhere to go for help. Jesus said, **"Come to me all you who are weary and tired and I will give you rest."** (Matthew 11:28) God does that at Standing Stones Retreat Center. Pray for all who work in His kingdom.

Lord, bring hope to all who serve You in this world.

OCTOBER 27

The prophet Isaiah lived among God's chosen people, and he was alarmed. So many of the men, women and children God wanted as His own had abandoned the faith, living in the wickedness and decadency of their pagan culture, becoming rebellious and prideful.

God said He was planning the destruction of the wicked because of their sins, and Isaiah heard the Lord when He asked, **"'Whom shall I send, and who will go for us?' Isaiah said, 'Here I am! Send me.'"** (Isaiah 6:8)

There is much wickedness in our world today, especially in places where they should know better. Churches and missionaries have brought the Gospel of Jesus to western nations for 2,000 years, yet Western Christians today seem least receptive to the Gospel.

Who, then are those who want to hear about Jesus? It's the people of many African nations, the "untouchables" of India, and the people of China, that's who. The greatest growth of the Christian Church today is among those people.

God is working in our world to bring hope to the hopeless and help to the helpless. He has given great resources to Western Christians and urges us to be faithful in using what He has given us. The greatest challenge to us is not only to find resources, but to use what we have better.

Isaiah was moved to help and became a great prophet of God. May we also serve Him.

Lord Jesus, help us be willing to serve others.

OCTOBER 28

Pastor Joe was wondering what others thought of him. He'd felt well accepted by his congregation, but was unsure about other pastors. Acceptance by his peers was important.

Joe had made a short presentation at a conference and he felt it was a flop. As he sat down, Gary, an older pastor, leaned over and said, *"Good work, Joe. You did well."* At coffee time, Gary complimented him again, *"Joe, you're a natural at the ministry. People listen to you."* *"Are you sure?"* Joe asked. Gary said, *"When you speak, people listen."* Joe was amazed.

People like Gary have the biblical gift of encouragement. They can see when a person is feeling down and will offer a hopeful word. Such people are a blessing, better than those who offer only criticism and think that's enough.

Jesus experienced much criticism during His ministry, mostly from Jewish leaders. When a woman was criticized for anointing His feet, He said, **"Leave her alone. Why do you trouble her? She has done a beautiful thing to me."** (Mark 14:6) The woman was very grateful.

There are times when a critical comment can help, but at other times a compliment can do more. Paul wrote, **"Encourage one another and build each other up."**(1 Thessalonians 5:11) This isn't to make the speaker important, but to help the one who hears. We all need to hear a compliment now and then.

Lord, help us give people compliments, not complaints.

God sometimes stops us in our tracks and points us in a different direction. It's up to us whether we will keep following our plans, or God's. Apostle Paul once had plans to go to Troas, but God in a dream said go to Macedonia. When he awoke, he went and found a large group of people eager to hear the Gospel. (Acts 16:7-10)

After eleven successful years at a larger congregation, Pastor Joe felt it was time for him to go. He'd been leading a Bible Class that gave examples of people following what God was doing rather than making one's own plans and going that way. When Joe announced his departure from his church, some members were confused and unhappy.

Having no plan after his farewell but to rest, Joe was counseled to start a new church at a town twenty miles south. Construction was booming there and people would need another church. With no money and only a few interested people, Joe held his first worship service two months later. When he retired after eight years, Joe was ministering to over four hundred people in his new congregation.

God sometimes stops us in our tracks and points us in a different direction. He uses us to bless other people. Pastor Joe is my "alter ego." I often use his name to tell my stories. God led me to start that new church.

Lord Jesus, thank You for Your blessed guidance.

OCTOBER 30

This time of year can be conflicting to some Christians. Tomorrow, October 31, is Halloween when children and even some adults don costumes and beg for candy or attend a party. Tomorrow is also Reformation Day, the day to recall how God led a troubled German monk to write down his concerns for debate about the direction the church was heading. There's nothing wrong with observing Halloween, but Reformation should not be totally ignored.

When it appears the Bible and society are in conflict, what should we do? Today's political trends may be a problem to some. Regardless of our political leanings, Christians need to do a "faith check" to make sure they are following God's Word. What is popular, even supported by the majority, does not mean it is correct.

What does God's Word tell us? Peter was arrested and told to stop preaching about Jesus, continuing to do so would cause the people harm. Peter knew he had a choice, and yet felt he didn't. He told them, **"We must obey God rather than men."** (Acts 5:29)

In our modern world it is easy to think majority rule solves all problems. It may help, but it is not always right. The majority of the crowd wanted Jesus to be crucified, but they were wrong. God the Father, however, made their wrong choice a blessing to the world. We always need to remember to obey God rather than men.

Thanks for going to the cross for us, Lord.

OCTOBER 31

Today is Reformation Day recalling Luther's posting 95 articles of debate with Roman church leaders on a church door. Here are 10 things about the Reformation you may not know:

#1. The purpose of Luther's 95 Theses was not to change church doctrine, but to stop the selling of indulgences as the forgiveness of sins.

#2. Luther's translation of the Bible helped the masses learn to read and formed basis of the German language that is still used today.

#3. Luther never chose to leave the Catholic Church. He regarded himself a member always and disliked the term, "Lutheran."

#4. Pope Leo X, of a family of bankers, used the new indulgence to repay loans for cousin Albert's purchase of the Bishopric of Mainz.

#5. Martin chose his name, "Luther." Original spellings varied from Luder to Ludher.

#6. The parsonage came from marriage of Luther and Katy. Prior to that time priests were single and usually lived with other priests.

#7. Luther, as eldest son, had several brothers and sisters, his closest being brother Jacob.

#8. Luther was no saint. He wrongly backed the marriage of Landgrave Phillip to a second wife, but later repented of this sin of bigamy.

#9. The Reformation changed more than the church. Modern ideas of democracy grew out of Luther's idea of the priesthood of all believers.

#10. Luther's writings made printers wealthy.

Lord, thank You for the ministry of Martin Luther.

EVERY DAY WITH JESUS
in November

NOVEMBER 1

Every year on November 1, All Saints Day, I recall the faithful, God-fearing people who have influenced my life. A "saint" is made holy by faith in our Lord Jesus. Today I will name some of them. Many are with the Lord, some still grace the living, and there are more.

Theodore, Leland, Henry, Chris, Walt, Craig, Joe, Don, Roger, Roy and Millie, Doran and Hazel, Glenn and LaVern, Alvena, Leonard and Helen, Art and Peggy, Bud and Irene, Gaylon and Carol, Ray and Mollie, Lowell and Judy, Garth and Carol, Leon and Lori, Darrell and Wanda, Harry and Donna, John and Ammini.

Rich and Sharon, Rick and Kathy, Dan and Carol, Jim and Debbie, Gordon and Joy, Al and Betty, Howard and Marlene, Herm and Kathy, Dave and D'wayn, Dave and Amy, Mark and Sherry, Denice, Ila, Garry and Jan, Ken and Dottie, Gene and Danette, George and Bobbi.

Carol and Sandy, Chuck and Debbie, Brian and Kersta, Ed and Martha, Edward and Betty, Bill and Marian, Fritz and Wilma, Bill and Lou, Bill, Emma, Marie, Harley, Maude, Judy, Randy, Dean, Karen, aunts, uncles, nephews, nieces, cousins and neighbors.

This is my list. What's yours? Who has God placed in your life as a blessing? **"To all who did receive Him, who believed on His name, He gave the right to become children of God."** (John 1:12)

Lord, thank You for all those You've given me in life.

311

NOVEMBER 2

In 1963 my friend Harley called me to meet him a few miles north of his Dad's farm. *"They've dug a big water hole there."* he said. *"Let's go see it."* We met at an enormous hole thirty feet deep, freshly dug by bulldozers. As we climbed down into it to explore, Harley said, *"See those sticks? Scientists say they're 10,000 years old."* We picked up a few pieces of mud-covered wood and decided we'd better obey the signs that warned us to stay out.

The newspapers reported that thousands of years before, a glacier covered a small stand of red cedar trees and sealed them in clay. After cleaning my little stump, I put in my drawer and forgot about it. Years later my artist brother Bill made it into handles for two metal letter openers. He named mine, "Methesulah."

We don't know all the facts about times past. God made our world with secrets we will never all learn, but we know He's the one who made human life. **"I will praise You for I am are fearfully and wonderfully made."** (Psalm 139:14)

We need not fear what we will learn about the earth, so long as we remember its God-made origin. Despite those who will never admit otherwise, elements, time and chance are not responsible for delicate marvels in the body's heart, blood vessels, tissue and brain. Humans have a Creator, and thankfully, also a Savior. In His time He will show us Himself.

Thanks for knowledge, Lord, and all You've given.

NOVEMBER 3

As winter appears, those seeking a handout on street corners seem to disappear. We may struggle whether or not to give money to someone holding up a sign, but in every age, we know there are people in need.

Jesus was talking to the disciples after they'd returned from going in pairs to surrounding villages, when a lawyer asked, **"What must I do to inherit eternal life?"** Jesus had him quote the law of serving God and neighbor. But the man asked, **"But who is my neighbor?"** He might have phrased it, *"Who is worthy of my neighborly acts of kindness?"*

Knowing He was being tested, Jesus told him a story of a traveler who was beaten and robbed on the road between Jerusalem and Jericho. The victim was ignored by two busy religious people who made their living working in the Temple. But he was helped by a passer-by who happened to be a Samaritan.

Some listening to Him may have gasped, since the Jews thought they were much better than Samaritans. The Samaritan could have paid someone else to help the victim, but he tended the wounds himself, put him on his donkey and took him to a roadside inn. He even gave the innkeeper coins to further care for him.

Jesus came into a world of people in need, and did what they needed. He showed by His suffering how He was willing to help us.

Lord, help us also be willing to help people in need.

NOVEMBER 4

Life can surprise us when we least expect it. I once hopped in my car for a quick trip home while the local classical music station played a pleasant number very loudly. It was a bright, peppy Vivaldi symphony, and few blocks into my ride, I heard some notes in it I knew didn't belong there. But they were in correct pitch and tempo, so I ignored them. A few blocks later I heard those notes again. Who was playing Vivaldi that way?

It wasn't the orchestra. I had forgotten to put on my seat belt and the car's warning system was "dinging." I was hearing "Vivaldi a la Ding Dongs!" I didn't let it happen a third time.

What surprises has life tossed at you lately? I hope they were as pleasant and entertaining as mine was that day.

Saul of Tarsus was a rising star among local Pharisees, and he felt good arresting the followers of Jesus. But Jesus knocked him off his horse, turning his life upside down and inside out. **"Who are you Lord?"** He asked. **"I am Jesus whom you are persecuting,"** Jesus said. (Acts 9:5)

When we feel in charge of our own life, we might be surprised by God's changes. Are we ready to listen for God's voice, and are we willing to follow Him? Or will we ignore Him?

Paul's blindness stopped him in his tracks. God often has to do that with us so that we will listen to Him. Following Jesus is an adventure.

Lord, help us listen for Your voice today.

314

NOVEMBER 5

A recent "Aerial America" episode told a brief story about Plymouth Rock, traditionally thought to be the place where the Pilgrims landed and set foot on America in 1620. When shown the memorial that now covers Plymouth Rock, one is surprised how small it is. It didn't used to be that way. Visitors over the years have chipped pieces off it, reducing it to a quarter of its original size.

That has also happened to the original crucifixion rock called Calvary. Christians over the centuries have taken pieces of it home, reducing it from a small hill to a little hump.

Apostle Paul referred to Jesus as a Rock. He told how the Israelites drank water from a rock in the wilderness, **"For they drank from the spiritual Rock that followed them, and the Rock was Christ."** (1 Corinthians 10:4) Jesus never changes (Hebrews 13:8). He is the solid Rock on which we can build our lives. (Matthew 7:24)

The Church is the Body of Christ and Jesus Himself is its cornerstone (Ephesians 2:20-22) Years ago Madeleine L'Engle wrote, *"It's a good thing to have all the props pulled out from under us occasionally. It gives us some sense of what is rock under our feet and what is sand."*

Plymouth Rock has an interesting historical significance for our nation. However, Jesus is our Rock what is never shaken, the cornerstone on which Christianity is founded. We praise Him for all He has done for us.

Lord, keep us rock solid and faithful to Your Word.

315

NOVEMBER 6

Most of my relatives were farmers, and while there are fewer of them now, our family's roots are deep in the soil. It was a nice surprise when I saw a billboard saying, *"If you ate a meal today, thank a farmer."* Those who produce our food do deserve our thanks. They do the hard work of tilling, planting, harvesting and selling the food that keeps us all from starving.

Most every farmer will give thanks to the Lord for His blessings of the sun, soil and water that make it all possible. God has given us all the needed elements to create our food. He has also endowed people with the ability to produce more food through improved seed, fertilizer, implements and technology, including GPS.

The Psalmist says, **"The earth is the Lord's with all its abundance, the world and all who dwell in it."** (Psalm 24:1) He has chosen us to be stewards, caretakers of the soil and resources.

God has also made us stewards of society. How we set up government, how we treat people, how we exercise our freedoms all show our commitment to caring for the world. That means we obey the laws we've made, pay our taxes, vote in elections and honor those in authority. We obligate ourselves to respect all others from different stations in life.

One thing we must do, however, is to give God thanks and praise for all of this. He alone is the one who makes it all possible.

Lord God, help us be good stewards of the earth.

NOVEMBER 7

C. S. Lewis once said that religious concepts are like soups: *"Some are thick and some are clear."* God's Word is not all clear. In Paul's letter to the Romans he gives us a heavy idea: **"God has mercy on whomever He wills, and whom He will, He hardens."** (Romans 9:18). That means God has control over His creation, and will do things we can't always understand. Yet Paul also says, **"The just shall live by faith,"** (Romans 1:17) which is quite simple and clear.

Lewis would agree with John Cameron, a 15th century Christian, who wrote, *"In the same meadow the ox may lick up grass...the bird may pick up seeds... and a man may find a pearl. So in one and the same Scripture passage are varieties to be found for all sorts of conditions."*

The Bible may seem to us a shallow answer book, but it's also a challenge to the reader. It is filled with treasures, knowledge and wisdom to help us grow in our faith to the Lord.

In a lake, fish will swim, a horse may wade, an elephant may walk and a child may play. But all are benefitted by the grace of God. The same is true of Holy Scripture. Not all of us will use it the same way, nor even understand it. But by the grace of God, it benefits us all.

How have you found the Bible useful? What lesson from it stays with you most? What gem have you found that blesses you most often? What is your favorite flavor in the soup?

Jesus, thank You for giving us your Holy Word.

NOVEMBER 8

Today is "International Day of Prayer for the Persecuted Church." There are so many examples of deadly persecution in our world today, and some are almost unimaginable.

In 2006, a woman and her six children were forced to witness an attack on their husband and father. Terrorists tried forcing him to deny Jesus and his Christian faith, but he refused. He continued to speak of his faith in Jesus and died praying for his family. His wife said they were determined to follow Jesus always.

Another man was sentenced to three years in prison for allegedly insulting another religion. He had been an outspoken believer in Jesus, and his wife and children were faithful to Jesus as well. Another man was beheaded when he refused to renounce his faith in Jesus.

Persecution in the world is just as real today as it was at the time of the Early Church. Christian and Jewish churches are regularly being bombed, and believers are subjected to all manner of suffering. They often must pray, **"May the God of all grace, ... after you have suffered awhile, perfect, establish, strength and settle you."** (1 Peter 5:10) Being a believer is not easy everywhere.

"Open Doors USA" encourages persecuted Christians and asks that we pray:

+ *For the safety and faith of secret believers.*
+ *For the courage of believers in prison.*
+ *For those who have lost loved ones for the faith.*

O God, help all who suffer for their faith worldwide.

NOVEMBER 9

What did you have for dinner last night? A burger? Tuna salad? Tacos? What if you were told that tonight your meal would be baby food? Do you think you'd look forward to a meal of that bland, mushy stuff?

Babies may have to eat mashed food but adults don't. Babies don't have teeth, and even some who do cannot digest the tougher foods adults can eat, such as meat or raw veggies. As they get older, babies will eat solid food, chewable vegetables and finally adult food. But they need baby food at first.

In the same way new Christians, those not familiar with the Bible, first need simple verses and concepts. If we want to understand the Bible, we don't begin by studying Revelations. The Gospels tell us what we need first. Then we move on to what Jesus' disciples wrote about Him and our relationship to God.

But some Christians, don't want to hear more difficult Bible passages. *"Keep it simple!"* they say. But a wise pastor or teacher knows that more depth of faith requires more depth of Scripture. If children are to grow stronger, they need solid food, meat and grain. The same is true of a stronger faith. We must have the solid teachings of God's Word for our faith to grow.

We can tell the physical age of people by how they appear. One's spiritual age can be seen by how they deal with good and evil.

Lord, help us seek to know the Bible in a deeper way.

NOVEMBER 10

Louis Armstrong was well known for his smiling face, raspy voice, white handkerchief and incredible ability to play the jazz trumpet. His childhood, however, was filled with pain and poverty. Abandoned by his father, he was put into Reform School at age 12. But that place became a turning point in his life.

A music teacher named Peter Davis came to provide music lessons for the boys. Soon Louis excelled on the cornet and became leader of the boy's band. His life was changed there, and he became a world famous entertainer.

Louis "Satchmo" Armstrong's life could be an example for Christian parents. The Bible says, **"Train up a child in the way he should go, and when he is old he will not depart from it."** (Proverbs 22:6)

All kinds of experiences come our way when we're young, and bad turns can set a good life onto a bad road. In the case of Louis, a talent and training resulted in a lifetime as a virtuoso musician, bringing joy to people.

Parents are teachers. As they provide instruction to their children, they should encourage them to pursue their interests and talents. This is an important step which must not be left only to schools or friends. Parents are the best teachers of what children need to know in life. Parents and children both need to know they are all forgiven by our Savior Jesus when they sin.

Lord, help parents to be good examples to all.

NOVEMBER 11

November 11th is Armistice Day, recalling the 1918 Armistice that ended World War I. On this day, as well as July 4th and Memorial Day, we pause to remember and give thanks for the men and women who have given their time and lives for our freedom.

In my ministry, I've had the privilege of presiding over the burial of many veterans, and one who comes to mind today is John Lipski. He served at the end of World War II in two branches of service. After the war serving in the Army, being unable to get a job to feed his family, he was a cook in the Navy for two more years.

After his second discharge, John went to work for a new company developing a rocket. Although having no formal training after high school, John was a clever, inventive and artistic man whose abilities served him well in the fledgling field of space aeronautics. During the next three decades he was instrumental in designing and developing of several key items which made rockets fly.

During his free time John also made items of wood, including the cherry wood pectoral cross I and other pastors often wear on our gowns. The Psalmist says, **"Serve the Lord with gladness; come into His presence with singing."** (Psalm 100:2) John wasn't a singer, but he served God and his country with joy. We honor him and others for doing so.

Lord, protect all serve You and us wherever they are.

NOVEMBER 12

Although I've become a writer later in life, people often ask me for advice on how they can get their work into print. I usually have the same answer:

1) Have a Purpose for your work,

2) Have a Message to say, and

3) Have an Audience you hope will read it.

I also tell them there's more to write than only fiction or novels. Non-fiction can also be fun to write and beneficial to both writer and reader.

Although Apostle Paul didn't write much, he was still a writer. His words were recorded by Luke and other companions, and he once said of all Christians, **"You are an epistle of Christ, not written with ink but by the Spirit of the living God, not on tablets of stone, but on tablets of flesh, the heart."** (2 Corinthians 3:3)

Our stories are often displayed by how we live rather than what we write. Lewis Bayly, Chaplain to King James I, wrote, *"One man in a thousand can write a book to instruct his neighbors,... but every man can be a pattern of living excellence to those around him."* He was, of course, referring to Christians.

Our lives are like a book about Jesus, and we can influence others more in this way than we think. Parents teach children more from how they live than what they tell them. So can we all.

We may never write a book, but we can all be one. How we live our faith will be an open book to all who know we trust Jesus Christ.

Lord, help us show our faith in our words and deeds.

NOVEMBER 13

A young woman told me that in becoming a bank teller, it was necessary to learn how to recognize counterfeit paper money. In doing so, she closely examined both fake money and real money, looking for the differences in real money and comparing it to the fake. *"You don't look for similarities, but differences,"* she said.

Apostle John wrote to people having troubles with false teachers who said Jesus was not God, just a good teacher. John said Antichrists will appear in the End Times, claiming to have Christ's power but being fakes. He gave three marks of Antichrists: 1) They leave the fellowship of believers, 2) they deny Jesus is the Messiah and 3) they draw others away from Jesus also. **"No one who denies the Son has the Father. Whoever confesses the Son has the Father also."** (1 John 2:26)

John urged them to protect themselves by relying on the Holy Spirit who would tell them of the true Christ. **"But you have been anointed by the Holy Spirit, and you have knowledge."** (1 John 2:20) Knowing the truth of Jesus and being in fellowship with other believers, they could have the strength to resist false teachers.

We too can protect ourselves from those who say Jesus is not God's Son, nor that He came to forgive sins. Read and study the Bible and rely on its truth instead of following those who would tell us otherwise.

Jesus, help us trust You, for You are our Savior.

NOVEMBER 14

Ruby Bridges was an important little girl in our nation's history. She was the first elementary student to attend an all-white school in the south. On November 14, 1960, escorted by her mother and U. S. Marshals, she first attended Frantz Elementary School in New Orleans, and was the sole student of Barbara Henry, the only teacher willing to instruct her. Ruby was escorted by Marshals everywhere, even to the bathroom.

On her way to and from school, angry adults taunted her. A school psychologist discovered her secret in dealing with this. Every day Ruby prayed, *"Dear God, please forgive them because they don't know what they're doing."*

Our Lord knew Ruby's taunts, for **"He was despised and rejected by men, a man of sorrows and acquainted with grief."** (Isaiah 53:3) Jesus gave His life for us, and opened the doors to salvation for all who believe. Our nation has come a long way since 1960, but there is still much hatred and anger towards those who are different from us.

Ruby graduated from Nichols High School, attended school and became a world travel agent. She married and had four sons. She established the Ruby Ridges Foundation to help parents take a more active role in education. In 2007, the Children's Museum of Indianapolis unveiled a display of her life. Few of us could say we are part of history like Ruby, but we can still follow her example of forgiving those who hated her.

God, forgive us when we are hateful towards others.

NOVEMBER 15

Every year I try to rid our backyard of weeds, branches and dead plants. Every year we also conduct a housecleaning to remove dust, unneeded papers and old clothing from home and closets. It's done to make our home a nicer, cleaner and healthier place to be.

Sometimes God takes part in the yard work when He sends a strong wind that blows up the branches, dead leaves and hidden stuff. When He is done, then my cleanup work begins!

God also sends stormy weather into our lives, shaking loose ugliness and sin that needs to be cleansed. Sometimes God's winds reveal what should long ago have been removed, a bad habit or old hobby that needs replacing. Some old things can become a waste of time and resources.

Jonah, the Old Testament prophet, had to get rid of some things when God's wind blew him away to a strange land. Despite his trying to run away in a ship, Jonah landed inside the belly of a big fish. From there the prophet prayed, **"I called to the Lord out of my distress and He answered me."** (Jonah 2:1)

Jonah's stubbornness and hatred for the people of Nineveh had to be removed so God's love could move them to repent.

Our yard trash reminds me of my bad attitudes things I do that cause harm. We can replace old anger, bitterness and sloth with love, joy and peace.

Lord, help me clean house in my heart often.

NOVEMBER 16

The Bible speaks much of the fear of God. "Fear" is a combination of nervous respect, awe, admiration and, yes, some actual fear. After all, He is God and we are the creatures He's made.

Fear always means being afraid to some degree. PGA golfer Padraig Harrington says fear is his motivator. In 2008 he won both the British Open and the PGA Championship golf tourneys. He said, *"Fear is a big part of me. I'd like to say that I have all the trust and patience and I'm relaxed on the course, but that's not my makeup. Fear pushes me on. It gets me to the gym. I have to work with it and use it."* Harrington learned a good lesson.

Fear of failure can be a motivator. Fear of not making our goals can push us to do better and more useful things in our professional lives. Christians may also be helped by fear. The Bible challenges us to have a reverential respect for God, which is the best kind of fear there is. It causes us to be concerned about obeying Him and living according to His will.

God's Word tells us, **"The fear of the Lord is the beginning of wisdom; all who practice it have a good understanding."** (Psalm 111:10) When we have a respectful fear of God, we will understand wisdom and knowledge. We will see the world for what it is – His marvelous creation that only He could have made. Fearing God can be the first step towards true faith in our Savior Jesus.

Lord, help us fear You because we need You.

NOVEMBER 17

Ly Keohavong and his Laotian family came to North Dakota in 1980, sponsored by one of my congregations. He had served as a driver for American soldiers during the Viet Nam War, so he needed asylum for his family. As they awaited to go to their new home, he and his family were placed in a refugee camp in Cambodia for two years. It was not an easy place to be since most of his children were teens or pre-teens and could have been negatively influenced by others.

But Mr. Ly, as we called him, was not bitter about staying in the camp so long. He said, *"It gave me time to tell people there about Jesus."* Years before, Mr. Ly had become a believer and despite his stutter, he had willingly shared his faith, often leading worship services in the refugee camp. After two years with us, he took his family to New Iberia, Louisiana, where he also preached in Laotian Christian churches. He and his wife Chanh are with the Lord now.

Right after receiving the Holy Spirit, Peter and John were speaking of Jesus as the Savior of all while in the Temple. The Temple leaders told them they must stop. However, the two men insisted on telling others, no matter what the cost. They said, **"We cannot but speak of what we have seen and heard."** (Acts 4:20)

When Jesus becomes your Savior, life is not the same. Fear is replaced with His love. He is so important that you want to tell others.

Lord, show us how to share Your love with others.

NOVEMBER 18

There is something about a wedding that captures the mind and heart. In a remarkably elegant and joyful wedding, Prince Harry of England wed American actress Meghan Markle, in a ceremony viewed by perhaps a billion people worldwide. What made it lovely was not only the beauty of clothing and pageantry, but the centrality of Jesus and God's Word.

Weddings are notorious for both beauty and troubles. So much planning goes into the details that trouble can occur. The bride is the center of attention, and the groom appears only when he is about to be joined to her in marriage.

When Jesus chose His disciples and began His ministry, his cousin John already had a number of disciples. They came to John one day and said things that seemed to show jealousy of Jesus: **"He is baptizing and all are coming to Him!"** (John 3:26) What should they do?

But John was glad to hear this. He had come to prepare the world for Jesus and said, **"I have been sent before Him. The friend of the groom who stands and hears him rejoices greatly because of the bridegroom's voice. Therefore this joy of mine is fulfilled."** (John 3:28-29)

John also said of Jesus, **"He must increase, but I must decrease."** (John 3:30) John had done his work. His ministry was no longer for himself. Jesus now must take center stage. Such humility is hard to find these days.

Lord, help us also be humble as we serve You.

With storms, volcanoes and earthquakes rattling the rafters of our world, it's easy to forget there is still much beauty all around. Yellowstone National Park, for instance, is filled with geysers and hot pools painted so colorfully by algae and minerals. Yet visitors are standing on top of one of the most active and powerful volcanoes on the planet. Should they think of the danger there, and run, or be grateful for the beauty?

Reading the Book of Job is like visiting Hawaii's seething Kiluea volcano. Job was enjoying a rich life and didn't realize the disaster that was just around the corner. He trusted that God was his "hedge" from disaster. But when that hedge was removed and Satan was let in, Job felt like his life had exploded.

A friend of mine was attacked by a mysterious nerve disease that left him nearly dead and paralyzed for life. But like Job, my friend and his wife are accepting life as it comes, each day as a gift of God and giving thanks that they still have each other and God to help them.

Job had the faith of a giant. Faced with such loss and pain, he said of God, **"Though He slay me, yet will I trust Him."** (Job 13:15) That passage helped me when I lost my first wife and life turned very bad. I read Job and knew that if he could trust God with all his losses, then I could trust Him also. We must trust Jesus all the way. That is best.

Lord, help us trust You with our whole heart.

NOVEMBER 20

Andy Warhol, 20th Century pop-art painter of American images like "Campbell's Soup Cans" and "Chelsea Girls," is also famous for stating that in the future everyone will be famous for 15 minutes. After a life of influence, controversy, wealth and celebrities, he died after surgery at age 58.

Andy Warhol's "15 minutes of fame" prediction never happened. Billions of people worldwide will never have their moment in the spotlight. Most of them will spend their lives working hard, raising families, praying to God, sharing their faith, helping others or simply making it through each day.

Most people will never be recognized outside their family or circle of friends, but God knows each of them. He knows of their faith and obedience. He also knows their sins and forgives them for Jesus' sake.

Apostle Paul says, **"Whether we are at home or away, we make it our aim to be well pleasing to God."** (2 Corinthians 5:9) Andy's cousin, Rev. Paul Warhola, is a friendly Denver pastor who may not be well known, but he has influenced many people who have grown from his chaplain ministry. That's the best kind life to have – ministering to people and being blessed by it.

God's approval is our reward, but it doesn't get us noticed by Hollywood. It enriches our lives, as we are reassured that He loves us.

Lord Jesus, show us what You want us to do in life.

NOVEMBER 21

As Thanksgiving approaches, our thoughts may be turning to food. How much would you be willing to pay for a piece of fruit? I read that somewhere in Japan a man paid $6,000 for a Densuke watermelon. It's grown only on the northern Japanese island of Hokkaido, and is a rich dark green the size of a bowling ball. That 18-pound watermelon was one of only a few available in the world each year, so it was very expensive. Being rare can make things expensive, but it cannot bring us blessings.

Christians get far better food at no cost! Apostle Paul speaks of "Fruit of the Spirit" and lists them as, **"Love, joy, peace, patience, kindness, goodness, faithfulness, gentleness and self-control."**(Galatians 5:22-23). This fruit from God is absolutely free. Such fruit is found wherever God's people gather to worship Him, hear His Word, and serve each other.

God's fruit blesses whoever has it. It may not fill the tummy, but it fills the heart. This fruit will give us genuine love and peace. It will make us kind, patient and good. It will help us be gentle and self-controlled. With God's Spiritual Fruit, we will never hunger again.

Rare fruit may bring a high price at the market, but the blessings of Jesus are freely given and received as the Holy Spirit lives within our hearts each day. Therefore, we can share them with others. What a bargain!

Lord, thank You for such wonderful fruit!

NOVEMBER 22

We may know the first official Thanksgiving in America was proclaimed by President Lincoln in 1863 during the Civil War, but what is the reason for us to give thanks? It is to let God know how much we appreciate what He has done for us. Thanksgiving is best done by talking about it. As G. B. Stern wrote, *"Silent gratitude isn't much use to anyone."*

People need to be taught gratitude. Parents need to show their children how to send a note of thanks (by card or email), or speak to the giver by phone or in person.

Uncle Bill, one of my baptismal sponsors, started sending me a $20 bill for my birthday when I started school. He faithfully gave it each year, and I'm sure I thanked him at first. But one year his gift stopped. When I mentioned it to my mother, she said, *"Maybe it was because you stopped thanking him."* That was a lesson I never forgot. We should always say thanks, whether for a cup of water or a $20 bill.

We need to do it. W. A. Ward said, *"Feeling gratitude and not expressing it is like wrapping a gift and not giving it."* God is the great Giver and we are His recipients. The Bible says, **"It is more blessed to give than to receive,"** (Acts 20:35). It also says, **"Give thanks in all circumstances, for this is the will of God in Christ Jesus for you."** (1 Thessalonians 5:18) Thankfulness cannot be a silent thing. It needs to be openly expressed.

Lord, help me be grateful for all gifts that I receive.

NOVEMBER 23

When George W. Bush was president, he made a surprise visit on Thanksgiving Day to American troops deployed overseas in Iraq. Due to their daily schedule, their Thanksgiving meal began at 6 AM. In a gesture few there would ever forget, the President of the United States helped serve his troops turkey, mashed potatoes and gravy, cranberries, corn and pumpkin pie. A reporter covering the event wrote it was too bad the soldiers couldn't save their meal as a souvenir, because, *"It's not often that a soldier gets served by the President."*

Every soldier, sailor or airman knows he or she is there to serve their nation. So when the Commander-in-Chief, their highest ranking officer, serves them food, they knew they were being honored for their service.

While most seek to serve others, some only want to be served. Scripture tells us some of the disciples thought following Jesus would give them special status. This once led to them arguing about who was the greatest.

But Jesus set them straight. **"The Gentiles want to lord it over others... It shall not be so among you... Whoever desires to be first shall be the slave of all."** (Mark 10:43-44) He was training them to be servants, not masters. Good leaders must first learn by being good servants. It's the best way to serve other people, and it's the way Jesus taught.

Lord, show us how to serve Your people as You do.

During a Thanksgiving service, a pastor led his people in an unforgettable prayer. Instead of being a thanksgiving prayer, it was one of confession. On their behalf, he confessed how they complained of want, even though they had far more than enough. He said they got angry when things didn't go their way, even though most of the time they did. They sought gifts from God rather than giving them. As members of a large church, they wanted to be served, not to serve. He ended, *"Forgive us our lack of gratitude for what You have given us."*

Having an abundance of goods can make people be unthankful. Our sinful human nature can move us to think we have more because we deserve more. Fortunately, though, most of God's people are grateful.

When Nehemiah brought a large group of Jewish exiles back to Jerusalem to rebuild its walls, they first gathered to confess their sins. They prayed, **"Neither our kings nor our princes, our priests nor our fathers, have kept Your Law, nor did they turn from their wicked ways."** (Nehemiah 9:34,35) Only after confession and forgiveness were they ready to serve God by rebuilding the city walls.

Thanksgiving is best offered with clean hearts and hands. When we think we deserve our blessings, we are in danger of losing our faith in God who gave them to us.

O God, help us appreciate all You've given us always.

NOVEMBER 25

Writer Anne Cetas tells of attending a family Thanksgiving dinner in which each person was asked to share what he or she was thankful for. Starting with the youngest, each person spoke: 3 year-old Joshua was thankful for music, and 4 year-old Nathan was thankful for horses. Prayer stopped for a moment when 5 year-old Stephen said, *"I'm thankful that Jesus loves me so well."* The boy's simple faith was wonderfully expressed in his gratitude that Jesus loved him personally.

Apostle Paul wanted the believers at the church in Ephesus to understand how well God loved them. His prayer was: **"[I pray] that they are able to comprehend with the saints what is the width and depth and height of the love of Christ."** (Ephesians 3:17-19) He prayed they would always be rooted in God's love.

To be rooted in God's love requires we remain connected to Him by worship and prayer. It is helpful to be reminded of all the blessings God has bestowed on us. Memorizing simple verses can help us do that. We memorize so much. Bible verses are best because they give God's blessings.

It's helpful if we take a few moments each day in prayer to give God thanks and adoration for all He's provided us. Thankfulness comes with practice. If we give God our thanks, we will put that thankful attitude into action, usually by helping others in need. Showing our thanks is a way of life we need to learn.

Savior, help us show our thanks to You always.

NOVEMBER 26

Growing up among relatives in a large immigrant family, our Thanksgivings were huge. Uncles, aunts and cousins all attended the same church, and Thanksgiving dinners were held in the biggest house.

There were 5 of us and a dozen cousins, plus parents and other adults. It took at least two rooms to set everyone down, adults in the dining room tables, and kids on card tables in the kitchen. *"You have a hollow leg, Bobbert,"* Uncle Ernest said of my appetite. We all had pet names for each other in those days, some not so good. I smile thinking of them now and then.

All attended church first, except for the few who'd stayed home to cook. We'd all pray the table prayer and then pass the potatoes. What a feast of tasty, rich food! I miss those days. After our huge meal the women cleaned up, older guys smoked or passed a football in the yard, and younger kids played upstairs.

We were thankful for Jesus, but also for harvest, food and health. God seemed more real to us then. He'd brought the old ones from the Old Country, and the young ones home for the holiday. The war was over, churches were full and the Sixties hadn't found us yet. Everyone seemed hopeful that the best was yet to come.

God is with us yet, but barely visible amid noise and technology. Jesus would've enjoyed being with us at Thanksgiving. In fact, He was.

"O give thanks unto the Lord, for He is good!"

Anna Anderson's husband died young, leaving her to raise their 3 young daughters. Although trained as a teacher, she lacked credentials to work in the Philadelphia schools, so she took in laundry, ironed clothing and scrubbed floors. Racial prejudice closed doors to her, but Anna trusted the Lord to give the four of them what they needed.

Her favorite passage was, **"Trust in the Lord with all your heart and don't depend only on yourself. In all your ways acknowledge Him and He will direct your paths."**(Proverbs 3:5-6) She taught her daughters to depend on the Lord and always be thankful.

When her firstborn, Marian, rose to become an internationally acclaimed opera singer, Anna kept praying for her. When reporters asked her how she felt hearing her daughter sing in Carnegie Hall or with the Metropolitan Opera, she said, *"We thank the Lord!"* She meant every word.

When hard times come, it is easy to feel sad and wish for a better life. But rich or poor, we are never without reasons to give thanks to God and the blessings He has given us. Rather than lament what we don't have, we give thanks for what we do. God makes it all possible.

Jesus gave thanks to His Father in His prayers, and God blessed His ministry and the work of His disciples. He loves to hear us say, *"We thank the Lord!"* It shows Him our faith.

Lord Jesus, we thank You for everything we have!

NOVEMBER 28

Francis Asbury was the first Methodist "Circuit Rider" in America. It's estimated he rode a horse 6,000 miles a year for 45 years. That's over a quarter million miles on horseback. Despite weather, health or bad roads, he tirelessly took the Word of God to early settlers in his adopted country, planting churches wherever he could.

When he arrived in New England in 1771, there were 600 Methodists in America. When he ended his ministry 45 years later, there were 200,000. During his ministry, he recruited 700 more pastors, and despite having little formal education, he even founded some schools.

Asbury was like the Apostle Paul who also planted churches with the Gospel wherever he went. Paul wrote, **"From you the Word of the Lord has sounded forth, not only in Macedonia and Achaia, but also in every place."** (1 Thessalonians 1:8)

"Circuit Riders" are rarely found in America today, but in Canada the Lutheran Association of Missionaries and Pilots (LAMP) flies Gospel messengers and nurtures churches in small towns among the northern native people. In Africa and Australia, train pastors are sent into the bush, often using only the radio to teach.

Circuit riders are still a blessing to people. Like Paul, they want everyone to hear of Jesus. Each of us can also be a missionary to an unbelieving friend or co-worker.

Lord, help us to share Your hope with others.

After Mom and Dad sold the farm they'd owned for 40 years, they moved into town. They bought a small but snug two story house near church and lived there 15 years before moving into the nursing home. Their marriage was a model of caring for each other.

The picture of them I carry in my mind is this: When it was time for bed, Mom would start up the stairs and Dad would walk right behind her, his arms spread wide as he held both handrails in case she should stumble or lean back too far. He'd had both railings installed to support her in case she fell backwards. Coming down, he would walk slowly in front of her.

It reminds me of Solomon's advice for us: **"Two are better than one, because they have a good reward for their toil. If one falls, the other will lift him up. But woe to him who is alone when he falls and has not another to lift him up!"** (Ecclesiastes 4:9-10)

God seeks our good by giving us spouses, friends and neighbors who can help. After creation, all was good for people except being alone. Thus He said, **"It is not good for man to be alone."** (Genesis 2:18)

God reaffirmed this when He said, **"I will never leave you nor forsake you."** (Hebrew 13:5) Jesus was with His disciples in ministry but He was alone suffering for us on the Cross. He promises we will never need to be alone again.

Thank You, Lord, for always being with us.

NOVEMBER 30

Sir Francis Bacon said, *"Men fear death as children fear to go into the dark."* Shakespeare wrote, *"Cowards die many times before their deaths; the valiant taste death but once."* The writer of Hebrews said, **"Man is destined to die once and after that to face judgment."** (Hebrews 9:27)

All mankind has some concern about what happens at death, for we are no longer in control. In that moment, we trust that God is with us. No one can avoid death. Physical death is a certainty to all, so we trust God to be with us.

When sin came into the world, mankind died, both physically and spiritually. With sin came separation – from God, from nature and from each other. In Jesus, we are re-united with God. He is the bridge that connects us to the Almighty. He is the fullness for the emptiness we all have due to our sins. Sin may separate us, but in Jesus we are re-connected.

In Jesus, we are certain that all is not lost when death comes. As we pass from this earth, remember: **"[Jesus] Himself partook of the same things, so that through death He might destroy the one who has the power of death, that is, the devil. He will deliver all those who through fear of death were subject to slavery."** (Hebrews 2:14-15)

There is so much we may not know, but in Jesus we know we will be rejoined to the Father. It is a blessing we all await.

Lord, hold our hand until we're in heaven with You.

EVERY DAY WITH JESUS
in December

✂

DECEMBER 1

Advent means getting ready for Jesus' first coming at Christmas, and His Second Coming in Judgment. During the winter my parents often had their farm neighbors to play cards on weekday nights. They kept no calendar and yet always knew whose turn it was to be host.

One day Mom handed me a broom to sweep, saying, *"The Olsens might be coming tonight, and I want to be ready."* "Why not call and ask?" I said. *"We'll be ready in case they come."* Mom said.

The Olsens came that night to play "Five Hundred" in the kitchen. I was in another room, reading or watching our snowy black and white Philco. I heard their laughter, smelled the coffee, and was invited to eat with them before they left. The next time it would Mrs. Olsen's turn to be ready in case the Taslers came.

Advent is a time for us to be ready. Jesus told His disciples He was going away and would come back unexpectedly. He said, **"Blessed are servants whom the master finds awake when He comes. He will serve them."** (Luke 12:37) God's Son will return and serve those ready for Him. Being ready comes through worship, prayer and service. That's Advent!

Lord, help us be ready for Your return at any time!

DECEMBER 2

While sitting on a bench in a shopping center, the divine scent of freshly baked cinnamon pretzels wafted my way. It was coming out of an oven twenty feet away so I quickly bought a fresh pretzel. Hot cinnamon bread – Mmmm!

This shop showed some Biblical knowledge. One of their posters said, *"The Sinful Taste of Cinnamon."* Next to a picture of a pretzel it said, *"The Original Sin."* On the paper bag was, *"Moderation has a time and place. This isn't it!"* In a world that lives on shaded truth, it was a breath of fresh air to see honesty. Somewhat like a sign held by a smiling young man on the corner that said, *"Why Lie? Out of Beer. Donate Here."*

Jesus understood sin of all kinds, but He despised the hypocrisy of religiosity hiding behind deceit. To religious experts He said, **"Woe to you, scribes and Pharisees, hypocrites! For you shut the kingdom of heaven in people's faces."** (Matthew 23:13)

Honesty and truth are needed for a culture to remain strong. Lies and deception can be poisonous. Jesus said lying is Satan's tool and it seems the Devil is working harder these days.

After enjoying our cinnamon snacks, Carol and I got turned around and ended up on the wrong parking lot. We finally found our car and went home, but only after I'd stopped by the stand to get another fresh pretzel in hand. Can't let a good thing get away!

Lord, help us be honest in all we say and do today.

342

DECEMBER 3

One of the joys that grandparents have is seeing little ones in a Christmas program. No matter where they are held, the place is abuzz with family and friends, all awaiting the program to start with cameras at the ready.

When the children come in, some look at the teacher, but most look at the audience, hoping to be seen by a familiar face. They'd been reminded to pay attention, but they're looking elsewhere. This is their time. They wave when they see us, then sing or speak together when it's their turn. It may be a program about Christmas, but children feel it's about them.

Some adults feel the same about church. Instead of doing a good deed for their Lord or His people, they want people to pay attention to them or help provide their needs. Christians can be self-centered. That's why we need Jesus.

After the resurrection Peter heard Jesus tell him he would be required to give his life for Him. He wasn't sure this was fair, so he pointed to John, **"What about him?"** Jesus said, **"What is that to you? Follow me!"** (John 21:22)

It's easy to be distracted by what others are doing. We may think we have a better plan than God does. We may even wonder why others are doing so well and we're not. But God's plan for each of us is the same: to trust and follow Jesus. The Christian faith really isn't about us, it's all about Jesus.

Lord Jesus, help us follow You, no matter what!

DECEMBER 4

God is willing and able to answer our prayer, but if we pray, we should be ready for His answer. It will come at His timetable, and He will answer, even if it doesn't seem possible.

A hundred years ago, a young farmer's wife died, leaving him with four children. After a year, he realized he could not raise them alone. He prayed, but no answer came, so the man realized he had to do something about it. He got on his horse and rode to a neighbor's farm, where he asked to see their oldest unmarried daughter. When she came out, he asked her to marry him. Of course she refused.

The man then rode to a second farm, and again asked to see their unmarried daughter. She came out, and when he proposed to her, she accepted him. They were married over forty years until he died.

Amazingly, the farmer proposed both times without getting off his horse! He was a distant relative of my wife, an uncle through her father. God answered the man's prayers, but only when he did something about it.

Zechariah and his wife wanted a child, so they prayed. God said, **"Your prayer has been heard. Elizabeth will bear you a son, and you shall call him John."** (Luke 1:13)

God sent an angel to tell them to get ready. Their prayers were answered, but only after they did something about it.

Lord Jesus, help us be ready for Your answers.

DECEMBER 5

What's your favorite Christmas song? The Christmas season is filled with great music. Its message of God sending His only Son into the world in Bethlehem gives us joy and hope.

Pop-song artist Irving Berlin could neither read nor write music, only play it on the piano. When he was finished composing a song, his secretary re-wrote it into playable notes.

On January 8, 1940, Berlin wrote "White Christmas", and the next day he told his secretary, *"This is the best song anybody every wrote."* Hearing Berlin's new tune, his secretary agreed. Bing Crosby recorded it a year later in just 18 minutes. Many still think "White Christmas" is the greatest song ever written.

But as nice as it may be, it's only a song of sweetness and it lacks any message of Christmas. Isaiah the Prophet wrote, **"To us a child is born, to us a Son is given."** (Isaiah 9:6). The angels said, **"To you is born this day a Savior, Christ the Lord."** (Luke 2:11)

Snow memories and sweet music are nice but they don't give us true hope. God's son Jesus, born of Mary in a stable, is the source of Christmas peace and hope. Recalling a snowy Christmas gives us momentary nice thoughts, but the love shown us by God is our best source of joy.

Jesus came to Bethlehem to give His life for our sins. His great sacrifice is the best Christmas gift God could give us.

Thank You, Jesus, for coming into the world for us.

DECEMBER 6

How do you react when someone asks you what you want for Christmas? Most of us are stumped and can't think of a thing.

However, we've all wondered what it would be like if a genie popped out of a bottle and offered to grant us three wishes. Sociologists say there are "three-wish" stories in almost every culture, and most of them follow the same pattern: A genie says it will grant three wishes, but the recipient gets mixed up and usually ends up with nothing. That such stories occur so often suggests we all want something we can't get on our own.

There's a similar story in the Bible, but with a better ending. The Lord appears to young king Solomon and says, **"Ask what I should give you."** (1 Kings 3:5) Solomon, perhaps too young to consider fame, fortune and power as an adult might, asks for an understanding heart, humility and ability to listen so that he can lead his people well. God grants him his wishes, as well as the fame and fortune.

If God would ask you what you want, how would you respond? Would you want wisdom, love and a holy life? Or would you be foolish and ask for riches and power?

Jesus asked for strength to do God's will in His final hours. Because He did, we and all of humanity are blessed eternally. For this we give Him glory, honor and thanks at His birth.

Lord, give us faith and wisdom to live each day.

DECEMBER 7

One year during my ministry, member friends gave us a unique Christmas gift. It was an overnight at the Glen Eyrie Castle located north of Colorado Springs, Colorado. It is a beautiful old English Tudor style castle in a breathtaking setting near Garden of the Gods National Landmark.

Built by Gen. William Jackson Palmer, Glen Eyrie and its pristine gardens show the elegance and refinement Palmer sought when he established a city with his name nearby at the foot of Pikes Peak in 1872.

After settling into our snug guest room, we were treated to a dinner prepared and served in medieval fashion, complete with servants and a court jester. A few were dressed in period costumes, probably people from the staff to add authenticity to the evening. The show featured music and dancing of the Medieval style.

It was all a show, but we enjoyed ourselves, knowing we were being given a peek inside an era long past. All in all, there was good food, fun, music and lasting memories.

"O come let us worship and bow down. Let us kneel before the Lord our Maker." (Psalm 95:6) Christmas worship services and concerts are more than a show. They remind us of God's great gift of His Son born into the world. We worship and honor Him, giving thanks for all He has given to us.

Lord Jesus, thank You for coming to be our Savior.

DECEMBER 8

It's difficult to wait, especially if the line is long. A young pastor was installed at a large congregation in a huge city. The pastor who preached at his installation was a classmate who knew him quite well. He said, *"Joe, now that you're in a big city, you're going to have to learn to wait. There will be lines at the grocery, lines at the theater, lines at the gas station and even lines at the bank. Be patient and wait. Don't get anxious, because we are all waiting in those lines. We either learn to wait, or we can't live here."*

The wait for Mary and Joseph seemed long. They'd endured the whispers and stares of family and neighbors. They'd wondered if they could be accepted in their village. They may even have wondered if the angel's message was true. Then came the edict to register for the census. Waiting to take the trip to Bethlehem may have been the longest wait of all.

But God gave them what He'd promised. When a child is born, the first part of the wait is over. Now come the decisions: Where shall we live? How can we pay for expenses? What will we say to visitors? What is next for us?

When God calls us to follow Him, He also shows us the way. With each need, the couple had gift funds provided. With each question, there were answers. **"Do not be afraid, Mary, for you have found favor with God."** (Luke 1:30) God's favor means God's answers to our needs.

Lord God, answer our prayers and fill our needs.

DECEMBER 9

We may find it bothersome when we see so much attention given to things that people do which we know are wrong. Immoral lifestyles, legalized abortion and legal marijuana use come to mind. It could also be entertainers, athletes or leaders who thumb their noses at what has always been considered good behavior.

It would be easy to follow those who've lived before us. We could shake our heads in dismay, or try to stop such changes. But God gives us a better way.

The Psalmist says, **"Do not fret because of evildoers, nor be envious of the workers of iniquity."** (Psalm 37:1) David's advise is wise, especially when we are in the midst of a season recalling the birth of God's Son. But why should we not be upset with evildoers?

God says he will take care of them. *"God will one day balance the books,"* a friend said. Psalm 37 says, **"Fret not yourself; it tends only to evil, for evildoers shall be cut off."** (vs. 8,9); **"They shall fade like grass."** (vs. 2)

What we can do? We can follow God: **"Trust in the Lord and do good"** (Psalm 37:3), **"Delight yourself in God"** (vs. 4), **"Commit your way to the Lord, trust in Him and He will act."** (vs. 5)

We may not like what we see and hear in the world, but we mustn't forget God is in control. He will care for us. Trust in Him and do what's right. Above all, **"Don't fret about it."**

Help us, Lord Jesus, to give You all our worries.

DECEMBER 10

In <u>The Weight of Glory</u>, C. S. Lewis tells the story of a woman who gives birth to a son while confined in a windowless prison. As the boy grows, he cannot see the outside world, so his mother tries to describe it to him with pencil drawings. Later when the mother and son are released from prison, those simple sketches are replaced by actual images of the world.

This story could be used as a way to understand the Bible. No matter how clearly or descriptively Paul, John or David might write of heaven or God's glory, it would only poor sketches compared to the reality of God.

Paul realizes this as he wrote, **"Now we see in a mirror dimly, but then face to face. Now I know in part, but then I shall know and be known."** (1 Corinthians 12:13) He also wrote, **"The sufferings of this present age are not worth being compared with the glory that shall be revealed to us."** (Romans 8:18)

Even the peace and joy of the most perfect Christmas cannot be compared to the actual peace and joy of being with God in heaven. When Jesus' disciples were told He was going to prepare a place for them, they could have no idea of what that place would be like.

Our best dreams or most detailed mental pictures of God are mere sketches compared to really being with Him. Human artists may try to show it, but we see it best only in Jesus.

Lord, help us look forward to being with You.

DECEMBER 11

There are many small country churches in the Upper Midwest. A man told me that one year he and his wife saw a small white church next to the freeway with a huge sign on its side that spelled out the letters, "H-O-P-E". The lights alternately twinkled, then were solid, then twinkled, then solid, etc. They spelled out the meaning of Christmas for all who drove by.

In his letter to the Romans, Paul wrote, **"We rejoice in our sufferings, knowing that suffering produces endurance, and endurance produces character, and character produces hope, and hope does not disappoint us because God's love has been poured into our hearts through the Holy Spirit who has been given to us."** (Romans 5:3-5)

At this time of remembering Jesus' holy birth, God's hope comes to us and fills us with joy. The promised Messiah has come. He is the one who carried our burdens and sins to Calvary where they are buried forever.

Today we no longer seek hope in an infant. The holy child of Bethlehem has grown to become the source of all hope on earth, as well as our hope for the life to come.

As you consider decorations for your home this Christmas, a large sign saying "H-O-P-E" might be a good way to remind people why Jesus came. It's surely better than "Ho-Ho-Ho" with a Santa and reindeer!

Lord, give us hope that we can take with us always.

DECEMBER 12

On December 12, 2011, Aryann Smith, age 24, was crossing a street in West Valley City, Utah, when a city bus ran over her. She was pinned beneath the bus with severe leg injuries.

Officer Kevin Peck was the first responder on the scene. Seeing someone was under the bus, Peck crawled on the icy ground to check for a pulse. The woman was alive and asked him not to leave her. He assured her he would not let go of her hand until help came.

An emergency crew was able to jack up the bus, slide a backboard under her and bring her out. *"She was afraid she was going to die,"* the officer said, *"I just prayed she'd make it and told her I'd stay with her until we got her out."* The young woman lived, in part because the officer stayed with her through it all.

There may be times when we feel we are *"under the bus"* from bad health, a poor relationship, faulty finances or bad decisions. But Jesus will be there to help us through it all. He has promised to be our Immanuel - **"God With Us"** - every day.

We need not fear what will happen to us. Jesus will hold our hand and make sure we get the help we need. Jesus means Savior, *"One Who Rescues."* Trust Him and thank Him that He is with you when you need Him. He has told us, **"Never will I leave you, never will I forsake you."** (Hebrew 13:5)

Hold our hand, Lord, so that we will never stray.

DECEMBER 13

When Carol and I visited Israel in 1999, someone asked our guide, *"How far is it from Nazareth to Bethlehem?"* We had been talking about the journey Mary and Joseph made before Jesus was born. Our guide answered, *"Depends on where you live. If you're in Pennsylvania, it's about 9 miles and takes 10 minutes by car. If you're here in Israel, it's about 80 miles and takes about a week of walking."*

We may forget the distance they travelled, and also that Mary was pregnant. There were no hotels with a soft bed and warm bath. There was only a group of people to walk with and some food to eat that you carried and perhaps shared with others along the way. No McDonalds or Motel 6, just sleeping on dirt and eating dry, dusty food. Now that's hardship!

The journey for the infant Jesus was even longer. He left His place in heaven to come to earth and take on the life of humans. He walked the earth for over 30 years and never owned more than his clothing. At the end He was rejected, stretched out on a cross and killed. His grave was not even his own.

But His journey wasn't over. He descended to hell, rose from the grave and returned to heaven. Only then was He home again. As you make a journey this Christmas, think about His journey. He came to bring us to heaven, and He reigns there now so we can join Him later.

Lord, prepare our hearts by faith to meet You.

DECEMBER 14

I've always been amazed and delighted by what people give each other at Christmas. One year my father gave his brother-in-law, my Uncle Paul, a set of plowshares because Uncle Paul had loaned Dad his John Deere tractor and plow to do the fall plowing. I helped Dad carry the heavy box of iron to my Uncle's trunk after the Christmas Eve service that night.

The first peacetime Christmas after WWII was a time of plowshares also. The New York Daily News told its readers to expect an armada of warships in New York Harbor. *"Christmas Day will find a mighty armada, consisting of 4 battleships, 6 carriers, 7 cruisers and 24 destroyers,"* the article reported. But instead of war, the ships brought gifts for over 1,000 children, many of whom had lost loved ones in the war.

The children's sizes had been given beforehand so everything fitted nicely. Navy blue coats and woolen caps were gift-wrapped and given to the children aboard the ships. That day, carriers of death had been transformed into carriers of compassion.

Isaiah had predicted such a day when he said, **"They shall beat their swords into plowshares and their spears into pruning hooks. Nation shall not lift up sword against nation, neither shall they learn war anymore."** (Isaiah 2:4) Christmas reminds us that the Prince of Peace will one day bring global peace again.

Lord, we await that day with joy and longing.

DECEMBER 15

Christmas isn't always a happy time. Difficulty or loss can make us feel that Jesus has been stolen from us at Christmas. At such times we must somehow find ways to bring back the joy we've lost.

Before such displays became illegal on public property, the residents of Wellington, Florida, were proud of their lovely ceramic nativity set owned by the town. One year the newspapers reported Baby Jesus was stolen from the scene, so officials took action to insure it wouldn't happen again. The article told how they placed a tracking tracking device inside the replacement Jesus. Next Christmas, when Baby Jesus disappeared again, the signal led sheriff's deputies to the thief's apartment.

Apostle Paul gives us a sense of this in Romans 8 which is filled with so much hope. He says **"the Spirit intercedes with God for us"** (8:27), **"If God is for us, who can be against us?"** (8:31), **"If God so gave us His Son, will He not also give us all things?"** (8:32). Therefore **"Nothing will be able to separate us from the love of God in Christ Jesus."** (8:39)

Thieves or laws may try to keep Jesus hidden; War may separate loved ones; Disease may bring death; Strife may bring sadness; Greed or pride may steal our peace of heart. But the Christ child of Christmas can never be stolen from our hearts forever.

Lord Jesus, stay with us, no matter what happens.

DECEMBER 16

Why do we have Christmas? Why do we give gifts? Someone has said, *"God's presence is more important than our presents."* The Christian writer Oswald Chambers said it another way: *"It is not God's promises that we need, it is God Himself."* How very true!

This time of year, however, people work very hard to celebrate and give gifts as a way to remember God's gift to us in Jesus. Sending greeting cards, shopping, wrapping gifts, hearing the music and attending social events all put us in a holiday mood. But what we need are not all the trappings, but God Himself.

Certain parts of the world give gifts December 6th so they can have the rest of the month to focus on Jesus and the wonder of His birth. How many of us can say we want God's presence more than we want presents?

Our prayers rarely reflect adoration of God. Most of them are requests. *"Dear God, please help me… give me… show me… heal me…"* In our prayers, we say "me" much more often than "thee." Have we turned Christmas away from His presence to *"Give me my presents"*?

King David once wrote, **"In Your presence is fullness of joy."** (Psalm 16:11) Gifts may make us happy for a moment, but His presence makes the happiness last. True joy comes when we have a relationship with the baby at Bethlehem. What would Christmas be like without Him?

Savior, may we ever come to You in faith.

DECEMBER 17

From 1955-62, Hollywood Director Alfred Hitchcock hosted his own television show to tell his unique and often morbid stories. Each week as Charles Gounod's "Funeral March for a Marionette" was played in the background, the portly man walked on stage and said in his dramatic way, *"Good eeeeevening."* He then introduced his story of the week. His wry humor was enhanced by his distaste for commercials. In nearly every show he would say with a frown of distain, *"And now a word from our sponsor…"*

I don't appreciate commercials very much either. They are most irritating when you're not even sure what product they've talked about. If we must watch them, at least we should know what it is they are selling. Someone told me the same thing about a sermon, when he said to me, *"What's your point?"*

What's the point of Christmas? With all its commercialism, what's it all about? Where is the true story behind it, the baby born in a manger who came to forgive our sins?

You will usually find it clearly spoken in a Christmas Eve worship service. Whenever the timeless story is read from Luke 2, the people recall again, **"This shall be a sign for you. You shall find the babe wrapped in clothes and lying in a manger."** (Luke 2:12) With those words, we come into the presence of God, and we remember why this season means so much to us.

Lord, remind us of the reason You've come to us.

DECEMBER 18

A man finally admitted he needed to learn about computers for his business, so he bought one from a local store. He enrolled in a "Computers for Dummies" class and did manage to learn a few things, which made him quite proud. In the second class, however, he was trying to learn some easy commands when he was heard to say, *"Where's the 'Oh-Oh' button?"* The class burst out in laughter!

Have you ever done something seriously wrong and didn't know out how to "undo" it? Have you ever wished you could put your life on "pause" so you could "rewind" it and then "cut and paste" in the correct thing?

After Jesus was arrested, His closest friend, Peter denied he knew Him three times. The first two times were mere reaction to accusations, but the third time he denied Jesus, Peter saw the Lord looking right at him. He knew he was caught, so he felt there was nothing he could do but run away and hide.

But there was something better. After the resurrection when Jesus came to him, Peter faced up to his sins. When Jesus asked, **"Do you love me more than these?"** Peter said, **"Yes, Lord!"** Then he went and lived those words in ministry and witness.

Jesus came to forgive Sin. His birth signaled God's intent to give the world another chance. He restores and cleanses us to start life anew.

Lord, show us how we can restart life with You.

DECEMBER 19

I enjoy eating fruit. It's nourishing, tasty and a good source of fiber. Some tell us we should eat fruit in every meal. I'm not sure that's best.

The "Durian" is called the "King of Fruits." While many find it delicious, many do not. You either love or hate the Durian. Those who love it will pay a great price for it, but those who dislike it will it will avoid its odor at all costs.

If cost were no object, what would you give your best friend? The Wise Men gave Mary and Joseph expensive gifts. Besides honoring their child, their gifts put food on the table. Gold, frankincense and myrrh were not kept; they were sold to spend on basic necessities.

What kind of gift could we give our Lord? What would it cost us? Jesus told a parable of a wealthy man who gave money to his servants before leaving on a trip. He told them to "do business" with the gifts. To the two who increased his wealth he said, **"Well done, good and faithful servants. You've been faithful over a little; I will set you over much."** (Matthew 25:23)

The story was not about gaining wealth but being good stewards. Jesus said being faithful with what God has given us is a gift. To use His gifts for the good of others can be our gift to Him. Jesus was saying, *"Don't waste my gifts."*

As we give and receive gifts this season, think how they can bless both the one who receives and the one who gives.

Lord, help us give You gifts of worship and honor.

DECEMBER 20

On a moonless, cloudless night, you can see countless stars. Astronomers estimate a person with good vision could possibly see 5,000 of the pinpoints in our Milky Way galaxy. There are far more out there that cannot be seen.

In 1995, the "Hubble Deep Field Study" concluded that there are not just billions of stars, but billions of galaxies, each containing billions of stars. Someone has said in the universe there are probably more than 10 stars for every grain of sand on the earth.

God "brings out" these stars every night. Actually, He makes them show up brighter when the sun, our source of our light, is unseen behind the earth as it turns in its 24 hour rotation.

Isaiah explains it this way: **"Lift up your eyes on high and see: who created these? He who brings out their host by number, calling them all by name; by the greatness of his might, and because He is strong in power, not one is missing."** (Isaiah 40:26) Isaiah continues, **"Why do you say, O Jacob, and speak, O Israel, 'My way is hidden from the LORD, and my right is disregarded by my God'?"** (Isaiah 40:27) What wonderful words of faith!

If God can do all this, why can't He also know each of the billions of people who inhabit our globe? Because He can, we rejoice when we see the stars. God is watching over us! He sees us wherever we are.

Lord, help us believe and trust in You always.

DECEMBER 21

Amity Shlaes has written an insightful book about life during the Great Depression called, <u>The Forgotten Man</u>. The term was used for the thousands of individuals who were thrown out of work when companies closed their doors. Others had been wealthy people who lost everything when Wall Street tanked and banks closed.

A popular song at the time was, *"Brother Can You Spare A Dime?"* written by Harburg and Gorney, for the 1932 musical, <u>Americana</u>. It was made popular by Bing Crosby and Rudy Vallee who released their recordings just before the election of President Franklin Roosevelt. Its poignant words include,

> *"They used to tell me I was building a dream/ with peace and glory ahead. / Why should I be standing in line / just waiting for bread? / Once I built a railroad, / I made it run./ Once I built a railroad; / now it's done. / Brother can you spare a dime?*

In Galatians, Paul and Barnabas preached the Gospel and told others, **"Remember the poor."** (Galatians 2:10) As they shared Jesus as God's Son, they also gathered aid for the starving people in Jerusalem as they went from place to place. He urged others to follow his example: (Acts 11:29) **"The disciples urged, every one according to his ability, to send relief to those living in Judea."**

We may feel charities ask too much of us at this time of year, but it all started with Paul's generosity.

Lord, help us to be generous and giving to others.

DECEMBER 22

This time of year we might find ourselves needing help to find that one, last "perfect gift" for a loved one. We may resort to online gift lists (rather useless, I think), or advice from a friend (well-meaning for some things). But perhaps the best gift might be our time.

A boy gave his grandparents a car wash each week during his summer school vacation. A girl gave her big sister free baby-sitting once a month for a year. A man paid for coffee with his good friend whenever they met for a year. What gift of time could you give someone?

God the Father cares for His world so much that He sent His only Son, wrapped in soft clothes and lying in a manger. The shepherds knew this was an amazing gift. **"They went with haste and found Mary and Joseph, and the babe lying in a manger. And when they saw it, they made known the saying that had been told them concerning the child."** (Luke 2:16)

It is a great gift to share good news. A small child will tell anyone nearby that he has a new baby sister or brother. The angels that night were like children. They sang **"Glory to God in the Highest"** when Jesus was born. The normally shy shepherds went into town to tell people of the baby born in a stable.

Time spent with others is a fine gift. It says we are willing to give ourselves, not just our money. God gave us Himself. That's enough!

Father God, thank You for Your priceless gift, Jesus!

DECEMBER 23

After Pearl Harbor, Darrell Blizzard left the orphanage where he'd grown up and joined the war effort by enlisting in the US Army Air Corps. Although he'd never driven anything except a four-mule team to plow a field, he became the pilot of a four-engine B-17. Reflecting on this later in life, he said, *"We are all just kids flying those things."* Faced with responsibilities usually given to older men, those "kids" helped win the war.

In the Bible we often find God giving big responsibilities to young people. David was a teenager when he killed Goliath. Solomon was a boy when he was made king of Israel. Mary was a teenager when she became the mother of the world's Savior. Timothy was barely out of his teens when he accompanied Paul. Later when he became a pastor, he was told, **"Let no one despise your youth, but be an example to the believers."** (1 Timothy 4:12)

God values each person who comes into His family. With His strength and guidance, young boys and girls can he bolder in their faith than those older ones who may discourage them because they're "just kids." God's people, old or young, can have the faith God seeks.

Jesus said, **"Let the little children come unto me, and do not forbid them. To such belongs the kingdom of God."** (Matthew 19:14) May God continue to bless children of all ages. They have tasks God wants them to fulfill.

Lord, help us follow You, no matter how old we are.

DECEMBER 24

Missionary Allen Konrad and his wife served in Africa, and we've corresponded for 40 years. Mary Lu sent us a Christmas letter from Missionary Carlos Winterle of Mozambique:

NO CHRISTMAS TREE IN MOZAMBIQUE

Fir trees don't grow here, so a tree is not traditional.

There are no lights in houses or shops because most villages don't have electricity.

No sweets or cookies are on the tables. Most families don't even have tables in their straw huts.

There are no gifts to buy for children because there is no money to buy them.

There's no big Christmas meal, a plate of rice might be there, but probably food made of white corn flower.

No Santa Claus. "Father Christmas? What's that?"

No last minute gift shopping at the Mall because there are no Malls, and their needs are mostly food.

BUT THERE'S STILL CHRISTMAS THERE!

Christmas songs are sung with joy when Christians gather to celebrate the coming of Jesus, the Savior.

Christmas prayers express thanks because Jesus the Light shines on those who were formerly in darkness.

Christmas is full of hope when the Nativity Gospel is read and promises of God's love are heard again.

Christmas is full of love when family comes together after worship to share a pot of rice and maybe some meat.

Christmas is centered on Christ, not traditions. Those are good, but the Gospel of God's love is more important.

"I bring you good news of great joy that will be for all the people. To you is born this day in the city of David a Savior who Christ the Lord." (Luke 2:10-11)

Thanks, Jesus, that You came to be Savior to us all.

DECEMBER 25

Weather nearly cancelled Christmas in a rural North Dakota town one year. It had been a lovely autumn, and Thanksgiving had been warm. Crops were in, fall plowing was done and everyone looked forward to Christmas.

The first snowstorm hit the second week of December and the second, even bigger, came on December 22, heavily snowing for two days. Christmas Eve worship was cancelled for sure and maybe even Christmas Day. December 25 was sunny and clear, but few were out except to shovel blocked roads. Everyone stayed home.

December 26 was a Sunday, so one minister had an idea. There were five churches in town, so he told folks his church would open Dec. 26 for Christmas worship at 11 am.

Word spread, and when the sun came up, people began shoveling their sidewalks, most of them not members of his church. At 10:30 am ladies from another church brought coffee and goodies, and people began arriving.

As the service started, two men brought in a nativity and set it in front of the altar. Two hundred people packed the pews, mostly from other churches, and all walked to get there. It was a Christmas people talked about for years.

It was wonderful to be part of that service. Neighbors from all churches, all sitting together singing, all hearing the Good News, **"Unto you is born this day a Savior who is Christ the Lord."**

Lord, please give us such Christmas joy this year.

DECEMBER 26

Almost every Christmas Eve during a worship service somewhere, I like to sing a verse or two of "Silent Night" in German, the native language of my mother and father. I sing it softly so as not to bring attention. I just want to remind myself of my heritage, and how God sent His Son for all people of the world, including Germans.

I once read of a man named Simon who emigrated to the United States from the Netherlands. His wife Kay and their three children were all born in the U.S. Daughter Jenny grew up and married Roberto from Panama, son Bill married Vania from Portugal and son Lucas married Bora from South Korea. They had quite an international family.

On Christmas Eve, the entire family with all their children gathered and sang songs. After singing traditional carols in English, they finished with "Silent Night" and each one of them sang it in their native language. It was a lovely sound with the sweet words mixed together, praising God that the Lord of heaven came into the world to save us from sin.

The angel said, **"Behold, I bring you good news of great joy which shall be for all the people."** (Luke 2:10) Today nearly 2.5 billion people worldwide know of Jesus and trust Him as their Savior. Who could have known that night, except the angels, that the birth of a baby could change so many lives?

Lord, come into our hearts every day with joy.

DECEMBER 27

In preparation to write my children's book, The True Story of Silent Night, I learned about the conditions under which the beloved carol was written. Father Joseph Mohr labored among his small Austrian flock during the bitterly cold winter of 1816, the "year of no summer" due to the world-wide ash cloud from the explosion of the Mt. Tambora in Asia.

Father Mohr saw his people suffering and hungry, so he tried to help them with food, warm clothing and God's hope in Jesus. During his many trips through the freezing snow he became very sick, but he kept on ministering.

Each evening at the rectory he knelt in prayer before a picture of the Holy Family in which Jesus was a curly blond like the boys of his native Austria. He then wrote a new hymn describing the *"Virgin mother and child."* When he showed his verses to Franz Gruber, a new teacher and friend, Gruber wrote the melody. After Mass on Christmas Eve, 1818, Father Mohr, also a musician, played the guitar as the two men sang "Silent Night" for the first time.

The angel said, **"To you this day is born in the city of David a Savior, who is Christ the Lord."** (Luke 2:10) Our beloved Christmas song was written by devout believers who lived much as we do, dealing with life's problems and trusting that God will deliver them from this world to their heavenly home.

Lord, thank You for giving us songs of Your birth.

DECEMBER 28

It seems today that wherever we go, there are stations where we can clean our hands. Whether wet wipes as we enter a store or foam cleaner in a restaurant, people are cautious and careful not to spread germs. The last church I served even had a small jar that would pump hand cleaner as you went to pick up your coffee and donut. Some really clean Lutherans!

Just as the vigilant cleaning of hands will hinder the spread of germs, so also a clean heart can hinder the spread of sin. David spoke of this when he said, **"Who may stand in His holy place? He who has clean hands and a pure heart."** (Psalm 24:3-4)

David wasn't referring to personal hygiene but to spiritual cleanliness. Regular cleansing from sin is vitally important. That's why in most worship services, the pastor begins with a period of repentance and forgiveness, called "confession and absolution."

To stand before God should move us to want to be clean. We have dirty hands and hearts; He is goodness and purity. We have guilt and regret; He is grace and forgiveness.

In coming to earth, Jesus lived as we did and took the punishment for sins we deserved. In taking us into His family through Baptism, God made a *"silk purse from a sow's ear."* There's no greater honor than that we become children of God. As John said, **"And so we are."** (1 John 3:1)

Savior, hold us in Your hands all through our life.

DECEMBER 29

An article I read stated that in 1971, Ray Tomlinson was experimenting with some ways people and computers could interact. When he sent a message from his computer through a network to a different computer in his office, he had sent the first E-mail.

Today, decades away from that event, a billion or more E-mails are sent each day. They contain news, events and messages from family, friends and co-workers. But some contain unwanted ads or even a destructive virus that can do damage. A basic rule of using E-mail is, *"Don't open it unless you trust the sender."*

In the Bible, God has sent us many messages about His plan of salvation in Jesus. We've just passed the celebration of an integral part of that plan, that God's Son was born on earth, so that **"All who believe in Him shall not perish, but have eternal life."** (John 3:16)

But do we trust the Sender? Are we willing to believe the Word being sent to us? Perhaps we should ask, *"What better Word is there? What else in the world gives us any hope?"*

Hope is not hope if it hopes in nothing. Of all the objects of hope, nothing is better than to hope in a loving God who made us, and in His Son who was born to save us. The writer of Hebrews says, **"In these last days God has spoken to us by His Son."** (Hebrews 1:2) Those words alone give us great hope!

Lord, keep us hoping in what You've done for us.

369

DECEMBER 30

As the time drew near for the birth, Mary and Joseph must have been excited. Things would be different when the baby came and the wait was finally over. People are always excited when they successfully finish something.

It feels good to be completing <u>Every Day With Jesus</u>, my fourth and final daily devotional. Though writing and publishing less than ten years, I now have nearly a million words published. I praise God for this, but I'm also thankful to be slowing down.

It's wonderful to write about the blessings God gives us at Christmas. The story of God's love through His Son coming into the world is timeless, and its mystery is unfading. Like the flower on the apple tree each spring, the story of the Christ child opens its beauty to us each year at Christmas and shows us God's beautiful love inside once again.

Even the secular world with its eye on the bottom line finds joy and peace in this story. Science may discount it as being just another tradition mankind has fabricated, but it can never be removed from the hearts of young or old. God is greater than human reason.

The message, **"To us a child is born, to us a Son is given"**(Isaiah 9:6) transcends human reason and brings God back into the world He created. This story will not fade, because, **"The Word of the Lord abides forever."** (Isaiah 40:8)

Thank You, Lord, for staying with us forever.

DECEMBER 31

It's not often a popular author of westerns and short stories such as Louis Lamour comes up with a timeless sentence. But I believe this one closely reaches profundity:

"There will come a time when you believe everything is finished. That will be the beginning." (L. Lamour, <u>Lonely on the Mountain</u>, p. 1)

Tonight is the end of this calendar year, and many parties will be held to celebrate that end. Yet everyone knows it is a few hours away from the beginning of the New Year.

This is not profound, for it is done every year since God created time. For the Christian, however, the real essence of Lamour's sentence is a message for eternity: There will come a time for each of us when we believe our life is finished, but it will only be the beginning.

Earthly life is not all there is. We can't spike the ball and declare the game over. It's not a question of whether or not we will live again; it is all about where that life will be spent.

Whether with God in eternity or separated from God in perdition, all of us will live somewhere. It has been my desire to give people the hope of having a new life with God on that new heaven and new earth because they trust in Jesus whose mercy is new to us every morning.

"I am the Way, the Truth and the Life. No one comes to the Father but by Me." (John 14:6) These words of Jesus are the source of all hope.

Thanks, Father, for being with us this year, amen!

Rev. Robert L. Tasler

The author is a native of Windom, Minnesota, and a career ordained pastor in the Lutheran Church-Missouri Synod. A 1971 graduate of Concordia Seminary, St. Louis, Missouri, he has served parishes in North Dakota, California, Utah, Colorado and Arizona. Now retired, he and his wife Carol divide their time between Castle Rock, Colorado, and Casa Grande, Arizona.